Broadcast Journalism
A critical introduction

Broadcast Journalism offers a critical analysis of the key skills required to work in the modern studio, on-location, or on-line, with chapters written by industry professionals from the BBC, ITV, CNN and independent production companies in the UK and US. Areas highlighted include:

- Interviewing
- Researching
- Editing
- Writing
- Reporting

The practical tips are balanced with chapters on representation, ethics, law, economics and history, as well as specialist areas such as documentary and the reporting of politics, business, sport and celebrity.

Broadcast Journalism concludes with a vital chapter on career planning to act as a springboard for your future work in the broadcast industry.

Contributors: Jim Beaman; Jane Chapman; Fiona Chesterton; Tim Crook; Anne Dawson; Tony Harcup; Jackie Harrison; Ansgard Heinrich; Emma Hemmingway; Patricia Holland; David Holmes; Gary Hudson; Nicholas Jones; Marie Kinsey; Roger Laughton; Leslie Mitchell; Jeremy Orlebar; Claire Simmons; Katie Stewart; Ingrid Volkmer; Mike Ward; Deborah Wilson

Jane Chapman is Reader in Journalism Studies at Lincoln University. She has worked extensively in the industry as a television producer (with Chapman Clarke Films), as an on-screen news reporter for national breakfast television (TV-am), a TV news senior journalist (Granada TV), an assistant producer (BBC Panorama and Newsweek), a news sub editor (HTV), a BBC Radio 4 freelance reporter (You and Yours) and a staff researcher (Southern TV). She is author of *Comparative Media History* (2005) and *Documentary in Practice* (2nd edition, 2007).

Marie Kinsey is Course Leader for the MA in Broadcast Journalism at Sheffield University and won the 1990 Financial Broadcaster of the Year Wincott Award. She has worked in broadcasting since 1979 with BRMB in Birmingham, Independent Radio News, LBC, Thames Television and the BBC. For 15 years she specialised in business and finance, including posts as Deputy City Editor with IRN and Business Correspondent for BBC radio and television in the south east. She has presented live radio and television programmes and contributed to many networked programmes in both media. She is co-editor of *A Guide to Independent Radio Journalism* (1998).

Broadcast Journalism
A critical introduction

Edited by Jane Chapman
and Marie Kinsey

Routledge
Taylor & Francis Group

LONDON AND NEW YORK

First published 2009
by Routledge
2 Park Square, Milton Park, Abingdon, Oxon, OX14 4RN

Simultaneously published in the USA and Canada
by Routledge
270 Madison Avenue, New York, NY 10016

Routledge is an imprint of the Taylor and Francis Group, an informa business

Editorial Matter and Selection © 2009 Jane Chapman and Marie Kinsey

Chapters © 2009 contributors

Typeset in Janson by
Keystroke, 28 High Street, Tettenhall, Wolverhampton
Printed and bound in Great Britain by
Cromwell Press, Trowbridge, Wiltshire

British Library Cataloguing in Publication Data
A catalogue record for this book is available from the British Library

Library of Congress Cataloging in Publication Data
Broadcast journalism : a critical introduction / edited by Jane Chapman and
Marie Kinsey.
p. cm.
Includes bibliographical references and index.
1. Broadcast journalism. I. Chapman, Jane, 1950- II. Kinsey, Marie.
PN4784.B75B74 2008
070.1'9—dc22
2008024930

ISBN 10: 0–415–44154–4 (hbk)
ISBN 10: 0–415–44155–2 (pbk)
ISBN 10: 0–203–88645–3 (ebk)

ISBN 13: 978–0–415–44154–4 (hbk)
ISBN 13: 978–0–415–44155–1 (pbk)
ISBN 13: 978–0–203–88645–8 (ebk)

Contents

Contributors

Jim Beaman is Course Leader for Broadcast Journalism at the University of Gloucestershire and has worked as an instructor with BBC Radio Training. His broadcasting career includes presenting, reporting and producing for BBC Radio. He is the author of *Interviewing for Radio* (2000) and *Programme Making for Radio* (2006).

Jane Chapman is Reader in Journalism Studies at Lincoln University. She is the author of *Documentary in Practice* (2007) and *Comparative Media History* (2005), and of articles and chapters on the journalism of Narmada Dams controversy and the literary journalism of George Sand. She was TVam's first North of England reporter and has made over 200 factual programmes and documentaries.

Fiona Chesterton is Director of Television at Skillset. She worked for seventeen years in BBC News and Current Affairs before her appointment first as Deputy Commissioning Editor for Current Affairs at Channel Four, then as the station's first Commissioner for Daytime Programmes. She returned to the BBC as Head of Education Commissioning and is a fellow of the Royal Television Society.

Tim Crook is a Senior Lecturer on Media Law and Ethics at Goldsmiths, University of London. During a career in journalism of more than thirty years he was Britain's first specialist broadcast legal affairs correspondent for Independent Radio News and LBC, campaigned against courtroom secrecy, and won for journalists the right to challenge crown court reporting bans.

Anne Dawson is Deputy Head of the Department of Media and Communications at the University of Gloucestershire. She began her broadcasting career in independent radio, then joined the BBC in Southampton as a television reporter. She worked for ITV in the 1980s, first in Southampton, then in the Midlands, where she presented *Central News at Six* for fifteen years.

Tony Harcup is the author of *The Ethical Journalist* (2007) and *Journalism: Principles and Practice* (2004). He has been a journalist within mainstream and alternative media for thirty years and is currently a columnist for *Press Gazette*. He has taught at the University of Sheffield since 2005 and his research has been published in *Journalism Studies*, *Journalism* and *Ethical Space*.

Jackie Harrison is Professor of Public Communication and Head of the Journalism Studies Department at the University of Sheffield. She has published extensively on the study of news and European communication and audiovisual policy. Her publications include *News* (2006) and *Terrestrial TV News in Britain* (2000), and her papers have appeared in *Journalism Practice*, *Journalism Studies* and *Communications Law*, among others.

Ansgard Heinrich is studying for a doctorate at the Department of Media, Film and Communication, University of Otago, New Zealand. Her research interests are global journalism and the new global news media infrastructure. Previously she worked as a freelance radio journalist for local radio stations in Germany. She is an honorary research fellow at the University of Melbourne, Australia.

Emma Hemmingway is Senior Lecturer in Broadcast Journalism at Nottingham Trent University. Her doctorate covered BBC regional news production and new media technologies. She is the author of *Into the Newsroom* (2007). Previously she worked as a television reporter and producer for BBC Television at regional and national level.

Patricia Holland is a writer, researcher and Senior Lecturer at Bournemouth University. She has worked as a television editor and producer and has published widely in the fields of television, visual culture and popular media. Her most recent book is *The Angry Buzz: 'This Week' and Current Affairs Television* (2006).

David Holmes is Course Leader for the MA Print Journalism at the University of Sheffield and worked in newspapers and radio for more than twenty years. His research interests include convergence, the newspaper of the future and journalism education.

Gary Hudson has reported on television from around the world – including the first Gulf War. He was BBC TV's chief news reporter in the Midlands. His other work includes football commentary on radio and sports reporting for ITV and Sky Sports News. He teaches broadcast journalism at Staffordshire University and is the co-author of *The Broadcast Journalism Handbook* (2007).

Nicholas Jones was a BBC industrial and political correspondent between 1972 and 2002. His books include *Soundbites and Spin Doctors* (1995), *Sultans of Spin* (1999) and *Trading Information: Leaks, Lies and Tip-offs* (2006).

Marie Kinsey is Senior University Teacher at the University of Sheffield, where she leads the MA Broadcast Journalism. She is an academic fellow with the Centre for Inquiry Based Learning in the Arts and Social Sciences and co-author of *Key Concepts in Journalism Studies* (2005). She has more than twenty-five years' experience as a journalist in newspapers, radio and television and holds a Wincott Award for Excellence in Financial Journalism.

Roger Laughton is a broadcasting consultant. He began his career at the BBC, in Bristol, Birmingham, Manchester and London. He became the first chief executive of ITV broadcaster Meridian and later led United Broadcasting and Entertainment. A former Head of Bournemouth Media School, he was commissioned by the BBC to review their West Midlands Local TV pilot in 2006.

Leslie Mitchell is Senior Teaching Fellow and Director of Learning and Teaching in the Department of Film, Media and Journalism at Stirling University. A former BBC radio and television producer, independent producer and vice-chair of the

Scottish Section of the Royal Television Society, he is also author of *Freelancing for Television and Radio* (2005).

Jeremy Orlebar has over twenty-five years' experience with BBC Radio and Television, producing and directing programmes. He now runs his own production company and works in higher education as a senior lecturer in media, and as an examiner. He is the co-author of *The Television Handbook* (2005) and author of *Digital Television Production* (2002).

Claire Simmons is a Senior Lecturer in Broadcast Journalism at the University of Gloucestershire. She has more than twenty years' experience as a journalist across national newspapers, BBC Radio and Television news and online. She has a master's degree in Mass Communication (University of Leicester) and her specialist research areas are celebrity journalism, news values and media ethics.

Katie Stewart has taught broadcast journalism on BA Journalism Studies at the University of Sheffield since 2004. She has worked extensively in radio and television as a presenter and reporter, most recently with Yorkshire Television's regional news programme *Calendar*.

Ingrid Volkmer, University of Melbourne, is the author of *News in Public Memory: An International Study of Media Memories across Generations* (2006) and '"Foreign" Journalism in the Global News World', in S. Allan (ed.), *Journalism: Critical Issues* (2005). She is also associate editor of the *Encyclopedia of Globalization* (2007).

Mike Ward is Head of the Department of Journalism at the University of Central Lancashire. The department is a leading provider of digital development services to UK news organizations. His book, *Journalism Online*, has been used internationally as a core text on the subject and has been reprinted in several languages.

Deborah Wilson is Programme Leader for the BA courses at Lincoln University and a freelance broadcast journalist. She has published on journalist Martha Gellhorn and has given research papers on broadcasting and journalism at national and international conferences. She is currently researching the development of community radio and civic journalism.

Part I
The shape of broadcast news

Introduction

Jane Chapman

The chapters in Part I offer explanations and analysis of the various contexts in which broadcast journalism operates. This essential information provides much more than a mere background description of the complex media landscape within which TV, radio and online news is located. An understanding of the terrain – past and present – enables readers to position themselves along with the point of time at which they come to this book in a broader historical and geographical trajectory.

At the same time, this section of the book allows readers to acquaint themselves with the debates and academic research about current issues relating to broadcast journalism. All of the chapters that follow in Part I fulfil the promise of our subtitle – 'A critical introduction'. What this means is that the resultant familiarity with broader contexts also gives added value in the form of food for thought, and an opportunity to reflect on a range of interpretations about the nature, evolution and practices of broadcast journalism.

There is also a further purpose to this opening section: it introduces themes that continue as undercurrents in future, more specific skills-based chapters. The limitations of space here mean that I will allude to some, but not all, of the arguments presented in individual chapters. I have selected points to mention that seem, to me, to fulfil this generic function of underpinning the more detailed information relating to specific aspects of broadcast journalism that comes later.

The first chapter uses a broad brush to tease out certain themes from TV and radio history, thus helping us to understand the nature of the mediums and how the industry has reached its present position. Using the past, we can even speculate on the future, although the latter is a cognitive activity that historians tend to shy away from. It may be more useful for us to ponder on trends and to take a longer-term view on themes such as media 'revolutions'.

For some time, people have talked about the digital revolution in terms of computers, but I advance the argument in the first chapter that, considered over a longer time span, the moving image has created the real revolution. Obviously, from this, one can conclude that the broadcast journalist needs to understand how to work with pictures and time-based recording; but the underlying message of broadcast history, with its separate development of radio then television, is also more fundamental. Despite, or even because of, convergence, it is imperative that we unpick the various component skills that make up broadcast journalism. If a news story has to be compiled for a variety of transmission platforms with a range of versions, then history can teach us about the essence of the mediums and therefore how to make the best of the various adaptations.

Roger Laughton underlines the importance of history in Chapter 4 when he focuses on the major part played by both politics and geography in the development of local broadcast news during the twentieth century, while Ingrid Volkmer and Ansgard Heinrich (Chapter 5) stress that this is still the case during the current century. In fact, history provides a salutary reminder of the struggles that broadcast journalists have faced when bringing their stories to various audiences. Nothing worthwhile in life comes easy – a truism today when it comes to finding the money to fund good research and reporting.

Thus, in Chapter 2, Deborah Wilson demonstrates that we should all be concerned about funding issues and that we should not consider public service broadcasting (PSB) as being immune from market forces. Every broadcast journalist needs to be aware of the bigger commercial picture – well illustrated by the fact that when it first started, a broadcast of Britain's favourite horse race, the Grand National, cost the BBC £175. Compare this to the total cost of the Corporation's news services today – some £112.6 million. In Chapter 4 Laughton also reinforces a point made first by Wilson in Chapter 2 – that cost factors determine levels of service, in this case provision of local news.

Interestingly, Laughton includes newspapers in his analysis of local services in the digital age. This is because of the increasing importance of convergence – a theme that recurs regularly in nearly all the chapters. The landscape that is described by both Laughton on local news and Volkmer and Heinrich on global coverage is a complex one, with both chapters raising the question of how to define 'local'. The other question that the contributions of Wilson, Laughton and Volkmer and Heinrich all beg is how future broadcast journalists will survive in this scenario. The message seems to be that flexibility is needed in order to move between sector suppliers, be they radio, TV or local newspaper groups requiring video journalists.

The implications of Volkmer and Heinrich's study is that we need a form of cross-media education to prepare journalists for working in a convergent newsroom – something that scholars have been pointing out for some years (Pavlik, 2000). The broadcast journalist needs to be sufficiently multi-skilled to move around the industry, but Volkmer and Heinrich also urge us to think big. The future may be local but it is also global. This touches on a huge debate within the academy about global versus local, summarized in Chapter 5. An appreciation of international, national and local structures that comprise both 'horizontal' and 'vertical' networks can underpin our work as practitioners. This is not merely an abstract point: globalized geography, aided by technology (as mentioned in Chapter 1) impacts on traditional journalism by facilitating trends such as 'citizens' journalism' via the Internet.

Therefore, as we negotiate our way through the broadcast journalism maze, we will probably take with us skills, a flexible attitude and an understanding of the past that helps to explain the current picture. There are two other factors that will complete our toolkit of critical understanding: appreciation of audience and of prevailing news values. In Chapter 3 Marie Kinsey discusses the battle for the audience in the context of changing consumer habits and in relation to convergence and the deregularized multi-channel environment. She examines how audiences are identified, selected and targeted, how broadcasters are managing the challenges thrown up by the Web, and how audiences are measured, and asks whether these methods are relevant or even accurate in a multi-platform world.

Whenever a journalist steps into a new organization, s/he is faced with the task of understanding the individual culture and how this impinges on news values. In the final chapter of this section Jackie Harrison enables us to do just this. She also provides clear indicators about the factors that influence decisions on what is covered, what is not and the prominence given to individual stories within the running order. News values are not set in stone; they are subject to much discourse and analysis by scholars. Harrison's chapter emphasizes that debates relating to news values are subject to constant adaptation, variation and change.

News values are always present but sometimes difficult to analyse – the very reason why they are subject to much discourse. Harrison quite correctly underlines the fact that they cannot be separated from ethical considerations such as accuracy and the search for truth, although we should be constantly aware of the conflict between the ideal and the real, for an analysis of news values is central to an understanding of reporting and writing practice, and as such underpins all of the chapters that follow.

In essence, the aim of Part I is to flag up the way that macro-changes influence the working lives of broadcast journalists at the local level, relating global change to specific environments both inside and outside the traditional newsroom. By introducing us to the nature of discourses on news production at different levels, this section also establishes the importance of the critical study of the profession and how it has a direct bearing on the way that journalists understand and execute their role.

Reference

Pavlik, J. (2000) 'The Impact of Technology on Journalism', *Journalism Studies*, 1(2): 229–37.

Broadcast journalism

Yesterday, today and the future

Jane Chapman

Introduction

The past helps us to understand the nature of broadcasting as a medium and the changing nature of the work and contexts within which the journalist operates – but the way that historians view these elements is always coloured by the present. As we progress through the twenty-first century, broadcast journalists are facing a challenge to the discrete identity of broadcasting and its very survival. Broadcasting now involves media that previously were used for non-broadcast purposes – different communications media are merging their functions.

The computer is at the heart of this revolution: it too has become a medium for broadcasting. The digital revolution and convergence have meant that TV and radio can be received using a variety of platforms. Gradually sector-specific definitions – for instance, between audiovisual and e-commerce industries – which historically had guided understanding of mass communication, are becoming eroded by technology and cross-media ownership. Therefore, this chapter aims to provide a counter-current to present trends. I use history as a tool to unpick the over-arching characteristics of radio and television as they emerged in the past, to tease out the strengths and weaknesses of words and pictures, and their contextual importance.

The ability to create the convergence of two different media in the same box was first established in 1927 with the radiogram and there have always been certain overlaps – such as sound with its shared mechanical features in radio, TV and film. However, the common binary code of digital technology means that media are now *interchangeable* so that each can assume the characteristics and functions of the other. Interchangeability can result in a single body of material being packaged for a range of outlets and delivery. Content then becomes paramount, and method of delivery secondary, but portrayal of content will be influenced by the same tools – words and pictures.

Broadcasting is a social application, varying with different cultural contexts, but always of such importance that it may well be feasible to conclude that the real media revolution of the twentieth and twenty-first centuries is not computers, but moving pictures. The ascendancy of the latter was helped by the inheritance of radio's institutional frameworks. The basis of this argument is that technology does not determine social use, but that broadcast journalists interact with aspects of society; their role is to reflect, to mediate and interpret political, economic, social or cultural phenomena.

From the 1920s onwards, first the words and sounds of radio, then the words and pictures of TV have always been present in the here and now of the listener and viewer and of the world that surrounds them. They have served to bridge public and private, with the reporter building an interactive relationship between them. As a medium, broadcasting provides 'the most rapid, broad and cost-efficient participation in anything unfolding moment by moment . . . broadcasting creates a sense of contact with other members of the dispersed audience' (Ferrell Lowe and Hujanen, 2003: 16).

The struggles of radio news

Radio's development over the years has been very much a function of its potential social usage as a medium. The arrival of phonograph, film and the 'wireless' all offered the reporter a tool for presentation that challenged existing communication of time and space, but this was not immediately obvious at the time. In fact, their ultimate application differed from their intended purpose. Early pioneers such as Marconi saw radio not as a mass medium but as a means of one-to-one communication! Broadcast journalism emerged only after a systematic struggle for acceptance within the media – not just by inventors and pioneers of equipment, but by reporters and broadcasters. The techniques that are used for reporting today are not automatic or set in stone. They took time to develop.

Often there was opposition to many of the now accepted tasks that broadcast journalists presently undertake on a routine, daily basis. Technical breakthroughs throughout the twentieth century relentlessly increased the potential for immediacy and hence drama through recording and reporting that have always aimed to appear as 'live' as possible. However, the arrival of a new means of disseminating information and entertainment tends to destabilize the existing media system, thus radio posed a challenge to the historic relationship between wire services and newspapers. The press in both Britain and the United States lobbied heavily for statutory restrictions on broadcasting, for they wanted to ensure that it was *they* who carried breaking news first – despite the fact that radio was, in retrospect, a more flexible and instant medium for doing this.[1]

Early radio news was a prisoner to the press. When the BBC started its *General News* bulletins on 23 December 1922, the organization had no in-house journalists. They were dependent on the supply of copy from Reuters, which owned the copyright, announced as a prelude to each bulletin. The BBC was obliged to transmit radio news only after the appearance of morning and evening newspapers. Text-based information had to be converted into writing for listeners' ears, into a style suitable for radio, but there were no interviews, features or actuality.

Notwithstanding this, radio's take-off was swift and public enthusiasm for it peaked during the 'golden age' of the 1930s and 1940s. Millions used radio as the main source of both information and entertainment. News was just one element of a schedule among drama, soap operas, music, comedy and talks. The thinking was that audiences should enjoy the entire range of mixed programming output, from classical music through to drama and news. Audiences were not separated or differentiated. This coexistence has involved gradual adaptations towards more entertaining styles of news presentation.

The way that the BBC made a virtue out of 'less is more' in broadcast journalism provides a stark contrast to the hungry values of today's twenty-four-hour news. One day in 1930, it announced that there was no news to broadcast – end of story! What it meant was that there was no news of importance that day. Yet by 1936 the idea of a news angle was emerging and a new style of radio journalism was being fashioned to provide 'authentic' news. After pioneer David Dimbley reported a devastating fire live at London's Crystal Palace, he wrote to the BBC suggesting that they needed somebody like him, to be called a 'reporter' or a 'correspondent', to cover unexpected events such as big fires, accidents and major catastrophes 'in which the public, I fear, is deeply interested'. He argued that such news could be presented 'in a gripping manner and, at the same time, remain authentic' (Stroud, 1969: 41).

Radio blossomed during the Second World War because of the shortage of newsprint at a time when news was paramount. By now the BBC had a war-reporting unit of sixty-two with forty-eight correspondents, who were given priority access for D-Day coverage. More than 50 per cent of the population switched on to *War Report*, the nightly news programme. Reporters broadcast with the latest technology from as near to the front lines as possible, providing on-the-spot field reporting with a quality of immediacy, crafted to paint pictures with words. Good radio journalism was by now at its best, as is demonstrated by this transcript of a report from the beach at Arromanches on D-Day by Frank Gillard:

> At first sight everything round the beaches still looks chaotic – there's still so much wreckage and litter lying about. Smashed-up buildings, tangles of wire, heaps of driftwood, enormous bomb-craters, water-logged landing-craft just pushed out of the way . . . wrecked vehicles piled one on top of another . . . but despite appearances everything is thoroughly under control. To prove it there are those unending columns of men and vehicles pouring inland in perfect order.
>
> (*Ibid.*: 35)

As George Orwell pointed out, the reputation of the BBC for accuracy and reliability both at home and abroad was supreme during the Second World War (Chapman, 2005: 187).

The most haunting of all eyewitness reports came from Richard Dimbleby, one of the first people to enter Belsen at the end of the war. As he picked his way over corpses and moaning, abandoned people he said: 'I must describe this exactly, in all its horror, even if I feel ill as I talk.' Later he admitted that he broke down five times while recording his story of almost indescribable human suffering (Stroud, 1969: 43, 46; BBC, 1997).

Public service broadcasting (PSB)

Broadcasting utilizes the electromagnetic spectrum, an immense, but finite, phenomenon of nature (Ferrell Lowe and Hujanen, 2003: 11). The twentieth century has witnessed successive advances in our ability to use more frequencies for varied and improved communication, and there are applications within the spectrum such as radio telescopes and satellite surveillance mapping that go beyond the scope of our present concerns. In the past it was perceived that a finite public resource necessitated some form of regulation, and from this emerged the concept of broadcasting as a public service. Therefore, the spread of radio in the 1920s and 1930s was accompanied by a rapid institutional growth of a new form of media organization: broadcasters, who were communicating radio transmissions. Television built on the structures first developed for radio (Chapman, 2005: 221).

Such is its awesome communication potential that broadcast journalism has always formed part of a bigger picture. During the entire nineteenth and twentieth centuries there was one main motivation for media communication which was shared by every country: to use it to influence the political process in the public sphere. The dissemination of propaganda was exploited to the full throughout the twentieth century – another reason why broadcasting could not simply be left to market forces. The first director general of the BBC, John Reith, had to request permission from his minister – the Postmaster General – to handle controversial subjects, provided the BBC reported with impartiality and responsibility. The fact that the BBC was forced under its licence conditions to avoid controversial programming also led to a narrow form of reporting. During the General Strike in 1926, opposition and trades union voices were silenced and many listeners started to use the term BFC (British Falsehood Corporation) in protest (BBC, 1926).

In 1934 BBC News became an independent department, partly to encourage public confidence in its corporate ethic of neutrality, but the Second World War necessitated the government management of information, and this impacted on the institutional relationship between the media industries and the state. Radio was used for entertainment, information and propaganda by all sides, most dramatically in France. During the occupation the Nazis seized people's radio sets, but until liberation in 1944 the airwaves in France were the scene of a verbal war between Nazi, Vichy and resistance propaganda, with the latter emanating mainly from London, where Free French leader Charles de Gaulle was exiled.

Politicians like Churchill cut their teeth on radio, but simultaneously feared that broadcasting would replace regular democracy as a forum for debate to compete with Parliament. Hence the 'fourteen-day rule' from 1944 to1957, specifying that there could be no coverage of issues that were due to be debated in Parliament for fourteen days prior to the event. MPs were responsible for broadcasting regulation and policy. For their part, TV and radio lacked the technical ability to procure instant audience feedback: instead, much of the response was political.[2]

Thus broadcast journalism was plunged into a relationship with the public sphere. It has always been a love–hate affair of mutual dependency. The revelation of social problems can have a progressive, even democratizing effect. Yet it can also be argued that the lack of democratic accountability over broadcasting institutions means that commitment to journalistic integrity is liable to become subordinated to the interests of state and corporate elites (Allan, 2004: 44). In addition, PSB entails wider values associated with Western democracy: diversity, pluralism, universal service and the maintenance of cultural identity. More recently these values have been challenged by the prevalence of neoliberal, free market ideology and the increased competition of the multi-channel environment. Nevertheless, PSB has been crucial for its role in kick-starting new technology, taking risks when the commercial sector could see no profit, such as leading the development of black-and-white television in the 1940s. Similarly, public service operators such as the BBC have been in the forefront as providers of digital services that are not dictated by the vagaries of the market place, and this is important for the role of journalism in society.

The television revolution

The development of photography introduced a claim to accuracy and impartiality because of the apparent veracity of an image, but it was viewed at the time as an adjunct to print news reporting. In contrast, television fundamentally changed the media landscape for both practitioners and public. As the *Daily Mirror* stated in 1950, 'If you let a television set through the door, life can never be the same' (cited in Chapman, 2005: 207). Yet old media are never completely replaced by new ones, so at first television news was presented in almost the same way as radio. The BBC was afraid of personalizing the news, so presenters were off screen, voice only and anonymous – sober and quiet.

Nevertheless, the 'age of television' took off in the 1950s, using by and large the same technology worldwide, although its take-up varied geographically according to the affordability of sets. In Britain, the arrival of ITV following legislation in 1954 shattered broadcast journalism's mood of caution, for the BBC had been slow to appreciate the potential of the visual image. Gerald Barry commented in his *Observer* television column that: 'The sad fact has to be recorded that news on television does not exist. What has been introduced nightly into the TV programmes is a perfunctory little bulletin of news flashes composed of an announcer's voice, a caption and an indifferent still photograph. This may conveniently pass as news, but it does not begin to be television' (cited in Davis, 1976: 13, 14). As veteran broadcaster Robin Day later pointed out in his memoirs, 'It is an incredible fact of broadcasting history that in the very year that ITN began [1955] there had been a general election in which there was no coverage by BBC broadcasters of the campaign, *not even in the news bulletins.*' Sir Hugh Greene, Director General from 1960 to 1969, admitted that this was 'a tremendous abdication of responsibility' on the part of the Corporation (Day, 1989: 76, 181).

To his tremendous credit, ITN's first editor Aiden Crawley[3] succeeded in making the news more lively and human, even though he resigned soon afterwards because of the lack of air-time and resources allocated to the commercial provider. The new technology of lighter sixteen-millimetre cameras and sound helped location reporting, so ITN went for scoops, used vox pops and questioned public figures in a less deferential way than the BBC. Its local news was also an advantage as the rival BBC was more centralized at the time. In 1960 the BBC bounced back with the *Tonight* programme – a series that was on the side of the viewer and commanded audiences of nine million a night. By the early 1960s, TV began to replace radio and the press as the principal source of news, but watching TV never completely replaced listening to radio.

The power of television news

After the Second World War, the ascendancy of television, advertising and mass consumption prompted further discourse on public versus private within the media. In America, the growth of advertising, public relations and television as a communications weapon for politicians meant that the medium played a crucial part in elections. President Kennedy, for instance, would probably not have been elected without it. But as both Pierre Bourdieu (1998) and Daniel Boorstin (1963) have noted, the forms and conventions of production dictated the nature of both the viewing experience and the experience of those appearing on television. Politicians in America accepted the existing genres; they did not seek to change them.

By the late 1960s, the tone of news and current affairs was more informal and sceptical, demonstrating the democratizing trend of the era. Television has a levelling effect on rank, expertise and authority, providing viewers with a critical gaze. Relentless news coverage of civil disturbances and the Vietnam War highlighted the role of the media as both reporter and agent of rebellion in various countries. The Vietnam War was the first TV war, and journalists were criticized for encouraging opposition to American intervention. Meanwhile, protest against American intervention in Vietnam and support for causes such as peace and nuclear disarmament acquired a fashionable transcontinental appeal.

The effects of news coverage in this and other issues have been hotly debated, with claims that the American civil rights movement would not have existed without television coverage. Protests involving civil disorder tended to be newsworthy, but were said by some to be given more prominence by virtue of the attention given to them by the media. Similarly, students confronting tanks in Beijing's Tiananmen Square in 1989 showed that nations and governments cannot hide from their problems. When Mrs Thatcher referred to journalism as providing the 'oxygen of publicity' for terrorists, she highlighted contemporary debate about the effects of television. In the cases of coverage of terrorism and of missing children, the style of television treatment becomes part of the social policy process (Altheide, 1991) – a cautionary reminder of the power of broadcast news to influence policy-makers and citizens alike.

Pictures have an immediate impact that is temporal and specific, but audiences are encouraged by the medium to generalize – a single bomb can suggest an entire region at war, and tourism and investment will then be affected. At the end of the 1970s, TV news suggested that the whole of Britain was being torn asunder by strikes and social unrest, and the calming words of Prime Minister Callaghan to the contrary did not alleviate the impression that TV had implanted. 'Television embodies an old paradox: often the more we see the less we learn, the less we see the more we learn' (Crisell, 2002: 161). TV can encourage 'moral panics', such as those that arose over BSE and CJD. Furthermore, our sense of priority can be distorted by the pictures, because some news stories, such as earthquakes or floods, lend themselves more readily to protracted TV news exposure than slower processes, such as political oppression, unemployment or diplomatic and trade negotiations.

Radio's reinvention

A fashion for pirate radio and contemporary political thinking that supported the encouragement of community democracy influenced the BBC's concept of local radio, although there was no evidence of substantial demand. In Europe, three types of radio – national public with local services, independent and community – developed to meet the diverse needs of listeners. By the 1970s, radio was consumed in a different way – no longer collectively as a domestic fixture, but more personally, with different channels according to taste. The mixed programming of the BBC's cultural pyramid had given way to Radios 1–4 as sectors within the provision of public service (Radio 5 Live came later).

When the Conservatives were elected in Britain in 1970, they wanted to give commercial interests the opportunity to exploit radio, as they had done with TV in the 1950s. Independent local radio – ILR – was legislated for, with the first two stations opening in 1973. Modern VHF/FM technology allowed it to spread rapidly:

by 1983 there were forty-three stations covering more than 80 per cent of the population, although they were not necessarily profitable at first. Technology saved radio by enabling it to reinvent itself in a more portable and individualized way that ensured its worldwide survival.

Breakthroughs such as FM improved the quality of transmission and reception, and these were accompanied by changing radio usage within consumer lifestyles. The latter came to be affected by the profusion of transistor radios, hi-fi stereo tuners, car radios, Walkmans and other devices that made listening more flexible and adaptable. With the introduction of digital radio the number of channels exceeded the amount of programming available to fill them, a situation first encountered in early radio: in this respect, history had turned full circle.

Global and local trends

From the very beginning, television invention was an international affair, with big corporations emerging as dominant players in the manufacture of hardware. Yet, until the 1980s, newspapers and basic broadcasting systems tended to be nationally owned and regulated. The last terrestrial channel to be launched in the UK before cable and satellite arrived in the 1980s was Channel 4, and as such it did not require new viewing hardware. Welsh language activists threatened civil disobedience and hunger strikes if they did not receive their own separate channel, resulting in S4C. When it was first launched, Channel 4 embodied a new version of PSB, commercially funded yet with no advertising sales of its own, financed instead by subscriptions from the ITV contractors – a blend of PSB with the commercial model. In 1983 UK breakfast TV was launched, once more expanding choice, although the programming mix soon developed into a blend of trite and bland as Roland Rat replaced broadcast journalism's 'mission to explain'.[4]

From the late 1970s it was becoming clear that emerging media globalization was being facilitated by Cold War politics that had created frameworks of international support for the 'American way of life', as expressed by media products with business dominance. The privatization of communication systems and deregulation – an approach espoused by President Reagan in the United States, Margaret Thatcher in Britain, the International Monetary Fund and the World Bank – were accelerated by the development of new satellite and digital technologies. Some people, especially in the USA, hoped that cable would mean a more progressive future for television with greater access, while others were more concerned with the business potential. By the time the broadband environment had arrived, the business model had clearly triumphed.

At the same time, a closer link emerged between what audiences consume and what they pay for, a tendency that leads to more entertainment and less current affairs and news. However, the advent of digital terrestrial TV allowed the public services in Europe to champion a technological development that promised to free up the previously limited analogue spectrum. German, British and Italian public broadcasters offered the widest range of additional digital services, and the BBC launched a range of niche channels for children, the arts, youth and news, although audiences were initially small. The Internet and the broadband infrastructure offered the consumer enhanced functions, such as interactivity and personalization via cable

TV, but the question arose as to whether PSB could survive this trend. In particular, how were public broadcasters to provide a forum for the nation among all those narrowcast channels? This is the point at which history meets the future.

Conclusion: pictures win

Steve Jobs, co-founder of Apple, said in 1996, 'The Web is going to be very important, but it's certainly not going to be like the first time somebody saw a television . . . it's not going to be *that* profound' (cited in Stephens, 1998: 11). Like Jobs, historians take a long view. This present 'digital age' is said to be a revolution, but communications have experienced previous revolutions – the invention and development of writing and the invention and development of the printing press. Both of these demonstrated that it takes a long time to realize the potential, much longer than those living through the changes expect (*ibid.*: 9). New developments are usually attacked during the early stages, for, as radio and TV have both demonstrated, new forms of communication can change how we look at the world.

About half the world's population now spend the bulk of their leisure time watching television. In only eight years, TV penetrated more than 50 per cent of all American homes. The reach of computers has been slower and less profound (*ibid.*: 11). The moving image revolution could prove as powerful as its predecessors, for it is still young and will gain new power as it increasingly dominates the Web. 'There are indeed decidedly different kinds of thinking associated with moving images: jumpy, fast-moving, ironic, surface-orientated ways of thinking. Some we have seen – and already grown comfortable with. Some we have likely not seen yet' (*ibid.*: 12).

Meanwhile, convergence of media forms has been characterized by unaccountable oligopoly. Multinationals tended to expand using both vertical and horizontal integration, so a film, for instance, will spawn a soundtrack, a book and merchandising such as dolls and toys, with the potential also for CD-ROMs, video games, amusement-park rides and even a spin-off television show. Journalism and public affairs are less attractive, unless they serve business interests. As one journalist observed, 'We have experienced an expansion of technology but the agenda of the media has shrunk' (Pilger, 2001). Coverage of 9/11 demonstrated that although audiences are fragmenting, the potential for pictures to bring a nation together still exists. However, a small number of media conglomerates are competing over a limited range of big stories.

Much of the information revolution is about disseminating the news, not collecting it. Increasingly viewers are getting the raw elements of news as the end product. As the Internet shapes the media landscape towards a more decentralized and community-orientated form of publishing, media organizations are no longer gatekeepers of information like the BBC was in 1930. However, the lone consumer making choices at the computer will still need broadcast journalism to make sense of the world, to interpret, to work through consensus while exploring diversity. Broadcast journalists can use their skills and their medium to support the interchange of content and ideas between networked communities, but for this we must first understand the needs of communities – back to the social role of broadcast journalism.

Notes

1 For a comparison of the tactical opposition by the print industries in Britain and the United States, see Chapman, 2005: 154–8.
2 The BBC started audience research in 1936.
3 In the early days of TV journalism, the new profession had no existing career ladder, so leading figures often came from other walks of life. Crawley, an ex-Labour MP, was also well known as a Second World War Hurricane fighter pilot who had been shot down by the Nazis, escaped and been recaptured four times as a prisoner of war, and also helped others to escape. His wife, the author Virginia Cowles, was killed in a car crash and his two sons died later in an aeroplane crash (Day, 1989: 76).
4 Under Greg Dyke 100 newsroom journalists lost their jobs to make way for Roland Rat. The author was (commercial) TVam's first on-screen reporter for the North of England at the time.

References

Allan, Stuart (2004) *News Culture*, 2nd edn, Buckingham: Open University Press
Altheide, D.L. (1991) *Media Worlds in the Post Journalism Era*, New York: Aldine de Gruyter
BBC (1926) Memorandum by C.P. Atkinson, May, London: BBC Written Archives Centre
BBC (1997) *A Celebration of BBC Radio: 75 Years of the BBC*, London: BBC Worldwide
Boorstin, Daniel (1963) *The Image*, Harmondsworth: Penguin
Bourdieu, Pierre (1998) *On Television*, London: Pluto Press
Chapman, J. (2005) *Comparative Media History: 1789 to the Present*, Cambridge: Polity Press
Crisell, A. (2002) *An Introductory History of British Broadcasting*, 2nd edn, London: Routledge
Davis, A. (1976) *Television: Here Is the News*, London: Severn
Day, R. (1989) *Grand Inquisitor: Memoirs by Sir Robin Day*, London: Weidenfeld and Nicolson
Ferrell Lowe, G. and Hujanen, T. (eds) (2003) *Broadcasting and Convergence: New Articulations of the Public Service Remit*, Goteberg: Nordicom
Pilger, J. (2001) Speech to the Department of Journalism, London College of Communication, University of the Arts, London, 15 February
Stephens, M. (1998) 'Which Communications Revolution Is It, Anyway?', *Journalism and Mass Communication Quarterly*, 75, 1: 9–13
Stroud, J. (1969) *Special Correspondent*, London: Ward Lock

Paying the piper

Funding broadcast news

Deborah Wilson

Introduction

Why is there a need to consider the funding of broadcast news? What does it mean to those entering the profession? By considering how the specific nature of the funding of broadcast news and current affairs impacts on the profession and operations of the broadcast journalist, I will argue that it impinges on both the job market and the journalist's practice. To this end, I provide an overview of funding models for the BBC and commercial television and radio, followed by an evaluation of the current position of staff and freelance broadcast journalists, focusing on those increasingly operating in a multimedia and multi-platform environment. Finally there will be a snapshot of the threats and opportunities for broadcast journalists.

The ownership, and therefore finance, of broadcast journalism differs fundamentally from that of the printed press. While they both have to operate within the same legal constraints, the regulatory frameworks are different and the consumer has quite different expectations of political impartiality and ethical standards. It could be argued that it is the influence of market forces that has historically set broadcast news apart from print, but this distinction is narrowing. Newspapers' primary function has always been to sell their own product, but broadcast news has not been driven by the commercial imperative to the same extent, although it is becoming far more market driven and, particularly in the case of ITV news, has to satisfy both the criteria of the public service broadcaster and the need to make money.

Funding models past and present

It seems strange to broadcast journalists now, in the twenty-first century, to consider the challenges facing the pioneers of broadcast news, but the founding of the BBC and its unique source of finance has moulded the nature of public service broadcasting in the UK. The term 'broadcast' was, by default, radio in the 1920s and the initial discussions over the introduction of radio news in what was to become the BBC in the UK was subject to extensive negotiation. As Briggs (1961: 97) outlines, there was an emphasis that only 'bona fide radio manufacturing companies' could apply for broadcasting rights, effectively blocking the potential opportunities at that time for newspapers to expand into broadcasting, and the inclusion of a news service by any broadcaster was to be subject to greater scrutiny and further deliberations. The early plans drawn up in 1922 by the Wireless Sub-Committee of the Imperial Communications Committee, who were tasked to consider the way forward for broadcasting in the UK, detailed that 'the broadcasting of news not already printed was to be prohibited except by special permission' (*ibid.*; see also Chapter 1, this volume).

The Crawford Committee (1926) asserted that broadcasters should be free of commercial domination. The first BBC licence fee was ten shillings (fifty pence), it was paid by the owners of a radio receiver, and the aim was to raise revenue for the output rather than make a profit for shareholders. This remains the same in the twenty-first century. The main development over the intervening years is that the BBC, as with any public service broadcaster, must now justify its existence (and thereby its licence fee) while competing against a plethora of providers of broadcast news for a critical mass of viewers and listeners. The amount of revenue allocated to the BBC's news output in 1927 was minimal and was incorporated into the overall budget, not meriting a separate entry in the *BBC Handbook* of the time, the only costs noted being the 'royalties . . . for the news supplied by the news agencies' (1929: 50), although the cost of broadcasting the Grand National was 'approximately £175, made up of: hire of trunk lines, expenses of engineers, and the commentator's fee and expenses' (*ibid.*). Nearly eighty years later, the costs for delivery of BBC News in the UK were £89.5 million for newsgathering and £23.1 million for BBC News 24's 'additional costs', making a total of £112.6 million (figures for 2005/6; Ofcom, 2007b).

In the early days of the BBC, the licence payment was for radio only. This element of the BBC's licence fee would disappear in later years as the cost of collecting it became too great to be sustainable. But the payment for the first provision of news to the BBC was dependent on the number of licences and the BBC was not permitted to take news from any other sources for the duration of the agreement. It is interesting to note, considering the BBC has acquired a global reputation for its newsgathering and objective reporting, that the integrity of the BBC's news then relied on the fact that it was a summary of copy supplied by a number of news agencies. In its turn, the BBC began to investigate the potential of using the voices of those featured in a news item (not something a newspaper could do) or live commentary on an event (again, something not yet experienced by the public). The Press Agreement was waived during the General Strike of 1926, as most of the national newspapers could not be published, and it was this that led to the formation of a BBC News Service and the transfer of editorial control, expressed thus in the *BBC Handbook* of the time: 'The BBC has founded the nucleus of a Press of its own which will expand to be an important safeguard of, and auxiliary to, the microphone' (1928: 346).

Broadcast news in the UK is dominated by television, which, in itself, is dominated by the BBC. The other two main news producers are ITN and Sky News. The BBC provides news for its domestic consumers via its terrestrial television channels, both networks and regions, and on its rolling news service – BBC News 24 – and the Internet. The licence fee is constantly subject to debate, particularly at the time of the renewal of the Royal Charter. In an independent report prepared in April 2006 for the BBC Board of Governors on public perception of the continuation of the licence fee, it was suggested that although the fee was not universally popular with the British public, on balance the value assigned to the BBC's output outweighed any calls for alternative funding of the eighty-year-old institution, and that opinion remains remarkably steadfast in the face of continuing rises.

> There is a 'bigger picture' which emerges consistently from all research which presents the public with realistic policy options for the BBC and requires them to think carefully about their responses. In this 'bigger picture', the BBC is highly trusted, highly valued, and assumed to be the public's most important guide to the transition to a fully digital broadcasting world. To play this role, it will need enough resources and enough flexibility to adapt to changes in

markets, technologies, and the needs of society. Inevitably, the costly transition to digital (infrastructure, services, communication, and probably targeted help) will require a higher licence fee for the next few years than if these costs did not arise.

(BBC, 2006: 28)

ITN supplies television news to ITV1, Channel 4, More4 and Setanta Sports. Although ITN is a commercial provider, its clients must satisfy public service obligations, including the provision of news programmes to the regions. ITN now employs several hundred journalists and is an independent company owned by four shareholders: ITV plc (40 per cent); Daily Mail and General Trust (20 per cent); Reuters (20 per cent); and United Business Media (20 per cent). There is increasing online provision, with ITN 'On' providing multi-platform content for mobile phone operators, websites and more than 260 commercial radio stations across the UK on the IRN network (ITN On, 2008). ITN's facilities are used by GMTV, the breakfast channel, which is partly owned by ITV plc, but maintains its own newsgathering operation (Ofcom, 2007b: 18). ITN also supplies commercial radio via Independent Radio News. IRN's first bulletin was in 1973, when the service aimed to provide news, both text and audio, to the rapidly expanding local, regional and national commercial radio networks. Initial funding was in the form of cash payments from the stations, but this was replaced by advertising airtime in 1987 (IRN 2008). Now IRN produces a wide range of output, twenty-four hours a day, including text copy, audio, packages and full radio bulletins. Income is generated by short advertisements at the end of news bulletins.

Sky News, launched in February 1989, was the UK's first twenty-four-hour news channel. It started with just six staff but now has 500 based in the UK and abroad. Following the closure of the twenty-four-hour channel provided by ITV, Sky News is currently the only British independent all-day TV news channel. Sky spends more than £50 million on its news every year (Sky, 2008: 16). This does not, in itself, qualify as public service broadcasting but in supplying news to Channel Five it must comply in part with the obligations imposed on a PSB licensee.[1] In May 2007 it became the first twenty-four-hour news channel to exist in the virtual world. Second Life, a 3-D world which has been built and operated by millions of users, houses a replica of the Sky News studio. Users can read bulletins from the presenter's chair or operate the control room. News clips are offered on a virtual TV set (Ofcom, 2007c).

An unholy alliance: ratings and the news

The development of models of finance has been influenced by issues of ownership, accountability, governance and editorial influence, and the dominance of audience preferences has been increasingly unavoidable. Since competition began for the BBC at a national level with the launch of ITV and its dedicated news service, ITN, there has been an unavoidable symbiotic relationship between the audience and the viewing figures for news programmes and the finance of broadcast journalism. If viewing figures fall for a major news bulletin or current affairs programme, the agenda, style and choice of stories covered can be affected. Editorial teams are faced with the issue of ratings when a bulletin follows a less popular programme or its place in the schedules inherits poor figures. Despite efforts to increase ratings for current affairs programmes by popularizing the content, broadcasters have to contend with diminishing interest from the viewing public.

Meanwhile, in radio, as Niblock and Machin (2007: 191) found in their study of IRN, the sector is becoming increasingly market driven: 'there is a strong drive to produce news feed that is less for a public, but rather that fits particular demographics, which can be used to locate the world of news events in the lives of particular market-segmented groups'. Their study refers to lifestyle groups and outlines how the news process complies with these brand identities, and they found that 'newsworthiness is but one criterion in the selection and packaging of news, and operates alongside production requirements and market-awareness. This is vital for the survival of commercial news organisations' (*ibid.*: 202). It is perhaps more understandable that commercial radio increasingly employs marketing strategies, with advertising revenue falling and cuts being made to workforces.

Twenty-four-hour news

The greatest expansion in television news provision came in the 1990s. In addition to the growing digitalization of news production processes, television channels dedicated to twenty-four-hour news provision proliferated. With these channels, concerns about other programmes affecting their audience do not apply. These channels could be considered, once selected, to have a loyal audience. But the brand is dominant here, with, for example, BBC News 24 relying on the perceived integrity of the country's longest-established provider of broadcast news and Sky News establishing a reputation for swift reaction to news stories: 'We can't afford to be on background or analysis when there's a breaking story' (Nick Pollard, then head of Sky News, in Hudson and Rowlands, 2007: 396). But twenty-four-hour television news is already on the decline. Sky News is no longer to be found on digital cable and is only now received in satellite-equipped homes, while ITV's all-day news channel was closed in December 2005 (Ofcom, 2007b: 21).

Up to now, sponsorship has not affected news output, but it could creep into a number of areas of factual programming, as is the case in the USA. It was rejected as an option for the BBC in any form by the Department of Media, Culture and Sport (DCMS) in its review document *The Future Funding of the BBC* in 1999, along with advertising in any of the BBC's own branded channels and its online provision, acknowledging the EC Directive on Broadcasting banning sponsorship of news and current affairs programming. The Ofcom Broadcasting Code, which does not apply to BBC services, specifically prohibits sponsorship of 'news bulletins and news desk presentations on radio and news and current affairs programmes on television' (Ofcom, 2005: Section 9.1).

The working broadcast journalist – survival techniques

Funding is of paramount importance in two ways. How does it influence the job market? Can a newly qualified broadcast journalist get a staff job or survive as a full-time freelance journalist? And how does it impact on the practice of journalism, the independence of the news agenda, editorial control, the resources needed to carry out thorough, accurate, investigative research? The environment is constantly shifting, and this inevitably impinges on the work of the broadcast journalist. The profession, as it is practised in the UK, benefits from the tradition of public service broadcasting and the existence of a politically and commercially independent press. But the environment is increasingly competitive – both for the news organizations and for the journalists working within them – and all the major providers currently have to make economic cuts, which means job losses.

Certainly the job of broadcast journalist is not an easy one. They have to be jacks of all trades, working twelve hours a day in some cases, satisfying the demands of multi-channel and multi-platform output. Media and news organizations are focusing on exploiting media technologies to reach audiences and maximize value and cost effectiveness. Professional development and ongoing skills training are essential for the converged or converging journalist with an increasing blurring of the boundaries between print and broadcast and a growing expectation of multi-skilling.

There was already recognition in the 1990s that technological developments could be responsible for an increase in journalists' workloads and pressures as they would be expected to work in a multimedia environment, and that the quality of journalism would suffer as the quantity of news production increased (Cottle and Ashton, 1999: 33). Cottle and Ashton found that:

> the multiskilled environment of multimedia production, contrary to managerial statements of intent, appears to have compromised the ability of journalists to become familiar with, knowledgeable about, and responsive to local communities and their news reporting interests and needs ... [and] despite corporate and management claims to the contrary, contributed to the production of more standardised news treatments and formats, and led to more superficial journalist involvement with selected news stories and their sources.
> (*Ibid*.: 38)

However, there is increasing recognition that some BBC journalists welcome multi-skilling as a form of professional enhancement. BBC Video Journalist (VJ) Trainer Warwick Wise says:

> With video journalism, you are working harder, there's no getting away from that, but you're also seeing genuine benefits. It's not just about saving money. If you can edit and film yourself, all those things are going to feed into each other. From the manager's point of view, they're looking at the finances, and clearly it's much cheaper to send one person out than three. But from the bottom-up argument, the journalists themselves take to it very quickly, because it's such a good way of getting an intimacy and access in interview situations and allowing for a more character-based approach to storytelling in news.[2]

Threats and opportunities

Broadcast journalists

There has never been a time when the funding of the provision of broadcast news and current affairs has been so threatened as it is now. Cuts have been widespread, with a narrowing of provision for the consumer and the availability of staff positions decimated. The opportunities for freelance journalists and documentary-makers have been similarly restricted. In 2008, BBC News 24 announced its decision to cut senior posts as part of its cost-cutting targets following the licence fee settlement, halving its strand editors from six to three (Rushton, 2008). Unions are warning that ITV's plans to cut regional news programmes offered in England and Wales from seventeen to ten could mean the loss of hundreds of jobs. Executive Chairman of ITV, Michael Grade, said: 'the current investment of £120m a year was out of proportion to its commercial value and any public benefit' and claimed he was looking 'to make savings of between £35m and £40m a year' (Thomas, 2007).

A report was published by the regulator Ofcom in June 2007 on the prospects for television news in the UK. The research showed that the quantity of broadcast news was greater than ever before, and that consumers expected high-quality, well-funded television news across all the main public service broadcasters. But it identified 'significant challenges' for news programming in the UK nations and regions, and acknowledged that while:

> it is likely to remain in the interests of the commercial public service broadcasters (ITV, Channel 4 and Five) to maintain high quality UK and international news services in competition with the BBC . . . broadcasters accept that commercial challenges might impede the delivery of some in-depth and investigative forms of news programmes.
>
> (Ofcom, 2007a)

ITN and ITV trumpeted their six-year contract renewal in April 2007 – assuring them of the provision of news and the funding to modernize their studio complex. However, the National Union of Journalists (NUJ) has been negotiating alongside the broadcasting union BECTU in talks on changes to working practices and conditions. Their pay agreement of December 2007 incorporated the need for talks as ITN was proposing significant savings in staff costs (NUJ, 2008).

The government has so far protected the BBC's funding model. The DCMS, in its report on the future of the BBC's funding, was clear that news programming could suffer if the BBC joined the competition for advertising, sponsorship or subscriptions:

> The incentive on the broadcaster is therefore to deliver the largest possible audience at the lowest possible cost . . . advertising funding tends to encourage the production of programmes with shallow but wide appeal – for example, a game show or sitcom would be shown in preference to a news programme, classic serial or a listed sporting event – especially at peak viewing time.
>
> (DCMS, 1999: 206)

Investigative reporting is considered to be the cornerstone of 'good' journalism. As the most expensive of all forms of broadcast journalism, this naturally is the most threatened. Winston credits the success of the Watergate investigation to 'management's expensive decision to pay its reporters to spend far more time researching and writing' (2005: 391). This genre of journalism is arguably the form most jealously guarded by a democratic society, yet cash-strapped news providers, finding it the greatest drain on their resources, struggle to sustain its production.

Nick Davies (200: 62) summarises applying commercial logic to news as 'highly damaging, cutting out human contact and with it the possibility of finding stories; cutting down time and with it the possibility of checking; and thus producing stories in greater numbers at greater speed and of much worse quality'. This 'churnalism', as he terms it, prevails in regional television and radio newsrooms where staff cuts have been the greatest in percentage terms.

Independent current affairs production

The picture for independent producers of news and current affairs is mixed: while there is a healthy job market in factual programming and in info/docutainment, the body of independent producers is competing for declining slots. The game has become increasingly competitive (see Chapter 18), with an increased emphasis on marketing and pitching successfully for a slot of crucial importance.

But the picture is not all doom and gloom. According to the BBC's *Annual Report for 2006–7*, while the number of hours of news and weather decreased from 2,508 to 2,463 on BBC1 and from 673 to 558 on BBC2, current affairs output increased slightly on both channels in the same year (BBC, 2007). Meanwhile, BBC Radio saw a decline in news and weather on Radios 1, 2 and 5 Live and remained the same on Radios 3 and 4, but current affairs rose dramatically from 353 hours on Radio 2 to 504 hours. Radio 4 was very slightly down and Radio 5 Live up a little. The rise in news and weather on the BBC's Asian network was solely responsible for the overall increase in these sectors across the BBC Radio networks from 11,649 to 12,642 hours. Similarly, the same network's reduction in current affairs output forced the total across networks down from 3,803 to 3,470. News and current affairs as a whole therefore rose slightly from 15,452 to 16,112 hours. Costs per hour for the BBC fell in both news and weather and current affairs from £104,000 to £100,200.

Conclusion

In a time of rapid technological change, which affects broadcasting as much as any other industry, commercial factors determine its usage for more economically efficient newsgathering, processing and dissemination. The pressures, including both challenges and opportunities, this puts upon the practising broadcast journalist in terms of job availability and sustainability, working conditions and professional satisfaction have been outlined above. Any ideological perspective that more intelligent technologies can increase the effectiveness of the broadcast journalist, indeed of any journalist, has its flaws. The expectations of news managers that more can be achieved within the same time, that you can 'get more news for your money', may well compromise the quality of the journalism, no matter how advanced the technologies have become. The challenge now for journalists in an increasingly converged and competitive environment is to maintain high standards of accurate, well researched, responsible reporting and to guard against allowing the pressures of the need for speed, multi-platform delivery and unavoidable financial cuts to compromise those aims.

Notes

1 'Section 264 of the Communications Act 2003 requires Ofcom to assess the designated public service broadcasters, taken together, in terms of their delivery of the public service purposes set out in the Act. The designated PSB broadcasters are the BBC, ITV1, GMTV, Channel 4, Five, S4C and Teletext' (Ofcom, 2007b).
2 Interview with the author.

References

BBC (1928 and 1929) *BBC Handbook*, London: BBC

BBC (2006) 'The BBC Licence Fee Bid: What Does the Public Think?', April, at http://www.bbccharterreview.org.uk/seminars/2006/BBCGovernors-Independent_Report_%20Prof_PBarwise.pdf (accessed 23 February 2008)

BBC (2007) *Annual Report and Accounts 2006–7*, at http://www.bbc.co.uk/annual report/pdfs/reach.pdf (accessed 24 February 2008)

Briggs, A. (1961) *The History of Broadcasting in the United Kingdom, Vol. 1: The Birth of Broadcasting*, London: Oxford University Press

Bromley, M. (1996) 'How Multiskilling Will Change the Journalist's Craft', *Press Gazette*, 22 March, p. 16

Bromley, M. (1997) 'The End of Journalism? Changes in the Workplace Practices in the Press and Broadcasting in the 1990s', in M. Bromley and T. O'Malley (eds), *A Journalism Reader*, London, Routledge

Cottle, S. and Ashton, M. (1999) 'From BBC Newsroom to BBC Newscentre: On Changing Technology and Journalist Practices', *Convergence: The International Journal of Research into New Media Technologies*, 5 (22): 22–43

Cox, D. (2003) 'Public and Be Damned', *British Journalism Review*, 14 (13): 13–19

Davies, N. (2008) *Flat Earth News*, London: Chatto and Windus

Department of Culture, Media and Sport (1999) 'The Future Funding of the BBC', July, at http://www.culture.gov.uk/Reference_library/Publications/archive_1999/fundingh_bbc.htm (accessed 23 February 2008)

Hudson, G. and Rowlands, S. (2007) *The Broadcast Journalism Handbook*, Harlow: Longman

Independent Radio News (2008) 'A Brief History', at http://www.irn.co.uk/Contact Us.aspx (accessed 10 February 2008)

Independent Television News (2008) On Homepage, at http://itn.co.uk/on (accessed 25 February 2008)

National Union of Journalists (2008) 'The NUJ Has a Strong Presence at News Provider ITN', at http://www.nuj.org.uk/innerPagenuj.html?docid=668and string=broadcast (accessed 23 February 2008)

Niblock, S. and Machin, D. (2007) 'News Values for Consumer Groups: The Case of Independent Radio News, London, UK', *Journalism*, 8 (2): 184–204

Ofcom (2005) 'The Ofcom Broadcasting Code', July, at http://www.ofcom.org. uk/tv/ifi/codes/bcode/ (accessed 25 February 2008)

Ofcom (2007a) 'New News, Future News: The Challenges for Television News after Digital Switch-over', 26 June, at http://www.ofcom.org.uk/research/tv/ reports/newnews/ (accessed 23 February 2008)

Ofcom (2007b) 'Public Service Broadcasting Annual Report', March, at www.ofcom.org.uk/media/news/2007/03/nr_20070322 (accessed 28 February 2008)

Ofcom (2007c) 'The Communications Market 2007', August, at http://www. ofcom.org.uk/research/cm/cmr07/tv/ (accessed 29 February 2008)

Rushton, K. (2008) 'News 24 Halves Strand Editors to Reduce Costs', *Broadcast*, 13 February, at http://www.broadcastnow.co.uk/news/multichannel/2008/02/ news_24_halves_strand_editors_to_reduce_costs.html (accessed 23 February 2008)

Sky (2008) 'The Sky Story', at http://media.corporate-ir.net/media_files/irol/ 10/104016/TheSkyStory/BSBTSS07b.htm (accessed 27 February 2008)

Thomas, L. (2007) 'Bectu Slams ITV Regional News Cuts', *Broadcast*, 13 September, at http://www.broadcastnow.co.uk/news/bectu_slams_itv_regional_news_cuts. html (accessed 26 February 2008)

Winston, B. (2005) *Messages: Free Expression, Media and the West from Gutenberg to Google*, London: Routledge

Eyes, ears and clicks

The battle for an audience

Marie Kinsey

Most journalists have grown up with the idea that we tell people the news which we think they should be told. On demand news means that people can choose the news they want, when they want it. And they can interact with it, rant about it and contribute to it.

(Simon Bucks, associate editor, Sky News, 2007)

Introduction

News is for people. That should be a statement of the obvious, but in the heat of a breaking story and under the pressure of deadlines it's very easy to forget that there is an audience out there. There are real people listening to your radio programme, watching your television package, checking out your website. And increasingly that audience is talking back, via blogs, phone-ins, emails or text messages and contributing news. Journalism has come a long way from the days when the audience was perceived, if recognized at all, as a passive receptor of whatever information or story took the whim of an editor, or an editor felt the audience 'should know'.

Audiences matter because commercial broadcasters use ratings and audience profiles to attract advertising, while public service broadcasters like the BBC must justify the licence fee. News and current affairs programming is not exempt from this reality. In the early twenty-first century, measuring and analysing audiences for television, radio and the Web has become increasingly sophisticated, but the imperative of delivering an audience has never been stronger.

In Britain minute-by-minute television audience data is gathered by BARB, the Broadcasters' Audience Research Bureau. It was set up in 1981 as a not-for-profit organization, and it is now jointly owned by the BBC, Channel 4, ITV, Five, BSkyB and the Institute of Practitioners in Advertising. Radio audiences are measured by RAJAR, Radio Joint Audience Research, established in 1992 and wholly owned by the BBC and the RadioCentre, which represents Britain's commercial radio companies. In 1996 they were joined by ABC Electronic, a subsidiary of the Audit Bureau of Circulation, which has measured newspaper sales since 1931. ABCe audits website traffic to agreed definitions. It does not yet cover the whole sector, but most national newspapers have signed up, with some broadcasters periodically putting their figures through an audit. Website traffic is also measured by research surveys conducted by such organizations as Nielsen NetRatings, Hitwise and comScore.

This chapter will examine how broadcasters engage with their audience, how they determine what the audience is and how audience figures are calculated in a multi-channel, multi-platform environment. How are audiences identified, selected and targeted and how are audience measurement techniques changing to reflect the new multimedia world?

The environment

According to the broadcast regulator Ofcom (2006), the multimedia world in Britain is made up of more than 350 television channels, 40 of them broadcast on digital terrestrial television (DTT). There are more than 330 radio stations and 700 Internet service providers. BARB (2007a) says that by 2007 nearly nine million homes had satellite television and the same again had DTT. Two-thirds of the population had a computer at home, and half of these have broadband Internet access. According to RAJAR (2007), 20 per cent of the population live in homes with a digital radio. Now that people listen to the radio on a computer or via their television and pick up news via their mobile phones, finding, then keeping, an audience is not only increasingly difficult but of crucial importance.

In 2004 in a speech to the *FT* New Media and Broadcasting Conference, the BBC's then director of New Media and Technology, Ashley Highfield, invoked a well-known 1970s drinks advertisement to characterize the implications of this proliferation of provision and plethora of platforms. He called it 'Martini Media' – media that can be consumed any time, any place, anywhere.

Advances in digital technology have made this convergence possible, and journalism a global enterprise and a 'two way street' (Hargreaves, 2003: 242) where interactivity between journalist and audience is the norm. At the same time the sheer amount of choice available to listeners and viewers has made it more important for broadcasters to know not just how big their audience is, but what sort of people compose it. As radio and television stations invest more in their websites and traditional print media encroach on the broadcasters' territory, it is important to know how many people use them, how busy the site is, how often people visit, what they see when they get there and what they do.

The television audience

The most immediately obvious consequence of this amount of choice is declining audience numbers for individual television programmes, so-called audience frag-mentation. Highfield (2006) believes that by 2011 a prime-time hit will be 'anything that breaks through four million viewers'. In 1994, he said, 182 programmes reached more than ten million viewers; by 2004, it was just nineteen.

According to BARB data, we are each still watching about twenty-five hours of television a week, slightly less in the summer and more in the winter. It's a figure that has remained remarkably consistent in recent years. The big change has been the share of viewing accounted for by satellite and cable channels, which has jumped from just over three hours a week in 1998 to nearly nine hours a week in 2007. In the same period the BBC's share has fallen from over nine hours to seven hours and ITV is down from over ten hours a week to just over seven hours.

Television audiences are measured both quantitatively and qualitatively. BARB conducts a continuous Establishment Survey involving 52,000 interviews a year to monitor the pattern of television ownership and the demographic make-up of the population. From this information it recruits a panel it says is representative of the twenty-four million or more households in the whole of the UK and of the population in each BBC and ITV region. Presently the panel consists of 5,100 homes returning data from about 11,500 viewers.

Once a household has joined the panel, every television set and video recorder is monitored electronically via a black box the size of a hardback book. It automatically collects information about the programme and channel being viewed which is then uploaded to a data-processing centre every night. Individuals, including guests, have to register their presence in a room with a television set switched on by pressing a button allocated to them on a 'peoplemeter' handset (BARB, 2007a).

Apart from having immensely detailed numerical data, BARB is also able to provide detailed demographic and lifestyle data. The Establishment Survey monitors standard demographics such as age, social class, gender, working status and number of people in the household. In 2006 BARB undertook a Lifestyle Insights Survey which, according to its chief executive Bjarne Thelin, 'allows a dynamic analysis of television audiences reached by both programmes and commercials' (BARB, 2006). The survey covers general interests, leisure activities, holidays, travel, cars, newspaper and radio loyalty, home and business spending, computers and Internet usage.

If advertisers wish to target a particular group, data is available to examine their viewing habits. For example, the survey found that men aged sixteen to forty-four from the socio-economic groups ABC1 and with broadband computer access watched television for an average sixteen hours a week in October 2006 – noticeably less than the figure for all adults with broadband (BARB, 2007b).

The radio audience

'*Video Killed the Radio Star*' by the Buggles was the first pop video played on MTV on its launch on 1 August 1981, even though only a few thousand people on a single cable system in New Jersey could see it (Stuever, 2006). Hindsight suggests its sentiments were wishful thinking, as have been most of the dire predictions that the popularity and growth of television would see off radio, the so-called 'invisible medium' (Lewis and Booth, 1989).

Radio's heyday was arguably during and immediately after the Second World War. By the outbreak of war in September 1939 there were seventy-three radio licences for every hundred households in the United Kingdom (Briggs, 1965: 253). Millions tuned in to the evening news bulletin. Nearly seventy years later, according to RAJAR (2007), about 90 per cent of the UK population listen to the radio for at least five minutes every week. Unlike television, radio is almost invariably a 'secondary activity': we listen to it while doing something else – driving, the ironing, cooking. We may be engrossed in what we hear or it may barely register. This makes the radio listener a different animal to the television viewer, and analysing the audience is somewhat more complicated (Crisell, 1994).

RAJAR's audience measurement is entirely quantitative and, like BARB, is based on a survey. It publishes quarterly figures covering all radio in Britain derived from respondents filling in a diary. Diaries are personalized according to the radio stations available in any given area and listening is recorded in quarter-hour segments, where respondents are asked to note down any time they listened to the radio for more than five minutes, what station they tuned in to, where they listened and whether they were listening via the Internet, on a digital or analogue radio or via digital television.

Audience is calculated in a number of ways, including 'reach', 'share', 'average hours' and 'total hours'. A station's reach is the number of people who tune in at least once to a particular station during a given period. Share is the percentage of the total available audience taken by an individual station. Average hours are defined in two ways: as hours listened to a particular station averaged over the total number of *listeners*, or averaged over the total *population*. Total hours are the overall number of hours spent listening to a particular station (RAJAR 2007). RAJAR does not conduct qualitative research into audience lifestyles or interests – that's left to individual stations.

The numbers game

Both BARB and RAJAR ultimately derive their audience numbers from a sample of the population, and, as Starkey (2004) argues, broadcasters' faith in the data may be misplaced. Both organizations use non-random sampling techniques, which means they positively select different 'types' of respondents according to the population being surveyed. One concern is that certain demographics – young people, some ethnic minorities – may not be included in BARB's 'private households'. And if a station or programme is aiming at a particular sector of the market, then the final figures (in RAJAR's case expressed as a percentage of *all* adults) may not accurately represent its position within its target market. Success on the station's terms may not be reflected in the official figures.

Then there is the human factor. Both organizations assume that those taking part in the surveys remember their listening accurately or faithfully press the button to register their presence in a room every time they watch television. And, more fundamentally, both assume that the respondents tell the truth. A telephone survey of radio listening in New York (Frankel, 1969) found that the responses were only 91 per cent accurate – some people failed to identify correctly when prompted the station to which they were currently listening. Furthermore, a respondent may have 'heard' a programme but not 'listened' to it.

A study of households with BARB's set meters (Collett and Lamb, 1986) which placed video cameras inside television cabinets to record what viewers did while watching television found people doing a range of other social activities. 'There was a lot of sleeping, snoring, chatting, necking, wandering in and out, scrapping over the remote control' (*ibid*: in Beckett, 2001). More recently, *Guardian* journalist Andy Beckett (2001) found one household being told by the meter installation engineers that 'no one' prodded the control pad again if they temporarily left the room. One television was left unmetered: 'He did not bother with the television in the kitchen, which was high up on a precarious pedestal. "That's where we see the late night Channel 5 stuff that we don't want recorded," says [the viewer] with a half-joking smile.'

Sampling techniques take account of error because they are based on mathematical probability, and the larger the sample the less the impact of an error. But there is a point where increasing the size of the sample leads to only very small improvements in accuracy (Henry, 1990: 118). Counting actual viewers and listeners would be unrealistic, while costing a small fortune. According to Starkey (2004: 12): 'there is no practical way to definitively "disprove" the accuracy of audience research that has arguably been appropriately carried out by sampling.'

Radio

Both BARB and RAJAR have made changes to their methodologies and are planning more. In the case of RAJAR, for a time it looked as though the days of the diary system were numbered. As long ago as 2002 RAJAR was coming under pressure to move to an electronic system of measurement. Spectrum Radio, a niche station broadcasting to ethnic communities in London, claimed the diary survey distorted their listening figures because the sample size was too small. In 2004 Kelvin MacKenzie, a former editor of the *Sun* and former chief executive of the Wireless Group (now owned by UTV), launched a legal action against RAJAR in the High Court claiming the diary system was outdated and had consistently under-reported the audience of the group's biggest station, TalkSport, costing the company £60 million in lost advertising revenues (Tryhorn, 2004). MacKenzie lost, but in his judgement Mr Justice Lloyd acknowledged: 'It may be fair to say that each of the audiometers (electronic measurement systems) is much better than the diary system, but that does not help with the decision about which of the audiometers to adopt' (*ibid.*).

In fact, RAJAR began looking at electronic measurement systems as early as October 2000 on the instructions of its own board, and began its first tests in June 2001. In 2004 it launched an industry-wide consultation which reported early the following year, recognizing that: 'Concerns exist over the ability of the current survey to cope with industry change and the multi-channel radio future' (RAJAR, 2005). In January 2007 it began a two-year pilot scheme with the Arbitron Portable People Meter (PPM), a palm-sized, pager-like device. In a joint venture with BARB, RAJAR established an electronic measurement panel in the London area which would report alongside the quarterly sweep, with the aim of comparing the data obtained from both systems.

The difficulties with electronic measurement for radio are many. The devices work as 'audiometers' – they pick up radio signals and encode them, matching them to a particular station's output. But how much time counts as 'listening'? One minute or five minutes? How accurate are the devices in monitoring exposure to broadcast audio? Will people actually use them, particularly at breakfast time, when radio audiences are at their peak and people at their most busy?

RAJAR's own research found serious problems with early devices, mainly that they did not tell the whole truth, and it wants further evidence before committing completely:

> the uncertainty surrounding respondent compliance, and the lingering unanswered questions, mean it would have been irresponsible of RAJAR to convert to a meter-based currency. If we only have two thirds of the data for three quarters of the participating sample then we only have half of the truth. That may not matter, but we don't know that yet.
>
> (Kennedy, 2006: 3)

In April 2008 Rajar decided it knew enough to scrap the whole idea of electronic measurement. It announced it would pull the plug on its £3.5 million investment in June that year and launch an industry-wide review of radio audience research (RAJAR, 2008). It cited the rapid changes in the medium 'not only in terms of convergence and consolidation but also in terms of the rapid developments in mobile technology and the increasing significance of podcasting and time-shifted listening'. Instead, it decided to pilot an online version of the diary system aimed at increasing the scope of the survey and giving more in-depth analysis across all platforms. More significantly, and in recognition of media convergence, RAJAR's managing director Sally de la Bedoyere said: 'We would like to work more closely with organisations such as ABCe and JICIMS [Joint Industry Committee for Internet Measurement Systems] to encourage standard metrics and measuring of all station websites and traffic' (*ibid.*).

Television

BARB's present system has been running since January 2002 but this will change again to some extent from January 2010. In April 2006 the organization reported findings from an industry-wide consultation, 'Future into View', which identified three areas of concern: new forms of viewing, including via mobile phones, handheld screens and personal computers; out-of-home viewing; and in-home viewing. It identified new forms of viewing as the most potentially significant change not currently picked up by the survey:

> But these are not the only potential causes of change in our audience measurement. Other factors that might also require a change in the nature of the system, or the way in which we report data, include the increasing need to cope with ever smaller pieces of viewing and, perhaps most importantly, the willingness of the public to take part in research at all.
>
> (Bolus, 2006: 13)

From 2010 BARB's survey specification will be upgraded to include monitoring of video-on-demand, the viewing panel will be recruited for the first time by a separate organization and it will experiment with ways of monitoring viewing via computers. The sample design will encompass the UK as a whole instead of overlapping regions.

The Web audience

It's quite possible that 'audience' is the wrong word when it comes to discussing people's use of websites (see Chapter 12). People use and interact with the Web in ways quite different to how they interact with radio and television. The enormous investment made by news organizations in their websites in recent years has made it more important than ever to know how successful these sites are in attracting users. The holy grail is to bring in advertising. Web advertising is increasing rapidly: in 2004 it outstripped UK radio advertising for the first time (Timms and Milmo, 2005), taking 3.9 per cent of total spending against 3.8 per cent for radio. Two years later it overtook newspapers' share of the pie (Allen, 2007), with 11.4 per cent of total revenues against 10.9 per cent.

Measuring the success of your website has often been a matter of claim and counter-claim, and finding a way through a spider's web of definitions and methods that measure different things in different ways. It seems easy for website operators to claim millions of 'page views','visits' or 'unique users' and suggest that somehow they are ahead of the game. In 2006 *Business Week* described web metrics as a 'crapshoot' (Lacy, 2006).

Many organizations measure website traffic: Nielsen NetRatings, Hitwise, Alexa Internet, comScore and ABCe, to name but a few. Some use a survey system similar to that used by BARB, recruiting panels of up to two million Web surfers and recording their mouse clicks via a device attached to the computer. Others couple a survey with the use of tracking tags installed on a user's browser. In 2007 Nielsen NetRatings also started measuring the amount of time spent on a site. All acknowledge that Web metrics are in transition (Holahan, 2007).

The Joint Industry Committee for Web Standards (JICWEBS) has developed global definitions of terms such as 'unique user/browser', 'page impression', 'searches' and 'visits'.

Unique user/browser (How many?)
Does not measure a person, but the device through which a person interacts with a website or network, e.g. a computer or mobile phone.

Page impression (How busy?)
A file, or combination of files, sent to a user as a result of that user's request to a server. Non-requested files are excluded and one request should result in one page impression.

Visit (How often?)
A series of one or more page impressions served to a single unique user/browser within a thirty-minute period.

Search
The first page impression sent to a valid user when a search request from that user is received by the server.

In the UK ABCe does not work with just the research data but with the total activity the sites generate, including information gathered by the site operator. It published its first formal audit of website traffic using JICSWEB definitions for subscribing national newspapers in March 2007 and now its certification has expanded to include most national newspapers, some magazines and some broadcasters. Metrics have also been developed to measure streaming audio and video, email and chat.

The audience and the journalist

Broadcast journalists are always told to visualize a real person when they tell a story or read a bulletin, and in recent years market research has given newsrooms and programmes a much clearer idea of who the audience is. Harrison (2000: 116) notes that individual journalists tend not to talk about audience in terms of numbers, but to take a more 'organic and emotional' view by referring to types of people.

Most radio newsrooms will have a clear view of their target audience. For example, BBC local radio imagines a middle-aged couple, Sue and Dave. He's self-employed, she's a school secretary. Heart FM, with stations in Birmingham and London, sees its audience as mainly homeowning, intelligent, professional women who read tabloid newspapers and magazines like *Heat*. The Local Radio Group, with stations in the North East and the South, visualizes Jane, a married mum of two in her thirties who reads the *Daily Mail* and watches more ITV than BBC (Hudson and Rowlands, 2007). This means that stations will run stories that are relevant to their audience – or can be made to be relevant.

Television news tends to target a more universal audience, which brings its own set of challenges. Veteran American broadcaster Ed Murrow said the trick is to 'talk to be understood by the truck driver while not insulting the professor's intelligence' (in Ray, 2003: 70). The difficulty is that journalists tend to know more about a story than the audience does, so central to broadcast journalism is developing the skill of acknowledging the audience's intelligence but recognizing that they may not have the knowledge.

Vin Ray (2003: 71) of the BBC's College of Journalism urges all journalists to attend an audience focus group at least once in their career:

> For one thing it is encouraging to see that, by and large, people really want to understand. But it's also good to be reminded not just that 'real' people don't follow news the way you do . . . but the *extent* to which your audience doesn't follow news the way you do. Seeing this first hand will make you go back and work that bit harder to engage your viewers and really help them understand.

Conclusion

Finding and staying in touch with an audience has always been more than a matter of counting heads, important though that may be in making money or justifying the licence fee. Now that it's no longer possible to talk of 'the television audience' or 'the radio audience' or 'the Web audience' in quite such clear-cut terms, finding new and relevant ways of quantifying them is becoming more pressing. Ignoring the audience, or being ignorant of it, is no longer an option. At the end of the day, as Vin Ray (2003: 29) puts it: 'audiences have a habit of dividing [news] coverage into just two categories: interesting and dull'.

References

Allen, K. (2007) 'Online advertising share overtakes newspapers', *Guardian*, 28 March, at http://media.guardian.co.uk/advertising/story/0,,2044361,00.html (accessed 12 July 2007)

BARB (2006) *New 'Lifestyle Insights' Survey from BARB*, 5 December, at http://www.barb.co.uk/news.cfm?fullstory=true&newsid=149&flag=news (accessed 2 July 2008)

BARB (2007a) at http://www.barb.co.uk (accessed 2 July 2007)

BARB (2007b) *BARB Bulletin*, 13, February, p. 2

BARB (2008) *BARB Bulletin*, 15, February, p. 2

Beckett, A. (2001) 'Numbers game', *Guardian*, 20 November, at http://www.guardian.co.uk/media/2001/nov/20/broadcasting.g2 (accessed 2 July 2008)

Bolus, S. (2006) 'BARB UK television outlook – a view into the future', at http://www.barb.co.uk/futureIntoView.cfm?flag=futureIntoView (accessed 25 March 2008)

Briggs, A. (1965) *The History of Broadcasting in the United Kingdom, Vol. 2: The Golden Age of Wireless*, Oxford: Oxford University Press

Bucks, S. (2007) 'Blue sky thinking', *Press Gazette*, 25 May, p. 19

Collett, P. and Lamb, R. (1986) 'Watching people watching television: final report to the IBA', Oxford: University of Oxford, Department of Experimental Psychology

Crisell, A. (1994) *Understanding Radio*, London: Routledge

Frankel, L. (1969) 'The role of accuracy and precision of response in sample surveys', in W. Johnson and H. Smith Jnr (eds), *New Developments in Survey Sampling*, London: Wiley

Harrison, J. (2000) *Terrestrial TV News in Britain: The Culture of TV News Production*, Manchester: Manchester University Press

Hargreaves, I. (2003) *Journalism: Truth or Dare*, Oxford: Oxford University Press

Henry, G. (1990) *Practical Sampling*, New York: Sage

Highfield, A. (2004) 'The on-demand world is finally coming', *FT* New Media and Broadcasting Conference, 2 March

Highfield, A. (2006) 'On demand or over-hyped?', Edinburgh International Television Festival, 26 August

Holahan, C. (2007) 'Web rankings shakeup: it's about time', *Business Week*, 11 July, at http://www.businessweek.com/technology/content/jul2007/tc20070711_45 1666.htm (accessed 31 March 2008)

Hudson, G. and Rowlands, S. (2007) *The Broadcast Journalism Handbook*, Harlow: Pearson

Kennedy, P. (2006) *A Bewilderment of Meters*, London: Admap

Lacy, S. (2006) 'Web numbers: what's real?', *Business Week*, 23 October 23, http://www.businessweek.com/magazine/content/06_43/b4006095.htm? (accessed 25 March 2008)

Lewis, P.M. and Booth, J. (1989) *The Invisible Medium: Public, Commercial and Community Radio*, Basingstoke and London: Macmillan

Ofcom, (2006) 'The consumer experience', at http://www.ofcom.org.uk/research/tce/report/ (accessed 5 July 2007)

RAJAR (2005) 'The future of radio audience measurement', January, at http://www.rajar.co.uk (accessed 2 July 2007)

RAJAR (2007) at http://www.rajar.co.uk (accessed 2 July 2007)

RAJAR (2008) 'Rajar reviews future direction of radio audience research,' 28 April, at http://www.rajar.co.uk (accessed 15 May 2008)

Ray, V. (2003) *The Television News Handbook*, London: Macmillan

Starkey, G. (2004) 'Estimating audiences: sampling in television and radio audience research', *Cultural Trends*, 13 (1): 3–25

Stuever, H. (2006) '25 years down the tube', *Washington Post*, 1 August, at http://www.washingtonpost.com/wp-dyn/content/article/2006/07/31/AR2006 073101296.html (accessed 6 July 2007)

Timms, D. and Milmo, D. (2005) 'Broadband helps online advertising to overtake radio', *Guardian*, 5 April, at http://media.guardian.co.uk/advertising/story/ 0,,1452405,00.html (accessed 12 July 2007)

Tryhorn, C. (2004) 'MacKenzie faces £700,000 legal bill over RAJAR lawsuit', *Guardian*, 17 December, at http://www.guardian.co.uk/media/2004/dec/17/ rajarradioaudiencefigures.radio (accessed 25 March 2008)

'And now the news from where you are'

Going local

Roger Laughton

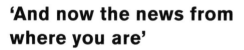

Introduction

Local news services have existed in Britain since the first newspapers were established in the seventeenth and eighteenth centuries. Print remains the medium through which most of us still receive news and features about our localities, about where we live.

It was the growth of first radio then television that enabled new regional news services to be established. As a consequence of spectrum scarcity and the perceived public interest, broadcasting in Britain was seen initially as a national public service, to be regulated in the interests of citizens rather than, as in North America, by the market place. Analogue broadcasting by radio and television is a 'one-to-many' medium. But the arrival of digital media at the end of the twentieth century enabled a range of different services, including more localized news services, to be supplied to consumers and citizens, a process that is still in its early days.

Defining 'local'

The term 'local' has been used in different contexts. In big cities, your neighbourhood can be local, although broadcasters describe a service targeted at the whole city as local. In rural areas, where you can drive ten miles to find a supermarket, a 'neighbour' may live in the next village. Many viewers currently describe their regional programmes as 'local'. Ofcom (2006: 1.17) recently defined 'local' services as 'any targeted at geographical communities ranging from a neighbourhood of a few hundred or thousand households to a major metropolitan area with a million or more inhabitants'. This definition includes communities of interest, like ethnic subgroups, within larger population areas. It is as good a definition as we have, and will be used in this chapter.

Local broadcasting in the analogue age

Politics and geography played major parts in the early development of twentieth-century broadcasting – particularly in their influence on the spread of local broadcasting. The contrast between the beginnings of broadcasting in the USA and Britain demonstrates this. Transmitters, enabling radio broadcasts to be received, need to be sited where optimal coverage of listeners can be achieved. Across the vastness of the United States, city stations emerged independently of each other. Local broadcasting was the norm. Often, as markets developed, too many signals competed for the same wavelengths, leading to poor reception – 'chaos', as it was described by a British observer from the Post Office in 1922 (Briggs, 1961: 68). Regulation of the airwaves in the USA was more a response to technical problems than a policy objective. The Federal Radio Commission did not meet until 1927, five years after the British Broadcasting Company had been set up. By contrast, in Europe, recovering from the most terrible war hitherto known to mankind, broadcasting development in the early 1920s started later than across the Atlantic. It was, from the outset, controlled and planned by nation states with the American experience as a lesson in what to avoid.

In Britain, a crowded country, in order to avoid the 'chaos' observed across the Atlantic, the British Broadcasting Company, owned by 'the manufacturers of broadcasting apparatus' was formed in 1922, receiving its licence from the Post Office on 18 January 1923. Its purpose was to provide a national service of programmes, centrally planned and funded by licence fees collected from owners of wireless sets. The supply of radio receivers was to be competitive, but not the supply of programmes.

The General Strike in 1926 presented the Company with its first major political crisis, a crisis it weathered successfully thanks to the leadership of its general manager, John Reith. It was his vision of broadcasting as a national public service which was to dominate the first eighty years of British broadcasting. In 1927, the Company became a corporation, with Reith becoming its director general and receiving a knighthood.

Local autonomy, the characteristic of early American broadcasting, was never an issue in Britain. Nevertheless, as a BBC memorandum of 1925 noted, 'those who have not been much in the Provinces cannot assess the extraordinary value placed upon the local station by provincial listeners' (Briggs 1961: 395–6). Indeed, eight provincial stations were specified in the Company's first licence. By the end of 1923, Manchester, Birmingham, Newcastle, Bournemouth, Sheffield, Cardiff, Glasgow and Aberdeen were up and running as parts of the non-commercial BBC. But they were then, as now, regional offices of a national bureaucracy, controlled centrally in London.

In England, BBC regional broadcasting came to be established around three mega-regions, loosely reflecting the divisions of Anglo-Saxon England – North, based in Manchester (Northumbria), Midlands in Birmingham (Mercia) and the West in Bristol (Wessex). The same landscapes that shaped human settlement in the ninth century formed the framework of effective transmitter coverage in the twentieth century. The BBC's Welsh services were based in Cardiff, its Scottish services in Glasgow and its Northern Ireland services in Belfast. These nations and mega-regions formed the framework of the BBC's network until the 1960s.

The arrival of advertiser-funded television in 1955 led to the establishment of an ITV network formed of fifteen regionally based licence holders. These were: London (weekday), London (weekend), South and South East, South West, Channel Islands, West, Midlands, East Anglia, Yorkshire, North West, North East, Borders, Southern Scotland, Northern Scotland, Wales and Northern Ireland. These licences, at the outset, were held by independent companies with local monopolies of advertising revenue. The companies came together to commission programmes, made by their own production arms, which were networked. But they each retained control of their own programme schedules. Licences were leasehold, not freehold, until the 1990 Broadcasting Act – a monopoly to 'print money', as one owner, Roy Thomson, put it, but not for ever.

The BBC's response to the arrival of a competitive television network, ITV, was to subdivide its television mega-regions to compete more effectively in news provision. Thus, for example, the West region, by the mid-sixties, had three television news sub-regions based in Bristol, Plymouth and Southampton.

The BBC's radio monopoly lasted until the 1970s. Shrewdly, with the support of a Labour administration, the Corporation introduced a network of local radio stations in 1969, ahead of the arrival of commercial competition and replacing its historic regional coverage. Now, there are around fifty local BBC radio services.

Commercial local radio began in 1973, under a Conservative government. Ten years later 60 per cent of the UK population was within range of a UHF signal. By 1988, there were sixty-nine commercial radio stations in Britain, many simulcasting on medium wave (MW) and high frequency (VHF). In that year, another liberalizing Conservative government permitted local stations to offer different services on their MW and VHF services. This led to a dramatic increase in the number of commercial radio stations and a significant increase in shared news services. Local services tended to fall under the ownership of larger radio groups during the 1990s, but there were over 300 different local stations by 2005.

Briefly, in the mid-1970s, the BBC considered a local television pilot scheme, based in Stoke-on-Trent, where, historically, its service had been weak. But the cost of developing such a service, alongside the continuing expansion of the local radio network, was deemed too high. The costs of providing local news services, as well as the technical problems of providing adequate coverage, have remained the most potent brake on their expansion up to now. Thus, the most salutary reminder that what is possible is not always affordable is the story of cable in the United Kingdom.

Cable is essentially the most appropriate delivery medium for local services, with the consumer able to receive a wide range of channels through a pipe that comes into the home. The trouble, as the British cable pioneers discovered, was that the capital costs of setting up a cable system were so hefty that the additional costs of establishing a half-decent news service could not be covered by the income from early adopters. So, pioneer news services in Greenwich and Swindon, which both opened in the early seventies, closed in the eighties. More ambitious ventures, like LIVE TV in London, were tried in the nineties, but these too did not generate a sufficient rate of return on capital for their backers. For a small country, satellite had quickly overtaken cable as the medium of choice for additional news and entertainment services. But satellite is not a cost-effective delivery mechanism for local services.

The 1996 Broadcasting Act made provision for a new form of local television service, licensed under the Restricted Service Licence (RSL) regime. RSLs were allocated unused analogue frequencies and broadcast to specific areas, like the Isle of Wight (Solent) and Oxfordshire (Six TV). Yet again, turning a good idea into a profitable business proved virtually impossible.

So the overall picture at the end of the analogue era was as follows.

- The BBC covered most of the country with its local radio services, all of which include locally generated content. Despite piloting local television services in the West Midlands in 2006, which is discussed later, no commitment to local television had been made by the end of 2007, although the BBC's local websites contained a higher proportion of video content than before.
- The ITV stations, most now under common ownership in England and Wales as a result of consolidation after the 1990 Broadcasting Act, continued to provide

regional news at the end of 2007, although the network had indicated that, when analogue signals were switched off, it intended to maintain only such regional and local services as were commercially viable.

● Local commercial radio continued to offer a range of news provision, with the smallest stations often taking a syndicated service from larger stations.

● In addition, by the end of 2005, Ofcom, the media regulator, had awarded sixty-two community radio licences, providing services on a not-for-profit basis to small geographical areas.

Opportunities in the digital age

In the analogue age, there were television, radio and print services. In the digital age, there will be content available any time and anywhere on a wide variety of platforms.

New digital technologies open up opportunities for a much wider range of services. In addition, convergence means that newspapers, like broadcasters, must adapt their services to a multimedia market place. The transfer of advertisers' revenue from print and linear television to the Internet means that there is an imperative for commercially funded news providers to publish their content on all available platforms. At the same time, the BBC, as it comes to terms with the digital age, has identified the need to review its regional and local news services in all media.

There are no longer major restraints on services as a result of spectrum scarcity. The costs of reaching citizens and consumers have fallen. Commercial models can be constructed which would have been unthinkable a decade ago. Public service models, based on linear broadcasting, need to be adapted to the needs of an increasingly interactive audience.

Until analogue broadcast services are switched off in 2013, it may well be unclear who the winners and losers will be in the digital age. But already most of the runners and riders can be identified.

Public service local digital content

Some commentators have argued that better communication links, virtual and physical, have weakened people's ties to where they live. But, in practice, detailed audience research (Laughton, 2006: Section 7) repeatedly uncovers a demand for more local news, as does the survival of so many local and community activities. People may belong to more communities than they once did, but their strongest ties are usually to their immediate neighbourhood (Ofcom, 2006: Figure 3.1).

Ofcom (*ibid.*: 3.43) has identified six distinctive roles for local digital content, fulfilling public purposes:

● Delivering enhanced services;
● Engagement and participation;
● Communication, access and inclusion;
● Providing local news and information;

- Supporting local production and training;
- Advertiser access to local markets.

Many of these roles are already being supplied by local newspapers. But it is also likely that consumers and citizens will benefit from the potential benefits of relevant digital content by the introduction of alternative voices and services.

One way of addressing this will be through the BBC's digital services.

The BBC embarked on a major initiative, Connecting Locally, between 2001 and 2004 in the BBC Humberside area. Over this three-year period, the Corporation invested over £25 million in a variety of new local services:

- A new news region;
- A new Open Centre, based in Hull city centre;
- Two BBC buses;
- Learn Express, a local education initiative;
- BBCiHull, an innovative broadband trial;
- A city centre big screen in Hull.

The investment increased audiences for the local news programme and was generally regarded by the BBC as a success. *Calendar*, ITV's regional news programme, lost viewers, but the *Hull Daily Mail*, the long-established regional paper, despite having major concerns about what it saw as unfair competition, did not appear to be adversely affected by the BBC's local competition.

In 2005–6, the BBC embarked on another pilot scheme, providing six distinctive local services in the area covered by its Birmingham-based regional news programme for the West Midlands. The trial was based on the existing infrastructure of local radio and 'Where I Live' websites and needed, on average, an additional six staff per service.

An independent review of the scheme reached the following two conclusions (Laughton, 2006: Section 12). First, the choice of the BBC's local radio areas as the spine of future BBC digital content delivery was endorsed. Second, investment in additional newsgathering in the local broadcasting areas enabled the BBC to offer added value for licence-fee payers.

However, uncertainties over the availability of future digital terrestrial frequencies over which linear local news programmes could be transmitted live and a lower-than-expected licence fee settlement led to the postponement of an early decision about how the BBC might implement new local digital content services. In any case, additional BBC services are not necessarily the only means of supplying public service digital content. Many would argue that the BBC's radio areas are too large to supply effective local news and information.

Broadband may well emerge as the most effective medium for delivering ultra-local content. Local authorities and the government have supported initiatives, like Carpenters Connect in East London, a community site serving a social housing estate. The Community Media Association has also identified a blueprint for not-for-profit local TV, based on the existing community radio model.

Other models will emerge before final decisions need to be made about whether and how there needs to be intervention in local media market places in order to add public value.

New commercial services for the digital age

ITV

The ITV network, originally a federation of regionally based stations, is now centrally managed and controlled from London. England and Wales are under common ownership, while the Scottish Media Group and Ulster Television control Scotland and Ulster, respectively.

In the last years of the federal network, new sub-regions were set up to provide more local services. Both Central and Meridian ran three separate news services in the 1990s. However, since the network came under common ownership in 2002, the trend has been to reduce investment in local services, because of their cost. As a result, and faced by increased competition in the overall market place, ITV has seen a sharper decline in its audiences for regional news than the BBC.

In 2006, ITV launched ITV Local in the Meridian region and has since committed to rolling it out more widely. This is an attempt to provide more local content on broadband, particularly more advertising and user-generated material. However, in 2007, Michael Grade, ITV's executive chairman, questioned the viability of regional news services after analogue switch-off unless the network receives additional regulatory benefits.

It seems unlikely that ITV will be a major player in regional or local broadcasting in the long term unless it finds a new commercial model for such services, possibly in partnership with other content providers.

Local commercial radio

Commercial radio interests, who already hold a strong position in the market for radio advertising, have shown little interest in providing original video content, although their websites could include it if they wished.

The most interesting experiment has been Six TV, operated by the Milestone Group and based in Oxford. Six TV holds an RSL licence, but its parent company has tried to build a multimedia regional company by buying newspapers and radio stations in the areas where its broadcast television signal can be received. The problem, as with other RSL licence holders, has been uncertainty as to whether the RSL licences will be extended and, most important, difficulties in establishing a commercially successful business plan.

Because of production costs, television broadcasters up to now have needed to be able to reach several hundred thousand viewers in order to run a sustainable service. Radio is commercially sustainable with lower audiences. But the problem for both media is that their historic strength has been the one-to-many relationship with a customer base. Digital broadcasting has a far cheaper cost of entry and offers interactivity, thus undermining older business models.

Local and regional newspapers

Local newspapers are the dominant and often the most trusted suppliers of local news. They have made a long-term investment in the raw material on which news suppliers depend – copy filed by journalists. Although local daily newspapers have faced serious circulation declines in recent years, local weeklies – often serving very small areas – have shown considerable resilience in the face of competition from the Internet and the broadcast media.

However, broadband services delivered over the Internet have presented the newspaper industry as a whole with a major challenge: 'Newspapers are making progress with the internet, but most are still too timid, defensive or high-minded' (*The Economist*, August 2006). As advertisers' revenue migrated to the Internet, the local and regional press began to show signs of coming to terms with the new medium in 2007. In Kent, the newspaper group KoS Media launched a regional TV news service, yourkenttv, in the autumn of 2007 – as well as eight new websites to accompany eight new free local newspapers. The Archant Group announced plans to develop a personalized online news service on its regional newspaper websites. Through geo-tagging, users would be able to prioritize the news they see online according to where they live. Johnston Press built a multimedia newsroom in Preston, prior to a national launch. It has also just completed a roll-out of an online family announcements service across all of its 281 newspaper websites. In addition to booking birth, marriage and death notices in the traditional way, users now have the option of an interactive, personalized Web page, as they might on an international social networking site like FaceBook.

Guardian Media Group's Channel M in Manchester has been the most ambitious initiative. Based near the offices of the *Manchester Evening News* and using the resources of an integrated newsroom, Channel M has attempted to dominate the news market in the Manchester urban area, using print, video, audio and online. The reach of the station – over a million viewers live within range of its analogue television signal – gives the initiative a chance to find sufficient commercial revenues to make money.

Different initiatives will suit different areas. The significance of these develop-ments is that the local press – whose owners have already invested heavily in local content production for its newspapers – has woken up to the need to protect its unique relationship with local consumers by offering interactive digital content, including specially shot video, in its local market places.

User-generated content

The rapid spread of user-generated content, using broadband distribution, remains a wild card. The BBC's West Midlands pilot scheme relied on such content, which comprised 25 per cent of the broadcast material. Local newspaper websites are increasingly trying to ensure they incorporate user-generated online material in their output.

It has been argued that new technologies have weakened local communities. But it now appears more likely (Ofcom, 2006: 3.1.13) that geographic communities are remarkably resistant to social change. What this means is that the Manchester

United fan who communicates via the Internet with a contact in Japan retains his or her local loyalties alongside a greater global awareness. The most recent market research (Ofcom, 2007b) showed how local TV, as an option for the future use of digital terrestrial spectrum, held its own against other options, like improved wireless home networks.

The threat to local news suppliers from the Internet is not the disappearance of local loyalties. It is a determined attack by major media players like Google, aware of the value of local advertising revenues, on the existing revenue base which sustains local content in Britain. Internet advertising rose by over 40 per cent in 2007. Local news suppliers must ensure they participate in this growth if they are to stay in business.

The future

Ofcom (2006: 3.58) proposed five public purposes for digital local video and interactive content:

- To inform ourselves and others and to increase our understanding of the world, with particular focus on issues relevant to our locality, through news, information and analysis of current events and ideas;
- To stimulate our interest in and knowledge of arts, science, history and other topics, particularly those relevant to our locality, through content that is accessible and can encourage informal learning;
- To reflect and strengthen our cultural identity, particularly that based on shared local identities, through original programming at a local level, on occasion bringing an audience together for shared experiences;
- To make us aware of different cultures and alternative viewpoints, through programmes that reflect the lives of other people and other communities, especially those within our local area;
- To support and enhance our access to local services, involvement in community affairs, participation in democratic processes and consumer advice and protection.

The debate now must centre on, first, whether these objectives can be achieved without public subsidy. Second, if subsidy is needed, how can it be best applied?

The BBC has moved on from its 2006 pilot scheme. Its newsgathering services are now under unified editorial control, thus ensuring its massive nationwide journalistic resource supports all its outlets in video, radio and online. Its local area websites now routinely include video inserts. With the future of the digital terrestrial spectrum still unresolved, no decision had been reached by the end of 2007 on whether, at some future date, there will be live, local news bulletins. ITV is unlikely to be a major local player unless it forms partnerships with other commercial news suppliers or discovers a new profitable business model. The most likely source of local digital news content remains those regional newspaper groups which have already invested heavily in local news provision.

Overall, it may well be that, at digital switch-over, a case will be made for some kind of public subsidy to enable local video news content to be made available, not just in those large urban areas (like London or Manchester) that can support local content without need of subsidy, but across the UK as a whole, ensuring universal availability of local digital content.

In the long term, high-speed broadband is likely to be the technology of choice for distributing local content. It remains to be seen whether subsidy, were it to be introduced, should support content creation, content delivery, or both.

Note

1 With the exception of Briggs, all references are reports produced for either the BBC or Ofcom.

References[1]

BBC (2004) *Building Public Value*

Briggs, A. (1961) *The History of Broadcasting in the United Kingdom, Vol. 1: The Birth of Broadcasting*, London: Oxford University Press

Laughton, R. (2006) *The BBC's Local Television Pilot in the West Midlands*

Ofcom (2006) *Digital Local*

Ofcom (2007a) *The Future of Radio*

Ofcom (2007b) *Choice, Competition, Innovation: Delivering the Benefits of the Digital Dividend*

CNN and beyond

5

Journalism in a globalized network sphere

Ingrid Volkmer and Ansgard Heinrich

Introduction

Over the last few decades, broadcast journalism as a traditional national media form has been transformed by a variety of developments and has become an important element of a complex and diversified globalized news terrain. Are the organizational structures of conventional broadcast newsrooms capable of adequate operation within a global sphere of information? This globalized terrain is no longer dominated by major transnational 'media empires' (Schiller, 1976) such as CNN and the BBC. An increasing globalized infrastructure of satellites in addition to virtual platforms enable national and even local news programmes to disseminate to a variety of world regions. It seems that we are only at the beginning of conceptualizing journalism within this enlarged sphere of political communication.

Although the majority of debates discuss journalism as a public discourse sphere of one society (often in relation to the US), more recent debates begin to capture important theoretical aspects of this new enlarged 'news' geography. McNair (2005: 156) argues, for example, that the globalized news sphere is in fact in the process of creating an 'emerging chaos' of a globalized news culture in the sense that the connection of 'the national', the 'transnational' and the 'global' spheres of public discourse produces 'unpredictable and largely uncontrollable outcomes'. Whereas McNair's model addresses new 'risks' of this globalized news territory, Cottle and Rai (2006) suggest a model of 'communicative architecture' and identify a number of 'communicative frames' of transnational journalism, such as terrestrial and satellite news reporting in a transnational context. Contributors to the debate, such as Stuart Allan (2004, 2005), consider online journalism as a new form of globalized news culture. Others relate these phenomena to debates in the theoretical framework of a globalized public sphere (Dahlgren, 1995; Sparks, 1998; Volkmer, 2005).

However, it seems that local and national broadcast journalism has developed transnational connections, a transnational connectivity which influences journalism practice on a variety of levels but in particular transforms conventional forms of 'domestic' and 'foreign' journalism. Whereas transnational connectivity has been conceptualized in the context of news agencies which allow transnational newsgathering for even the smallest news outlets (see Boyd-Barrett, 1980), it seems that new 'horizontal' and 'vertical' networks create the infrastructure of new forms of transnational journalism, far beyond conventional forms (and ideals) of 'domestic' and 'foreign' journalism. Whereas 'horizontal' networks describe new forms of transnational journalism, involving not only news agencies but a variety of international news outlets, the term 'vertical' networks relates to new forms of discursive 'connectivity' across technology platforms (audiovisual, audio and virtual platforms).

Such a globalized geography has an impact on traditional journalism as it creates on the one hand fragmented news cultures and, on the other, particular 'network' journalism cultures in various regions of the world: in Europe, the US, Africa, Asia, in developed as well as developing societies.

Traditional forms of 'domestic' and 'foreign' journalism can be traced back to the nineteenth century, when nation states were formed in Europe and 'the public' represented a new national sphere for political discourse. In the early days of radio broadcasting in the 1920s, the traditional European concept of 'public service' broadcasting linked terrestrial (government owned) relay stations within a national-cultural defined territory. Only one decade later, international radio broadcasters emerged, using shortwave radio signals for the delivery of news and political information to a transnational audience. Examples are BBC World Service, formed in 1932, which delivered its first foreign-language programmes in 1938 (Arabic and German); the Voice of Russia, established in 1939; and Voice of America, founded in 1942. These shortwave broadcasters aimed to deliver news and political information targeting audiences in a variety of world regions and extending national reach to a clearly defined transnational audience. These early forms of globalization of (radio) broadcast journalism reveal forms of transnational 'horizontal' networks through connectivity of local radio stations and technical relays in other world regions.

With early satellite technology in the 1960s the demand for 'live' video footage as well as for immediate access to news stories created new transnational network structures for broadcast news outlets which allowed the exchange of news material. Whereas during the era of shortwave radio international coverage consisted of either news agency reports or the stations' own reporters covering 'foreign' events, these emerging newspools not only facilitated international cooperation across one region but challenged national news frames, as material from other national broadcasters within one region could be used. In this sense, the boundaries between 'domestic' and 'foreign' coverage were blurred. One of these newspools is Eurovision, which was formed in 1954 as an outlet of the European Broadcasting Union and today has around 300 members around the world who contribute and use each other's news material. Asiavision was launched as another transnational newspool in 1984 by Asian broadcasters. These early forms of 'network' building have influenced the role of foreign journalism that could access and use journalistic material being made available in a particular transnational region.

Advanced satellite technology with new forms of newsgathering and dissemination modes in conjunction with virtual discursive platforms, providing continual updates via RSS feeds, blogs, podcasts and websites have, however, created a new 'news' geography. This is an important paradigmatic shift: a news geography which no longer positions 'journalism' conceptually in the centre of one society but integrates journalism into the communication culture of a world 'network' society (Castells, 1996).

Broadcast journalism in transnational connectivity spaces was also challenged by CNN. The station seemed to have gained world prominence through new forms of 'breaking news' coverage as well as a diversification of 'news' as a 24/7 channel. However, CNN's relevant change of journalism practice was the creation of different levels of transnational networks which have enabled it to develop new forms of newsgathering and dissemination – a new approach to globalized 'connected' broadcast journalism. CNN was launched in 1980 at a time when news and political information were not considered to be a commercially lucrative programme segment. The conventional US networks, ABC, NBC and CBS, had cut back their news programmes and those that remained were dominated by soft news and commercially sponsored anchor presentations.

Ted Turner, the founder of CNN, envisioned a twenty-four-hour channel solely devoted to news and information as thematic programmes aired in thirty-minute cycles, such as economic news, sport and entertainment. However, CNN's reputation has been gained through spectacular breaking news coverage. Because, in CNN's early days, satellite space was limited and only major networks (as well as news agencies) were able to utilize satellite capacity for newsgathering, the station was forced to develop its own international network. Whereas, before CNN's time, broadcasters used a small number of foreign correspondents, news agencies as well as newspools, the new channel developed a transnational network of broadcasters. Instead of sending its own correspondents abroad, CNN's (cost-effective) approach was to develop close relationships with international broadcasters who would exclusively deliver breaking news to CNN and in return would be able to use the channel's material in their newscasts. This network approach has become one of CNN's major strengths, and the formats of breaking news which were based on this network model have contributed to CNN's domination in the globalized news sphere for some time. However, CNN has built various types of horizontal networks. One of these has developed its own news agency which delivers breaking news stories to its subscribers (broadcasters in all world regions); another, widely unknown, is CNN's *World Report*, a cooperative news programme that airs news stories contributed by a network of about two hundred international broadcasters, national as well as local outlets. This journalistic format could be considered as the first global newscast (Flournoy, 1992; Volkmer, 1999).

Broadcast journalism in the network society: connectivity and convergence

CNN's influence as a transnational global player in distributing news faded as other transnational news outlets, such as BBC World, Zee-TV, Al Jazeera, Channel News Asia, Al Arabiya and France 24, started to emerge. These contesting global players have added different voices and new communities to the broadcast landscape, and digitalization has played a role in shrinking CNN's impact as a global news provider. More precisely, the 'network character' of digital technologies such as satellite and Internet remains a challenge for any broadcast outlet operating within the global news space. The new media infrastructure, in effect, has transformed the global media landscape as a whole.

With audiences 'active' users of news content rather than passive consumers (Deuze, 2004: 146–7), broadcasters are challenged in two ways: by users having a greater variety of news providers to choose from; and by users being increasingly technologically adept and able to access news content online, on their personal digital assistants (PDAs) or via mobile phones. The paths for obtaining information are characterized by a 'networked individualism' (Castells, 2001). Which path and provider – be it for local, national or transnational topics – are up to the user to decide, and he or she has a wide choice.

Broadcasters are acting in an arena that includes not only their presumably 'equal' competitors operating within the same medial framework. An increasing number of competitors in the global news market act via network platforms that 'provide global access to news from all parts of the world. Suddenly, newspapers, television, radio and other news providers find themselves in head-to-head competition' (Pavlik, 2000: 233). These new communication tools have enabled a great number of so-called 'citizen journalists' or 'amateur newsies' (Allan, 2004) and have laid the ground for new cooperation models of journalism. Independent journalists use new presentation formats such as weblogs or multimedia platforms on the World Wide Web to add to global information flows. Examples of the latter are media supersites such as Mediachannel.org that draw together material from mainstream as well as alternative media outlets around the globe and combine it with comment on (global) media issues, and the Back to Iraq blog launched by journalist Christopher Allbritton. Often these new players operating in a globalized news culture frame themselves as 'watchdogs' of mainstream media, shaping a new journalism sphere which utilizes advanced – and affordable – technologies in order to provide subjective angles on mainstream news stories. In a number of cases, these new 'news deliverers' have begun to feed their news pieces into mainstream broadcast media. Broadcast journalism has not only begun to utilize these new forms of newsgathering but is creating 'vertical' networks which allow the integration of news stories from a variety of technological platforms and channel them as news streams across outlets, such as television, radio and the Internet.

These vertical networks are used, for example, in the context of crisis coverage, a news sphere which was once dominated by CNN. The Boxing Day tsunami coverage, the Bali bombings and the images provided by mobile phone users from the London Underground 7 July 2005 all revealed the role of vertical networks for journalism practice. Another example is the coverage of the Virginia Tech shooting in April 2007. Benson and Eggerton (2007) comment on the material used by mainstream media after that atrocity:

> early media coverage was shaped in part by that most sought-after source of inside information: citizen journalists. While NBC grappled with issues involving killer Cho Seung-Hui's lurid videos, citizen journalism took center stage in relevance, thanks in large part to CNN's procuring of cellphone video shot by Virginia Tech grad student Jamal Albarghouti. With all other coverage beginning after the tragedy had concluded, Albarghouti's live view offered the only scenes of a drama unfolding.

CNN thus turned to its users to provide footage. Similarly, the public broadcaster BBC works with user-generated content which is gathered and distributed to various BBC platforms by staff based in London. In an interview conducted at the BBC, an editor estimated that about twelve thousand emails reach the Corporation's 'Interactivity News Desk' on a quiet day; bigger stories gather around fifteen thousand emails. During the Lebanon War in 2006 the BBC counted about 150,000 emails on Lebanon sent in by users.[1] The former 'receivers' have become 'deliverers' of information, with journalists turning towards their audience in order to gather comments, topic suggestions or footage 'directly from the hot spot'.

These examples indicate the first consequences that a global space of information flow has had for broadcast newsrooms. On the basis of the proliferation of information suppliers, new modes of connectivity are arising that are characterized by fundamental changes in the operation of newsgathering processes and that are based on new communication flows within a global space. McNair (2005: 151) has characterized this space as an 'environment of communicative turbulence' or 'cultural chaos'. Nevertheless, it seems inevitable that with proceeding digitalization cooperation models are required that reach further than launching user-generated content projects. This is because recent developments affect the ways in which news is gathered and produced, which means the fundamental structures of operation are altered.

Global broadcasters, like all other media outlets – be they national broadcasters or newspapers – are facing a structural transformation of the world around them in which the 'network' appears 'as a new globalization paradigm' (Volkmer, 2003: 12). Supported by the use of new technologies, networks are created that are far more complex and above all dynamic, leading to what Castells (1996) has termed a global 'network society'. On the basis of this, new global communication infrastructures take shape supporting a new social, cultural and political network infrastructure. Such a major transformation of society coercively impacts upon broadcasters. The 'network paradigm' thus necessitates the assembly of new information structures. In essence, broadcasting has to work according to the structures influenced by the 'network society' in which it operates. Broadcasters have to come to terms with forms of interconnectedness in a globalized environment characterized by a new transnational space, in fact a '"global" news sphere' (Volkmer, 2003).

This also raises the question of the roles journalists take on within this 'networked world'; roles that, according to Pavlik (2000: 236) 'must still take shape'. One such role can be for journalists to act as a communication node within this 'network society'. Castells (1996) describes the current global news infrastructure and its reorganization as a new 'network of nodes' (see also Volkmer, 2003). Within this infrastructure, journalism outlets can be viewed as taking on the shape of a node that draws together information from various sources: that is, other nodes. Newsrooms are in this sense interactive communication platforms that serve as 'supernodes' within a global news system and act as information hubs. News production in this space is accomplished on the basis of revised networks – a restructured information network that is triggered by the changes in the journalistic environment and embeds alternative sources, such as independent media sites or user-generated content, in the production process.

The collaboration within a rather open network and the integration of more or less 'untraditional' news sources are accompanied by revised collaborative work structures inside the newsroom as well, with an increasing number of journalists working cross-media. Multimedia competence is becoming a requirement for the journalistic profession (Barnhurst and Nerone 2003; Kawamoto, 2003; Pavlik: 2000).

The inevitable response to this is the creation of 'multimedia newsrooms' that are modelled on the idea of converging 'formerly distinct media operations' (Deuze, 2004: 141). Deuze provides a pragmatic yet concise definition of convergence in news media companies: 'Convergence is generally seen in terms of (increasing) cooperation and collaboration between formerly distinct media newsrooms and other parts of the modern media company' (*ibid.*: 140). In this sense, the convergent newsroom is a structural model paying tribute to the increase of content being shovelled from one media platform to the other and supports the structural change in the modes of networking in newsrooms. One example of a transnational broadcaster transforming into a multimedia newsroom is BBC World. In November 2007, the BBC adopted new forms of journalism practice in a 'vertical' network, facilitated by a multimedia newsroom maintaining the BBC News website, radio summaries and bulletins (except for Radio 1), BBC World Service news, BBC News 24, BBC World, BBC Breakfast and the bulletins on BBC1 at one, six and ten o'clock.[2]

The BBC's move towards an integrated newsroom that melds television, radio and online news into one vertical network entity can be viewed as one model of the transformation of transnational broadcast journalism. The convergence into a 'multimedia newsroom' is thus a step towards collaborative networking of journalists on various levels:

- it corresponds with the shift from audiences to technologically adept users of media who actively seek news on various media platforms;
- it enhances the capabilities of networking between journalists formerly operating in distinct media;
- it increases the opportunities of drawing more participants into the news production process from outside the newsroom; and
- it makes possible distribution of content via various platforms in ways that are appropriate for each medium.

Thus, instead of working against each other, former journalistic competitors are becoming colleagues standing on the same platform.

Technologies, then, support dynamic exchanges between newsmakers and whoever is connected within the 'network society'. New news production flows come into existence with journalism hubs profiting from a *multi-channelled, multi-layered information network* fed by numerous news deliverers. Journalists in convergent multimedia newsrooms have access to a broader network supporting processes of gathering, producing and distributing information. In a system of connected nodes, they act as the supernode.

It has to be noted that structural changes on this scale generate fear among journalists, who often see convergence as a means of increasing their workload, reducing staff and saving their employers money (Deuze, 2004; Singer, 2004). At the same time, news providers have had to create an organizational system that supports the work of journalists acting in a global space that is characterized by seemingly 'chaotic' global information (over)loads. Adequate journalism training thus not only has to focus on conveying journalistic knowledge for one medium as well as technological skills but has to prepare journalists to 'see the news' through more than one medium. Competences of multimedia journalists have to embrace what Deuze (2004: 148) characterizes as the 'shift from individualistic to collective and cross-departmental team-based newswork'.

According to McNair (2005), new global communication flows do not necessarily have to be viewed as a threat. The global communication flows at the beginning of the twenty-first century, however 'chaotic' they might seem, do also offer tremendous opportunities to obtain access to as well as to distribute information. It becomes a question of putting systems into place that help make the best of the material flowing between the plentiful nodes of the global 'network society'. The 'multimedia newsroom' is one option for the transnational system that some broadcasters operate.

Notes

1 The interview was conducted in April 2007 by Ansgard Heinrich as part of a series of interviews with leading players in the global media scene on the uses of new technologies in the newsroom.
2 Peter Horrocks, the head of the BBC Newsroom, announced the reorganization of the BBC on 12 November 2007 in his weblog on the BBC homepage. He also asked for user comments on the move of the outlet towards a convergent newsroom.

References

Allan, S. (2004) *News Culture*. 2nd edn. Maidenhead: Open University Press.

Allan, S. (2005) *Journalism: Critical Issues*. Maidenhead: Open University Press.

Barnhurst, K.G. and J. Nerone (2003) 'US newspaper types, the newsroom, and the division of labor, 1750–2000', *Journalism Studies* 4(4), 435–49.

Boyd-Barrett, O. (1980) *The International News Agencies*. London: Constable; Beverly Hills, CA: Sage.

Castells, M. (1996) *The Rise of the Network Society*. Oxford: Blackwell.

Castells, M. (2001) *The Internet Galaxy*. Oxford: Oxford University Press.

Cottle, S. and Rai, M. (2006) 'Between display and deliberation: analysing TV news as communicative architecture', *Media, Culture and Society* 28(2), 163–89.

Dahlgren, P. (1995) *Television and the Public Sphere: Citizenship, Democracy and the Media*. London: Sage.

Deuze, M. (2004) 'What is multimedia journalism?', *Journalism Studies* 5(2), 139–52.

Flournoy, D.M. (1992) *CNN World Report. Ted Turner's International News Coup*. London: John Libbey.

Franklin, B., M. Hamer, M. Hanna, M. Kinsey and J.E. Richardson (2005) *Key Concepts in Journalism Studies*. London, Thousand Oaks, New Delhi: Sage.

Gillmor, D. (2004, 2006) *We the Media: Grassroots Journalism by the People, for the People*. Sebastopol, CA: O'Reilly.

Gordon, R. (2003) 'The meanings and implications of convergence', in K. Kawamoto (ed.), *Digital Journalism: Emerging Media and the Changing Horizons of Journalism*. Lanham, Boulder, New York, Toronto and Oxford: Rowman and Littlefield.

Kawamoto, K. (ed.) (2003) *Digital Journalism: Emerging Media and the Changing Horizons of Journalism*. Lanham, Boulder, New York, Toronto and Oxford: Rowman and Littlefield.

McNair, B. (2005) 'The emerging chaos of global news culture', in S. Allan (ed.), *Journalism: Critical Issues*. Maidenhead: Open University Press.

Pavlik, J. (2000) 'The impact of technology on journalism', *Journalism Studies* 1(2), 229–37.

Powell, A.C. III (2003) 'Satellites, the Internet, and journalism', in K. Kawamoto (ed.) *Digital Journalism: Emerging Media and the Changing Horizons of Journalism*. Lanham, Boulder, New York, Toronto and Oxford: Rowman and Littlefield.

Schechter, D. (2006) *When News Lies: Media Complicity and the Iraq War*. New York: Select.

Schiller, Herbert I. (1976) *Communication and Cultural Domination*. White Plains, NY: International Arts and Sciences Press.

Singer, J.B. (2004) 'Strange bedfellows? The diffusion of convergence in four news organizations', *Journalism Studies* 5(1), 3–18.

Sparks, Colin (1998) 'Is there a global public sphere?', in Dayan Thussu (ed.), *Electronic Empires: Global Media and Local Resistance*. London, New York, Sydney and Auckland: Arnold.

Thelen, Gil (2002) 'Convergence is coming', *Quill Magazine*, July/August, p. 16.

Thussu, Dayan (1998) 'Infotainment international: a view from the South', in Dayan Thussu (ed.), *Electronic Empires: Global Media and Local Resistance*. London, New York, Sydney and Auckland: Arnold.

Volkmer, I. (1999) *News in the Global Sphere: A Study of CNN and its Impact on Global Communication*. Luton: University of Luton Press.

Volkmer, I. (2003) 'The global network society and the global public sphere', *Development* 46(1), 9–16.

Volkmer, I. (2005) 'News in the global public space', in S. Allan (ed.), *Journalism: Critical Issues*. Maidenhead: Open University Press.

Electronic sources

Allbritton, Christopher, 'Back to Iraq' (accessed 20 December 2007): http://www.back-to-iraq.com/

BBC Press Office, 'Press release: radical reform to deliver a more focused BBC', 18 November 2007 (accessed 20 December 2007): http://www.bbc.co.uk/press office/pressreleases/stories/2007/10_october/18/reform_news.shtml

Benson, J. and J. Eggerton, 'The impact of Virginia Tech on news', *Broadcasting and Cable*, 23 April 2007 (accessed 20 December 2007): http://www.broadcasting cable.com/article/CA6435500.html

Horrocks, Peter, 'Multimedia news', *The Editors Blog*, 12 November 2007 (accessed 20 December 2007): http://www.bbc.co.uk/blogs/theeditors/2007/11/multi media_news.html

Mediachannel.org (accessed 20 December 2007): http://www.mediachannel.org/

Exploring news values

The ideal and the real

Jackie Harrison

Introduction

The phrase 'news values' refers to two things. First, the normative use of the phrase, by which I mean accounts of what news journalists should do; and second, the descriptive use of the phrase, by which I mean accounts of the selection criteria for news used in the newsroom and by journalists in the field. Two points emerge: first an ideal–real relationship that helps clarify how the phrase 'news values' is used; and second, a clearer way of understanding what happens in practice and why that is the case – for what *should be* done and what *is* done may contradict each other.

Normative news values

If news is to be worthwhile, it should accord to something we value. It should have values which together explain why it is worthwhile. But what exactly are these values to which news journalism should accord?

Max Weber was kind to political journalists and to journalism in his essay 'Politics as a Vocation' (originally a speech at Munich University, 1918) when he said:

> The journalist belongs to a sort of pariah caste, which is always estimated by 'society' in terms of its ethically lowest representative. Hence, the strangest notions about journalists and their work are abroad. Not everybody realizes that a really good journalistic accomplishment requires at least as much 'genius' as any scholarly accomplishment, especially because of the necessity of producing at once and 'on order', and because of the necessity of being effective, to be sure, under quite different conditions of production. It is almost never acknowledged that the responsibility of the journalist is far greater, and that the sense of responsibility of every honourable journalist is, on the average, not a bit lower than that of the scholar, but rather, as the war has shown, higher. This is because, in the very nature of the case, irresponsible journalistic accomplishments and their often terrible effects are remembered.
>
> (Weber, 1918)

The war in question is the First World War, and the reference is to those German journalists who, with considerable courage, opposed or criticised the conduct of the war. The extent of Weber's regard for such journalism extends to his recognition of political journalism's explanatory, investigative and critical role, as well as the recognition that such journalism is always tempered by other factors. For Weber, the risks to critically independent journalism were obvious and easily identified as 'chain newspapers' that bred and encouraged political indifference, the loss of editorial independence, editors who were party officials or proselytisers, the demand for sensationalism (his word), the power of advertising and the political power of owners (he cites Lord Northcliffe).[1] And yet Weber's admiration for journalism is based upon what he perceives to be its depth of understanding, its brilliance to illuminate, to explain and to change things for the better.

More recently, Fred Inglis (2006: 13) explains that: 'the journalist discovers what we could not possibly discover for ourselves, and tells us what it is. He is faithful to his science, which is the history of the present.' Or, to put it another way:

> In these new circumstances, alike in Europe and North America, where the *grand récit* of democratic advance and equal economic progress has broken up, the rare journalist with the canonical attributes of moral conscience, literary ambition and public standing is conduit for two currents, both irresistible, flowing through her or him. The first is the appetite and energy for the story, the second the high tension of political solidarity.
>
> (*Ibid.*: 10)

There are, of course, many other endorsements of news journalism, alike in their depiction of what constitutes ideal news journalism. But following the logic and direction of the quotes above it is possible to recognise and appreciate that news journalism is, at its best for both Weber and Inglis, essential to democracy, to open political processes, to uncovering the details of contemporary events, to judging the significance of contemporary events, to public honesty and truthfulness and to clarity of understanding.

I would say that news journalism is at its best when undertaken by news journalists who retain their identity as critical interpreters of contemporary events and are governed by the desire to tell the truth and to be trusted, to be respected in the affairs of public life and to report contemporary events clearly, accurately and sincerely, while recognising that such events are set in the ambiguous and interpretative context of particular versions of space and time (Harrison, 2006 and 2007). To put the matter more simply, the normative values of news journalism can be represented as follows:[2]

Definition of news

- Truthful reporting and reports of contemporary events

Definition of news journalism

- Disposition towards truthfulness
- Interest in understanding contemporary events

The normative values of news journalism

- Disposition towards truthfulness:
    - Accuracy
    - Sincerity

- Interest in understanding contemporary events:
  - Critical interpretation of events located in relational and ambiguous space and time

I shall now look at these values in more detail.[3]

Accuracy and sincerity

The philosopher Bernard Williams (2002; 2005: 154–64) regards accuracy and sincerity as the two virtues of truth where, to quote Simon Blackburn (2007), 'Accuracy is the virtue of reporting how things are only when the report is the outcome of sufficient investigation to make it likely to be true, and sincerity is the virtue of communicating only how you take things to be.' Or, in Williams' (2002: 125) own words, accuracy 'lies in the skills and attitudes that resist the pleasure principle, in all its forms, from a gross need to believe the agreeable, to mere laziness in checking one's investigations'.[4] It is a 'passion for *getting it right*' (*ibid.*: 126) and this relies upon both the news journalist's will to do so – what Williams terms 'attitudes, desires and wishes, the spirit of his attempts, the care that he takes' (*ibid.*: 127) – and 'the methods that the investigator uses' (*ibid.*). That is, the news journalist achieves accuracy through an effective investigation of contemporary events, which balances both the desire for truthfulness with a way of going about things. But if accuracy is one virtue of truth, Williams argues that sincerity is the other. While sincerity, according to Williams, 'implies that people say what they believe to be true – that is, what they believe' (2005: 154) and as such is about 'trust and the abuse of trust', sincerity is also 'centred on sustaining and developing relations with others that involve different kinds and degrees of trust' (2002: 121). At the very least this involves the news journalist in expressing what he or she actually believes. It is 'trustworthiness in speech' (*ibid.*: 97). It is the disposition 'to make sure that any assertion one makes expresses a genuine belief' (*ibid.*). Sincerity is a disposition which, when shared, provides the grounds from which is built 'a modern understanding of what people deserve' (*ibid.*: 122), no matter how complicated or distant our relationship to another is. It is grounded in our social activities, our readings and our listening to others. This disposition is important to news journalism because it establishes for the news journalist (assuming they wish to be trusted) an attitude towards their job, and this, along with the need for accuracy, can be both taught and aspired to (Harrison, 2007).

So far, all we have said is that news journalists and their inquiries should be truth directed, assuming they wish to understand contemporary events and be trusted by their audience; and to achieve this they must be both accurate and sincere. But contemporary events are made up of complex and conflicting spatial and temporal stories. In fact, consideration of both space and time point to the constant difficulty for the news journalist of achieving accuracy, since both reveal ambiguities in the way contemporary events are inscribed by cultural and historical assumptions and ways of resolving issues of politics, membership and citizenship responsibilities, duties and obligations that may or may not be shared by the news journalist.

Critical interpretation, space and time

Spatial and temporal stories contribute to how our rhetorical responses and reactions to events are constructed. The participants in any contemporary event being covered by the news journalist are motivated and partly defined by their respective spatial stories (imaginative geographies) and by their respective temporal stories (multiple histories). Set in news reports, both spatial stories and temporal stories become the mediated identities which purport to represent the history, culture, politics and social life of a particular place through the language and images of news reports which claim to understand and report on people's 'ways of being' and 'ways of doing'. These mediated identities can lie in the foreground or background of a news report: they can be the report itself, or they can serve as its explanatory context. They are deeply judgemental as they transform specific events located in specific places and among specific people into expressions of: 'same or other', 'inclusion or exclusion', 'insider or outsider', 'member or stranger', 'right or wrong' and so on. These antinomies form the boundaries of differently mediated identities and are expressed in news reports through the use of authorities, experts, sources and the news journalists' own assumptions. Mediated identities are ultimately an attempt to come to terms with the complexity of a contemporary event: its manifold nature, its cultural context, its ideological pattern and rationale. As such, mediated identities in news reports are inevitable. However, and obviously, even though they are inevitable, they should still be assembled both accurately and sincerely.

All of this has to be understood by news journalists as both the background and the foreground of reporting a contemporary event, whether that event is large or small, occurs at home or abroad, involves a few people or many. Mediated identities should be assembled by news journalism openly to represent both the news journalists' assumptions that are built into the vocabulary about a particular event, and issues of a particular people's cultural and political practices, economic and social arrangements, moral and psychological attributes. In short, these are the reasons given for events or states of affairs being as they are. All of which requires that the news journalist is a critical interpreter of the event, the mediated identities assembled to explain the event and their own assumptions regarding that event. Only by becoming a critical interpreter and by undertaking news reporting accurately and sincerely can news journalism distinguish itself from propaganda, which in part consists of the wilful suppression by the powerful of the spatial and temporal stories of the powerless. Constant concern for the normative news values of news journalism – accuracy, sincerity and the critical interpretation of spatio-temporal complexity – is the news journalist's ideal *modus operandi*. But, of course, the reality is somewhat different.

Descriptive news values

The phrase 'descriptive news values' refers to accounts that purport to portray what really happens in the newsroom, or how journalists work in the field. That is, they offer accounts of how and which values influence the way news is selected. Here there are three dominant versions of the selection criteria for news. First, events are newsworthy because their news values fit into what a news organisation feels it stands for and the audience/readership it serves. In other words, news is selected according to the news organisation's *a priori* news values. Second, events are deemed to be self evidently newsworthy because they have certain characteristics that make them recognisably news. Thus, a contemporary event is newsworthy if it has certain intrinsic news factors. Third, real newsrooms have their own socialised dynamics that account for news selection. What counts as news is learned by 'doing the job' as new journalists acquire their understanding of newsworthiness from more senior or experienced members of the newsroom.

I shall look at each of these accounts of news values in turn to display their different ways of understanding news, although it is important to note that most studies offer combinations of these approaches rather than just one. To that extent, the separation is artificial.

News organisations and news values

Observational studies of news organisations have given us greater understanding of the way in which news is selected. Given the organisational complexity of news organisations, however, it is no surprise to note that accounts vary as to what factors most influence a news organisation's news values. Views about who exercises power in a news organisation, and therefore whose values dominate, range from: advertisers; consumers; owners; investors; to journalists themselves. Equally, views about news organisations and their values vary according to the theoretical approach adopted by the researcher. Those who maintain a critical or leftist approach see news organisations as reinforcing capitalism and its attendant ideologies where the interests of elites and media owners coincide. In contrast, some people emphasise that the market place for news ensures competition and creates the conditions for good journalism. Others say that the market place drives down standards and places news services in the hands of a few global media companies; and since they are mainly American or European, this gives an utterly Western feel to news. Complicating the picture even further is the view often held by politicians: the news organisations themselves are in control and shape the news. Some news organisations have countered this accusation by pointing to the prevalence of political 'spin' and the increasing difficulty in establishing facts in political stories. This debate leaves open the question of how far news organisations are themselves 'political players' with their own political values reflected in their news policies.

One thing though is certain: the news values of different news organisations differ. As I have argued elsewhere, news selection and presentation is adapted according to the designated style of each organisation and represents only one way of doing the job; or, to put it another way, reporting style is not universal (Harrison 2000 and 2006). David Randall (2000: 16) explains that the jour-nalistic culture which exists in a newsroom 'sets what editors and their executives regard as a good story or dismiss as "boring" and determines the subjects they think of as "sexy" and those that are not'; it also 'creates the moral atmosphere of a paper [or broadcast newsroom]'. In other words, different news organisations will, on news days not dominated by a major event, exercise different priorities which will result in different judgements about what is newsworthy. This is because the way in which a news organisation understands itself affects its news selection. For example, the way one news organisation might describe itself as impartial is very different from another that might describe itself as valuing 'objectivity, accuracy and a passion for the truth'. Of course, all news organisations seek to attract the reader, viewer or listener – it is a vital element of their function. But organisational studies show that motives vary as the competition for viewers/ readers increases. The sheer volume and diversity of news outlets now mean that any evaluation of the news values of a particular news organisation needs to take into account the cultural, political and economic setting of the news organisation itself. Increasingly, news provision is no longer simply the preserve of Western news organisations. The diversity of news organisations (as well as new communication technologies) needs to be taken into consideration before we can talk of dominant news values.

Intrinsic news values

Some researchers argue that the explanation for the selection of an event as newsworthy resides in the properties inherent in an event itself and not in the news organisation's predispositions or value system (see, for example, Galtung and Ruge 1965).[5] Agreement on major stories is a constant feature of news organisations. Indeed failing to accord to the 'common consensus' of what constitutes a major story can make a news organisation look either out of touch or quirky. But how is such consent or common agreement derived?

Rather than focusing on the context of journalistic practice (as a product of news organisations' own priorities) as an explanation for news selection, some researchers argue we should concentrate on intrinsic news values. Thus, news selection is regarded as something that occurs because of the inherent news values within an event itself which can be recognised by any trained news journalist. Metaphorically expressed, the event 'tells' the journalist that it is newsworthy and journalists 'hear' this and respond accordingly. What these intrinsic news values may be has been subject to considerable debate, and there are numerous lists to choose from, but most researchers would agree that they include:

- there are pictures or film available (television news);
- they contain short, dramatic occurrences which can be sensationalised;
- they have novelty value;
- they are open to simple reporting;
- they occur on a grand scale;
- they are negative or contain violence, crime, confrontation or catastrophe;
- they are highly unexpected; or
- they contain things which one would expect to happen;
- the events have meaning and relevance to the audience;
- similar events are already in the news;
- they provide a balanced programme;
- they contain elite people or nations;
- they allow an event to be reported in personal or human interest terms.

(Harrison, 2006: 137)

Accordingly, it is argued that the presence or absence of these 'intrinsic news values' in an event define whether it is newsworthy and therefore whether it is reported. While news journalists in the field do not refer to such lists, as some studies show, they do regularly refer to their ability to identify events as newsworthy or not, their ability to spot a good story and their ability to understand how other news organisations will respond to a particular event: namely, whether they will cover it.

As Harcup (2004: 34) observes, 'recruits to journalism tend to pick up a sense of newsworthiness and develop their "nose" for a story by consuming news and by absorbing news values from senior colleagues'. However, this only begs the question: how does this process of acquiring such practical knowledge occur? One answer is to focus attention on: the interpersonal and daily dynamics of the newsroom itself; and the degree of free agency news journalists have and the extent of their freedoms from a news organisation's own news values when doing their job.

News values and newsroom socialisation

How might one explain the balance between what a news organisation sees itself as requiring and the extent to which there is both editorial and journalistic autonomy and creativity that is free of interference and operates according to its own particular sense of news values? Researchers see the relationship between a news organisation and its journalists in terms of 'newsroom socialisation'. What they mean is that news journalists acquire an understanding of a particular news organisation's news policy and news values by being immersed in the news production process itself. This consists of: editorial decisions; editorial meetings; talking to and mixing with senior and more established colleagues; being subbed according to a specific house style; having reports accepted and more importantly rejected because they contradict the organisation's own news policy. These all combine to teach the news journalist to copy prevailing techniques and styles and to understand what is newsworthy in the newsroom and in the organisational setting in which they work. Thus, newsroom socialisation consists of both explicit (formal and managerial) and implicit (informal and collegial) ways of telling the journalist how to provide the 'right' kind of news. The net effect of newsroom socialisation is not the production of idiot drones but more pragmatically the realisation by news journalists that more publication and broadcast opportunities will usually be given to those who conform to organisational news policy than to those who do not. However, this makes the newsroom sound very harmonious, with everyone getting along and ultimately agreeing on news values. This is simply not the case.

Newsroom conflict primarily exists in the way management hierarchies work: that is, in the way the tiered relationships between the different levels of personnel in a news organisation are conducted. Conflict most frequently exists when there is a clash between organisational policy demands – for example, budgetary constraints or the introduction of new technology – and traditionally held journalistic ideals and views on the way to do the job 'properly'. In one sense this conflict is a common feature of newsrooms because it is so well understood by all taking part, so it might be viewed as routine or symbolic behaviour. The expression of such conflict does, however, show a degree of independent journalistic agency, and this sits uncomfortably with the idea that the news is entirely shaped or determined by forces beyond the journalist's control.

The extent to which such degrees of agency are exercised by journalists in modern converged newsrooms is subject to debate. A modern converged newsroom produces news for all platforms – television, print and Web – from a purpose-built central news hub which houses a central core of news journalists who are adept at writing for both print and the electronic media. These people work in teams, share one common set of archives, pool information and ensure that each platform carries different aspects of the story to facilitate cross-promotion and retain reader/viewer interest. In this way the three platforms (television, Web and print) seek to reinforce one another. The expectation is twofold: first, news journalists will be able to deal with all media and be truly multi-skilled; and second, fewer and better news reporters will be recruited. However, it is too early to tell what impact this type of newsroom will have on the more conventional newsroom socialisation and the balancing acts that occur between organisational values and independently held journalistic news values.

Conclusion

As was noted at the beginning of this chapter, when discussing news values it is important to distinguish the ideal (normative) from the real (descriptive); not that the distinction is a divide. Clearly the ideal can be what happens in the newsroom. As Weber and Inglis point out above, we can and do recognise good journalism as something of real value which is to be admired and emulated. Also, it is important to note that by separating the account of descriptive news values into three separate streams (Organisational, Intrinsic and Socialisation), there is perhaps a risk of oversimplifying what happens in real newsrooms. These three strands should be understood together (as they are for most researchers) and as overlapping with one another. In other words, newsrooms are mundane places of quotidian conflicts and compromises, but they are rarely places of high moral drama. By combining these three strands under the rubric of descriptive news values, that fact is revealed quite clearly. Descriptive news values help us to understand why the ideal forms of news journalism are sometimes not followed, or cannot be followed. They provide explanations for that and help us understand newsrooms as they both encourage and all too frequently frustrate good journalism in varying measures.

How sceptical you are about the current state of news journalism, or how good you consider it is, will ultimately influence how you regard contemporary newsrooms and the values to which they accord. Whatever the case, one thing is absolutely certain: analysing the complex nature of news values is central to understanding the practice, production and output of news journalism.

Notes

1   Alfred Charles William Harmsworth, 1st Viscount Northcliffe (15 July 1865–14 August 1922), is usually regarded as one of the British pioneers of tabloid journalism.

2 This is a further-evolved version of a diagram I have used previously (Harrison, 2006 and 2007).
3 The next two subsections follow the arguments made in Harrison, 2007.
4 Williams (2005: 156) adds that accuracy also resists 'wishful thinking' which 'lies in the quite general indifference of the truth to what the inquirer, narrator, recollector or informant would like it to be'.
5 See also Harcup and O'Neill (2001) for an update on the factors to be taken into account when determining news selection.

References

Blackburn, Simon (2007) at http://www.phil.cam.ac.uk/~swb24/reviews/Williams. htm (accessed 26 November 2007).

Galtung, J. and Ruge, M. (1965) 'The structure of foreign news', *Journal of Peace Research*, 2: 64–91.

Harcup, T. (2004) *Journalism: Principles and Practice*, London: Sage.

Harcup, T. and O'Neill, D. (2001) 'What is news? Galtung and Ruge revisited', *Journalism Studies*, 2(2): 261–80.

Harrison, J. (2000) *Terrestrial TV News in Britain: The Culture of TV News Production*, Manchester: Manchester University Press.

Harrison, J. (2006) *News*, London: Routledge.

Harrison, J. (2007) 'Critical foundations and directions for the teaching of news journalism', *Journalism Practice*, 1(2): 175–89.

Inglis, F. (2006) 'Letter from England: journalism, democracy, and American popular sentiment', Willard Thorp Lecture, University of Princeton, April, at http://nick-jones.com/fred/journalism_and_democracy.pdf (accessed 1 December 2007).

Randall, D. (2000) *The Universal Journalist*, 2nd edn, London: Pluto Press.

Weber, M. (1918) 'Politics as a vocation', at http://socialpolicy.ucc.ie/weber_Politics_as_Vocation.htm (accessed 10 June 2007).

Williams, B. (2002) *Truth and Truthfulness*, Princeton, NJ: Princeton University Press.

Williams, B. (2005) *In the Beginning Was the Deed*, Princeton, NJ: Princeton University Press.

Part II

The practices of broadcast news

Introduction

Jane Chapman and Marie Kinsey

The main message from this second section of the book is that research, writing, presenting and technical skills are of paramount importance in a diverse and fast-changing digital environment for both radio and television. While we acknowledge differences and similarities between the two mediums, we also recognize that the move towards multi-skilling has accelerated. The individual skills of video journalism, audio and video editing are all central to this section. We do not go into detail about the specifics of the equipment, concentrating rather on the concepts behind the skills. Broadcast journalism skills are also needed out of house in production situations involving only part of the process, or out-sourced facilities for feature magazine, current affairs and infotainment formats, as well as in newsgathering.

In this section we also focus on the existence of some specialist forms of broadcast journalism that require slightly different skills and knowledge, particularly politics, sports broadcast journalism and financial broadcasting. In the present multi-channel landscape, these are three areas of journalism that have expanded greatly, suggesting that, while a relatively large number of people studying journalism have some interest in sport, maybe too few of them understand how sports journalism differs from news. Specialist channels and twenty-four-hour news have enhanced the opportunities for political (Chapter 16) and financial coverage (Chapter 15). We also tackle specific issues raised by the reporting of celebrity (Chapter 17).

Thus Part II provides a range of incisive and challenging contributions covering the work environment, skills, culture and changing market that together constitute a body of essential knowledge for the aspiring broadcast journalist. This section works for the reader on a number of levels:

- there are tips and solutions relating to down-to-earth, everyday, practical problems;
- there is reflection on the meaning and potential significance of some of the ways of carrying out such tasks;
- there are insights into aspects of television and radio production that audiences may well take for granted – such as the myth of the so-called 'live' broadcast;
- there are projections and speculations about future trends; and
- there is a critical analysis of both practices and their interpretation by scholars.

In short, the pages that follow contain most of the essence of reflective broadcast journalism in its various manifestations. Part III will complete the picture with more information on specific areas and future plans.

There is a cogent reason why we need a range of chapters dealing with different aspects of the production process for both radio and TV: most tasks can no longer be dismissed as 'somebody else's job'. Journalists are increasingly responsible for gathering their own raw material for both radio and television, a trend that began with the establishment of commercial radio in Britain in 1973. It is now the norm for radio reporters to record and edit their own interviews and packages. Television has begun to adopt the same techniques in some situations, with video journalists shooting and editing their own stories. Online journalists also increasingly need to be familiar with using audio and video.

This section starts with Emma Hemingway exploring what she calls 'the various constellations of human and technological actors that in association with one another construct the daily news products of a specific organization' (Chapter 7). Instead of concentrating on the normal analysis of managerial hierarchies or political ownership that usually influence news agendas and, arguably, news content, the preoccupation of this chapter is to unravel the often complex and unpredictable relationships between the human and the technological elements at play in everyday routines of newsgathering and production. The routines of newsmaking may be technologically embedded, but they are not indifferent to meaning.

Hemmingway takes a regional BBC newsroom, a commercial national terrestrial newsroom and a digital twenty-four-hour rolling news station as her examples to examine some of the differences in structure, resources allocation and working practices. Her critical stance draws attention to certain features of news production that sometimes go unnoticed, such as the fact that in twenty-four-hour rolling news the audience appears to be ancillary to the organic flow of news events transmitted as and when they happen. Furthermore, rolling news is presented as if both the news event and the viewer share the same temporal frame. This chapter enables the reader to appreciate: the difference between the departments known as Newsgathering and Output; the layout of some newsrooms; the various jobs involved; the relationship between radio and TV in the case of the BBC; the routine and patterns of bulletin production; the extent to which news is crafted in different organizations; the extent of pre-planning involved in so-called 'live' reporting; and the extent to which broadcasters exploit 'user-generated material'.

Chapter 8 has two main parts, the first examining radio techniques and the second the relatively new and controversial field of video journalism, using the BBC's experience as a case study. It also examines claims that video journalism can make possible a different form of television journalism. The authors stress that, even with fast-moving twenty-four-hour news and digital technology, planning and preparation remain essential. They provide advice on how to research ideas, and conclude that 'there will never be any substitute for . . . getting out on location, talking to the people who matter and collecting the sights and sounds of the story'.

Some chapters in this section deal with specific aspects of a broadcast journalist's work, while others are generic to all forms of journalism, such as the art of interviewing. Jim Beaman and Anne Dawson's meticulous attention to the requisite skills (Chapter 9) provides a fascinating insight into ways of using what is probably the most important skill that a reporter has to learn. A good interview can make your career; a bad one can ruin it. They also leave us with a discursive issue to ponder: do traditional working practices amount simply to artificial manipulation resulting in manufactured material, or are they the application of creative post-production?

There are also specific considerations for television as a visual medium that need to be identified. By covering factual programmes and features as well as news, Jeremy Orlebar (Chapter 10) reminds us that the role of television is to bring the attitudes, views, opinions and expertise of people to the audience via the professional visualization of the programme-maker. But with this comes a caveat:

> The programme-maker's job is first and foremost to be conscious that the aim of the programme is to deliver a truth about the subject in a truthful way. This is not the same as being objective and balanced, which may also be appropriate. A truthful programme must not distort, change or alter any elements of the programme's implied truth.

Olebar argues that it is the job of the broadcast journalist to produce entertaining and enlightening production that satisfies the audience but does not compromise the implied truthfulness of the topic or people involved. He reminds us that the concept of 'writing' for TV is a broad one, involving a range of different activities and skills – both editorial and visual. He talks of the 'visually alert journalist', which seems a good phrase to describe the aim of the kind of work that his chapter analyses – particularly the discussion on how to use, or not use, television graphics. In addition, he raises the competitive spectrum of user-generated content or citizens' journalism, but argues fluently for the qualities that will ensure that a good broadcast journalist survives as a valued professional.

At the same time, radio's market is broadening. BBC Radio in all its many forms is where most crafted radio speech in the UK is to be found, but there is competition from Channel 4, and the Internet also brings quality speech from around the world within reach, such as NPR (National Public Radio) from the United States. Leslie Mitchell (Chapter 11) evokes the essence of good radio in his discussion of what constitutes a 'package'. He lists all the characteristics of good writing, recording and editing for radio, with examples of what to avoid and what to aim for. As he takes us through a proposed package on policing and the community, it is possible to imagine every detail in your head without even listening to a recording. He also suggests issues for further discussion that will enable readers to follow up on this key chapter.

Issues connected with user-generated material are discussed further by Mike Ward in Chapter 12: he examines the complete range of Web-based developments, including blogs and other opportunities for multimedia storytelling and argues that journalists should not see the various manifestations of citizens' journalism as a threat, but instead as an opportunity to extend their own professional tools, creativity, communications network and contact base. He also warns that professional journalists who ignore the opportunities offered by the Web do so at their peril. Another interesting point for those who aim to operate on a multi-platform basis is Ward's analysis of the differences in production techniques between radio, TV and the Web. We learn, for instance, that the much-used television 'talking head' shot does not work as well on a smaller screen or on a section of a screen. Quite simply, it loses potency.

The skills of the sports journalist specialist have never had a wider audience in British broadcasting than they do today, although sport is often viewed as 'soft' news. As Gary Hudson points out (Chapter 14), there is a difference between sports journalism and sports broadcasting: the former comprises writing, investigation and analysis whereas the latter often consists of the act of relaying sports events to the listener or viewer, which requires research and analytical skills and an on-air fluency for live broadcasting. The latter skill is analysed in Chapter 13, where Marie Kinsey stresses that good vocal delivery can be developed. It comes naturally only to a very small number of people; the rest of us have to work at it. Kinsey also points out that, while live programmes may give the journalist a buzz, they can be nail-bitingly stressful for the fixer or researcher who is waiting for a studio interviewee to arrive and dreading what will happen if they do not turn up.

The news cycle has speeded up, particularly over the last three decades, so it is hardly surprising that changes in broadcast journalism are of great interest to most contributors to this book. Nicholas Jones (Chapter 16) examines the increase in speculation and comment, in contrast to straightforward reporting of who said what in Parliament. A rapid turnover of stories has forced political correspondents to go behind the scenes to search for predictions of what might become an issue, such as speculation about the possibility of a surprise defeat for the government. The downside of this trend is that the flow of information has ended up in the control of political advisers rather than neutral civil servants, and 'Parliament itself has become another casualty'. Nevertheless, life as a political reporter is addictive, or so Jones claims.

Whereas the task of a political correspondent is to get beyond the adviser or spin doctor, celebrity reporters are forced to battle with the forces of PR. Here 'pseudo events' – planned promotional rather than spontaneous events in which stories are carefully manufactured – are the enemy. Claire Simmons (Chapter 17) offers guidance on how to navigate through celebrity spin to obtain the real story. The power of PR should not be underestimated – it can even extend to agents asking a journalist to sign a pre-interview contract, 'promising not to broadcast any negative coverage. If the contract is breached, the journalist can be sued.'

Inside the newsroom

Who's who and what's what?

Emma Hemmingway

7

Introduction

In this chapter I will identify and explore the various departmental, journalistic and technological roles and structures within different television newsrooms. This will help to unravel the often rather complex relationships that exist between constellations of media technologies and human resources which are responsible for constructing a particular organisation's news agenda and daily news content. When attempting to understand how a newsroom is constructed, organised and managed, it is often useful to think about less familiar concepts, such as flow, connectivity, association and contingency, rather than simply describing what have in the past been accepted and consistent or unchanging managerial or political structures that typify newsroom organisation and the behaviour of those who work within them.

While the growing number of empirical studies of newsroom organisation and management and the relationships such structures have to news agendas, routines and content have helped explain the somewhat elliptical news production processes that occur on a daily basis (Tuchman, 1978; Cottle, 1993, 1995; Schlesinger, 1978; Harrison, 2000, 2006), there is still a need for more sustained and detailed research into the actual processes of news construction. This should involve an exploration of different groupings or associations of media technologies and journalists. Any study of newsroom structures and practices thus necessitates a recognition that we need to map these detailed and often wildly varied associations between two distinct sets of actors: the technological and the human (Hemmingway, 2007; Van-Loon and Hemmingway, 2005). An individual newsroom is a far more complex, haphazard and often unpredictable arena than we might at first recognise, and our studies of news organisations should begin to acknowledge and explore these contingencies that occur at the chalk face of news production.

The majority of media analyses have focused on the political economy of media production, the semiotics of media texts or the socio-psychological effects of media consumption (Van-Loon, 2008). Empirical studies of media have thus tended to fix their gaze upon the way in which media industries are managed and operate, have explored audience consumption of media or have paid closer attention to media texts. All of this work has intrinsic value, and many of these studies have enabled us to glean far greater understanding of media organisations, media content and media consumption. But far less attention has been paid to 'processes of mediation', which is, after all, what is meant by 'media' (Van-Loon, 2008). With this in mind, we need to analyse what news is, how it comes into being and why it has evolved in the way it has. Far from being only a consequence of externally imposed forms of power, mediated by management, rules and procedures, professional cultures, hegemonic ideologies or threats, we need to begin to understand the routines of newsmaking as technologically embedded, but not therefore indifferent to meaning.

Accordingly, this chapter will concern itself with empirical studies of three television newsrooms in order to identify and explore some of the associations made between the technological and human actors within each, and to illustrate how different newsrooms operate at this specific level of everyday roles, practices and routines. The three newsrooms – a regional BBC newsroom, a commercial national terrestrial newsroom and a digital twenty-four-hour rolling news station – differ in size, resource allocation, target audience and ownership.

Newsgathering and output

A regional example

When exploring television newsroom structures there are some general characteristics that are fundamental to almost every broadcast newsroom in the digital age. The first of these is the significant division between the departments known as Newsgathering and Output (Van-Loon and Hemmingway, 2005). This division occurs in all newsrooms in some way, though the two departments might have different names. That said, the terms 'newsgathering' and 'output' are widely recognised within the BBC at both regional and national levels, as well as in BSkyB, ITN and BBC News 24.

Using the BBC regional television newsroom in Nottingham as an example, the newsroom can be best described as a large, open-plan but specifically demarcated space, wherein two separate departments which are denoted by two separate collections of desks oversee the newsgathering and the subsequent production – or output – of news. In the newsgathering department news is sought, identified and tracked down. Subdivisions comprising individuals or independent units are also located within the newsgathering department. These are: the planning department, known by those in the newsroom as 'futures', which is made up of one senior planning journalist, the assistant editor of creative futures, a second senior planning journalist and a third planning journalist; four specialist television correspondents; and the resources subdepartment, consisting of all the technical resources available to the newsroom, from satellite trucks to camera crews, studio lights and mobile edit facilities. Newsgathering also includes the personal digital production (PDP) operators, also known as video journalists. These are individual reporters, camera operators, VT editors or technicians who all have their own digital cameras and have been specially trained to film and edit their own material.

Situated on the other side of the room, opposite the newsgathering department, is the production department, normally referred to by those in the newsroom as 'output'. Here the news is written, produced and transmitted. This department comprises any of the production staff who may be on shift in the newsroom on a particular day. This would normally be a general production journalist, a senior production journalist responsible for the production of the shorter bulletins and the eleven-minute lunchtime bulletin, a lunchtime presenter, a weather presenter and two main programme presenters, as well as the main output producer, who is responsible for the production of the evening programme.

The output producer occupies the most senior position within the newsroom as he or she is responsible for all the daily editorial decisions regarding the construction of the main evening programme. He or she is answerable to the station manager, the Head of Regional and Local Programmes (HRLP), who is the BBC's chief management figure for each particular region. The HRLP is responsible not only for all of the television output but for the output of the region's radio stations and online services. Each of the radio stations also provides a dedicated Internet service which is located on the BBC's Where I Live sites. This is managed within the individual radio station by separate online editors but overall by the HRLP.

The newsgathering and output departments are crucially interdependent, and individual journalists, producers and technicians working within each have a shared tradition of knowledge, based upon experience and inherited working routines. Thus there is communal recognition of accepted output between departments, and both departments work towards a shared understanding of the specific news form (Hemmingway, 2007). A tradition of working practice is certainly commonly observed, but even the separate news departments, although they are similarly structured and may share both staff and resources, often adopt distinctive, unpredictable or even idiosyncratic approaches to individual stages of news production, as we shall see later in the chapter.

The regional terrestrial television newsroom is responsible for the transmission of separate news bulletins throughout the day. The early morning journalist known as a broadcast journalist (or BJ) produces and presents breakfast bulletins of four minutes duration every half-hour from 6.30 a.m. until 9 a.m. These have been written by the overnight journalist (a BJ) the majority of which is edited the previous evening. The lunchtime bulletin, which is eleven minutes long, is transmitted after the BBC's national lunchtime news, which runs from 1–1.30 p.m. The evening 'flagship' programme, *East Midlands Today*, is transmitted at 6.30 p.m. and is twenty-eight minutes and forty seconds long. All the regional programmes are transmitted immediately after the BBC's national news and are deliberately linked to the main national news programme by means of the national presenters handing over to the regional news teams, or within a national news programme, such as *Breakfast News*, from which the regional newsroom opts out for its four-minute half-hourly bulletin transmissions.

The regional television newsroom in Nottingham is shared by BBC Radio Nottingham and both are responsible for providing the BBC's national radio and television newsrooms with regional material, should they request it. The BBC in Nottingham used to operate as a 'bi-media newsroom', which meant that a television journalist working for *East Midlands Today* would be expected to provide material for the local radio bulletins by recording interviews and voice pieces while out on location filming his or her television package. However, this practice has been almost completely abandoned during the last two years, because of the implementation of PDP and the increase in the use of video journalists at regional level (Van-Loon and Hemmingway, 2005). But journalists within the two newsrooms, situated as they are in the same room, still work very closely together, often collaborating on stories at both the planning and the reporting stages.

Although the main local radio station is Radio Nottingham, the Nottingham newsroom also services what is known as a local radio cluster. The cluster for BBC East Midlands comprises five local radio stations, managed separately by local radio managers and at the regional level by the HRLP. The latter thus has managerial responsibility for the regional TV station at Nottingham as well as all the local radio stations in the East Midlands geographical area.[1] In the East Midlands the radio stations are BBC Radio Derby, BBC Radio Leicester, BBC Radio Lincolnshire, BBC Radio Northamptonshire and BBC Radio Nottingham. Each has an individual radio editor and is staffed by a team of local radio reporters. However, each station still relies on the newsgathering department of East Midlands TV, based in the Nottingham newsroom, to supply them with news that is being covered in their geographical area by TV reporters, even though formal bi-media practice has been more or less eradicated.

One of the most significant technological actors within any digital newsroom is what is known within the BBC as the 'media hub'. This consists of a matrix of connected digital interfaces, which are then connected to the entire technological infrastructure of the newsroom. This will include every desktop computer at every workstation, any adjoining edit suites, the main studio from where the programme is presented as well as the gallery situated next to the studio from where the programme is transmitted. The interface of the media hub is able to communicate with regional, national and international BBC television services and radio newsrooms. The BBC's networked, desktop information service – which was developed by the Associated Press and is known as the Electronic News Production Service or ENPS – enables journalists throughout the Corporation to communicate with one another and to share information and ideas. ENPS has more than twelve thousand users in the BBC and all staff are able to utilise the system for email communication, for the dissemination of ideas and information, for the creation of programme running orders and for writing scripts and links to programme items. In the Nottingham regional newsroom, the ENPS system is directly linked to the Quantel editing and playout system, which automates the input of audio and video media. It also provides communal browse and editing facilities online, as well as permitting access to archive material by means of a series of connected servers.

National commercial terrestrial news

ITN

Having outlined the structure and organisation of a typical BBC regional station, it is interesting to note some of the crucial differences in resources, staff roles and structural organisation of a much larger commercial station, such as the commercial terrestrial news channel ITN (Independent Television News).

ITN supplies the terrestrial news for the Independent Television Network, ITV, but it exists as a separate company in its own right. Its newsroom, which is based in central London, is shared by network ITN and the local news channel London Tonight.

While the same demarcation between newsgathering and output is recognized and adhered to within ITN's managerial structure, the newsgathering department is referred to here as 'input', and there is also a crucial division within the input department between domestic (or home) news and foreign news.

A single editor-in-chief and an assistant editor preside over each department. Editorial control is in turn then handed down to the head of output, who is responsible for liaising with the head of home news (input) and the head of foreign news (input). Beneath these positions, separate programme producers responsible for both input and output work a ten-hour shift pattern across the day with a team of individual reporters and producers working with them.

ITN has two flagship programmes which are directed at very different audiences. The first main news programme runs between 6.30 and 7.00 p.m. and is considered by journalists working within the newsroom as the main competitor to the BBC's early evening news, which runs from 6–6.30 p.m. In the daily prospects meetings which are held first thing in the morning and again in the afternoon, much of the discussion between journalists and producers revolves around how ITN news can approach the same news prospects as the BBC but from a deliberately and sometimes radically different angle. As one producer commented:

> The BBC may be our main rival, and they may have more resources than us, but because they are a public service broadcaster, they tend to do more issue-based stories. We work best on breaking exclusives, and this is a top priority for us. If we do cover the same stories as the BBC, we will always do it from a more human angle, whereas the BBC tends to concentrate on the underlying issue rather than the raw emotion of a story.
>
> (Chris, producer, ITN)

The second main programme is transmitted at 10.30 p.m. and is aimed at what producers describe as a much more professional and educated audience of AB1 viewers:

> The challenge with the late news is that the audience wants something more upmarket than the six-thirty programme. Therefore, we do more business and politics, so we need to use newsgathering resources to get these types of stories, but we are a much smaller outfit than the BBC and it is a real challenge. To overcome this, we try to choose very different stories from the BBC. And as I have no dedicated camera crews and no spare reporters I am on extremely limited resources. My job becomes all about balancing resources and the programme remit.
>
> (Steve, programme editor, ITN)

There is a direct correlation here between the technological resources available to the newsgathering and production teams for each programme and the choice of what issues or events are chosen as story prospects. The issue of resources, particularly with regard to the use of staff and technological resources from the eighteen regional ITV centres around the country, was raised on many occasions in interviews with ITN editors:[2]

> The BBC doesn't realise just how lucky it is with all its resources – and they also have much larger regional centres they can rely on. Sky doesn't have those regional centres. At ITV we try to get exclusives and we do go out on a limb to make different stories, but I just don't think we have enough resources outside London at night. At Sky they can't craft their bulletins as they're doing rolling news; they just really want to be doing lives all the time. Here I can craft my bulletin, but my main problem in doing this is my lack of resources.
>
> (Alan, programme editor, ITN)

The issue of ITN's limited resources in comparison with both the BBC and Sky has been highlighted by ITV's recent decision to limit its investment in the eighteen regional centres, which used to provide substantially more material to the national newsroom. A regional coordinator is still employed within the national newsroom to liaise with each regional newsroom and to consider the material produced by them, but the amount of regionally produced programme content and the ability of regional newsrooms to provide camera crews and journalists to cover local stories for national news have significantly diminished since this streamlining came into effect.

Newsgathering for twenty-four-hour rolling news

Sky

> We need to remember that people dip in and out of Sky News – unless it's a big story – so the planners are really the news editors of tomorrow. We need to keep asking ourselves: what would we do if we were editing the programme tomorrow?
>
> (Clive, deputy editor, planning, Sky News)

Unlike terrestrial television, where news is deliberately and artificially segmented into clearly demarcated programmes advertised at specific times during the day or night, the ethos of Sky News is that it is a continuous flow of news events that are both spatially and temporally unfixed within any recognisable boundaries. As the quote above suggests, the station's 'ideal' viewer almost stumbles across the news output by chance, yet discovers it continually presented as an organic flow of events transmitted as soon as they happen. The same temporal frame is thus perceived to be shared by both the news event and the viewer. Yet both the technical apparatus and the people who work with it to achieve this illusion are complex, haphazard and also dangerously unpredictable.

By examining the newsgathering routines of the planning department at Sky News, we can begin to recognise the separate but simultaneous time frames within which both people and technologies operate. First, the logistical arrangements needed for any forthcoming news event can be very complicated and need detailed study and preparation:

> We need to have a tremendous technical knowledge to plan properly. We need to know what our trucks are fitted with. Most of our trucks have a dual facility, which means they have two lines going into the truck, so we can do the press conference as it happens and a guest as well. The whole point about planning and newsgathering is that there are never enough resources so the expertise has to come from how to do the journalism by taking the right and necessary technical short cuts. It is kind of like playing three-dimensional chess with people – knowing what your newsgathering skills are technologically – so all of our researchers are trained in this.
>
> (Chris, deputy editor, planning, Sky News)

The paradigm outlined here places technological know-how at the very centre of newsgathering or planning success, something we will return to later in this chapter. But what is significant in terms of our exploration of temporal frames within rolling news as opposed to terrestrial news is the way that Chris describes a lengthy and complicated process of planning logistical configurations of vehicles, people, locations and technologies, all of which are essential for the successful enactment of the 'live' event but remain deliberately invisible during that event's transmission. If they were to be exposed, the re-presentation of the live would then store within it the separate time frames that all of these actors have occupied during this long process of configuring themselves and others in such a way as to make the so-called 'live' event possible. The process could therefore be described as literally 'time-consuming' – in more ways than one.

Newsgathering for twenty-four-hour news is complicated and therefore can take an inordinate amount of time to research and set up. But it must also – by definition of what it seeks to provide as a viewing event – *consume* the time it has taken in order to set up the enactment of the 'live' event.

In rolling news, the existence of all the qualifying modalities, such as the extra technologies, humans and machines, is not openly acknowledged. This has the effect of turning the content of the news event into a series of assumptions, instruments or skills, just as, in the same way, the viewer observing the 'live' news event accepts it as a normalised event and rarely questions its temporal framework or significance. Thus, the more the hinterland is standardised and concealed, the better (Law, 2004: 36).

User-generated content – a growing phenomenon

Another crucial aspect of today's television newsroom is the use of both the Internet and what is known as 'user-generated' material or content. At Sky News, £43 million has recently been invested in its online services, and twenty staff are dedicated solely to working on the station's Web pages, which are in turn advertised heavily by Sky News.

User-generated content refers to viewers' recorded material which they send into the newsroom for transmission. The terrorist attack on Glasgow airport in the summer of 2007 is a pertinent example of how user-generated material provided Sky with their entire footage of the incident. And, as staff point out, the genre of rolling news enjoys a crucial advantage over terrestrial news in terms of the use of user-generated material.

> This the biggest change in newsgathering in years – and it is the most important for twenty-four-hour continuous news channels. If you want to go big on a story, you may only have a graphic and a map, but now in literally minutes you can get stuff from people – you ask for it on the air. This ethos is spreading very quickly. Of course, if someone is very good they can certainly cheat us, so we do have to make a judgement. But here the advantages of twenty-four-hour news come in. The rapidity of the news makes it actually less likely that someone will be able to hoax you – you can't really mock up a burning jeep in less than ten minutes, which is what we had with the Glasgow attack, so rushing things to air ironically does guard against hoaxing as it doesn't give people enough time. But if we are handed material on a story that happened days ago, then we are less likely to run it, as we wouldn't be as trusting of its credibility.
>
> (Chris, senior editor, output, Sky News)

Once again every newsroom differs in both its use and in the resources it allocates to the retrieval and presentation of viewers' material. At Sky News there is a separate dedicated team of four journalists and two producers who are responsible for the gathering and checking of viewer material as well as a purpose-built area which has recently been constructed solely for the retrieval of this material. This is not the case at BBC News 24, which also uses viewers' material but has no separate department or newsgathering area dedicated to its retrieval. At Sky News, staff are keen to stress that the use of viewers' material does not compromise what they consider to be the editorial quality of the news they provide, and this is also one of the main justifications for dedicating extra staff and resources to its retrieval:

> We must make sure that we are not using viewer material as a vehicle for lowering standards. We must still decide about what stories are. We can ask people and encourage them to contribute, but we must editorialise. We do have a chief sub video – one a day – and he checks all the material that is coming in. And we would double up that role on a big news story day.
>
> (Chris, senior editor, output, Sky News)

Conclusion

Each of the examples presented in this chapter clearly demonstrates that technological agency – whether illustrated by the behaviour of a specific digital playout system, or the use of video journalists as opposed to traditional camera crews, or even the way in which recorded material is digitised by means of a central media hub – has to be explored if one is to understand how an individual newsroom operates. The media process, as the examples have indicated, comprises a range of interconnected human and technological actors in which distinctions between production and consumption are blurred and perhaps even become meaningless. We have seen how media are haphazard and often problematic assemblages of these two types of actors, and we need to map each individual association as and when we observe it if the newsroom structure and process are to be fully explained. This necessitates more careful and detailed empirical study as well as the crucial recognition and insistence on the contingent nature of human–machine interfaces and the networked nature of practices of mediation. We must recognise that we cannot simply predict how media processes in any newsroom will operate without first mapping those processes individually at the specific level of practice, and by taking into consideration the behaviour of many more of the human and non-human actors involved in the construction and operation of that particular newsroom.

Notes

1 Situated within the local radio stations are separate PDP bureaux, based at Leicester, Derby and Lincoln, each staffed by two PDP operators.
2 The eighteen ITV regions are: Anglia East, Anglia West, Border, Central Birmingham, Central Nottingham, Granada, ITV Wales, ITV West, Meridian Maidstone, Meridian Southampton, STV Edinburgh, STV Glasgow, STV

North, Thames Valley, TTTV Newcastle, UTV Ulster, WCTV Plymouth and YTV Leeds.

References

Cottle, S. (1993) *TV News, Urban Conflict and the Inner City*, Leicester: Leicester University Press

Cottle, S. (1995) 'The production of news formats: determinants of mediated public contestation', *Media, Culture and Society*, 17(2): 275–91

Harrison, J. (2000) *Terrestrial TV News in Britain: The Culture of Production*, Manchester: Manchester University Press

Harrison, J. (2006) *News*, London: Routledge

Hemmingway, E. (2004) 'The silent heart of news', *Space and Culture*, 7(4): 409–27

Hemmingway, E. (2007) *Into the Newsroom: Exploring the Digital Production of Regional Television News*, London: Routledge

Law, J. (2004) *After Method Mess in Social Science Research*, London: Routledge

Schlesinger, P. (1978) *Putting "Reality" Together: BBC News*, London: Constable

Tuchman, G. (1978) *Making News: A Study in the Social Construction of News*, New York: Free Press

Van-Loon, J. (2008) *Media Technology: Critical Perspectives*, Milton Keynes: Open University Press

Van-Loon, J. and Hemmingway, E. (2005) 'Organisations, identities and technologies in innovation management: the rise and fall of bi-media in the BBC East Midlands', *Interventions Research*, 1(2): 125–47

On the road

8

Gathering raw material

David Holmes, Katie Stewart and Marie Kinsey

Introduction

The stuff of broadcast news is actuality: pictures that show the viewer what's happening and audio that paints pictures in listeners' minds. Whatever the situation, the broadcast journalist is looking to bring a story to life. You want the right pictures, the eyewitness interviews and the atmosphere. Whether you are working in radio, television or online, gathering the raw material for a story is at the heart of the job. This applies whether you are a correspondent covering events that will become part of history or standing outside the local magistrates' court on a wet Wednesday.

It's not just the professional who gathers the raw material: it can come from viewers and listeners. The memorable mobile phone images of passengers walking down a tube tunnel during the terrorist attacks of July 2005 were one of the first uses of such material by mainstream broadcasters. And BBC 5 Live ran a recording from a listener's Dictaphone when police raided terrorist suspects after the bombings.

Technological literacy is more important than ever. Radio journalists are used to being responsible for the technical quality of their recording and editing but, increasingly, television journalists are being given a similar responsibility to film and edit their own material. Familiarity and trust in your equipment is crucial – make it your slave, not your master.

Online journalism has leavened the mix still further. It makes it possible to tell stories in a non-linear way, using a mix of text, audio, video and still pictures that allow the audience to choose how much or how little of a story they want to know. Each of these elements needs to earn its place in the story.

This chapter will look at the practice of gathering raw material on location for use in radio, television and online, and will pay special attention to videojournalism, where journalists are responsible for the pictures and the sound as well as the words.

Preparation

Whether you are covering a long-planned set-piece event or dashing out on a breaking story, organisation is crucial. It is always better to have more information about a story than you are going to need, so planning and research are essential; as is keeping up to date. News editors expect all their journalists to be aware of what's happening in the area. Reporters are expected to 'read themselves in' by browsing newspapers, looking through previous output and knowing what the opposition is doing. In small newsrooms, reporters do their own research, while in larger ones, particularly in television, there may be journalists whose job it is to set up interviews and provide briefings. But do not count on it! While the ideal briefing sheet might consist of details of where you are going, who you are interviewing, some suggested questions and a pile of cuttings, it is more likely to be a hurried conversation with details jotted down in your notebook, and you work out the rest on the way or when you arrive.

All newsrooms will have a diary and at least one daily meeting, usually in the morning. These meetings will consider a list of stories that might be covered, known as 'prospects', that will include diary items, follow-ups on previous stories and breaking stories. A local radio station will typically concentrate on hourly bulletins, with perhaps a news magazine programme requiring longer items. A half-hour regional television news programme will be looking for a mix of hard news stories and lighter items. There may be live guests, live location reports and pre-recorded packages. Some larger newsrooms, particularly in television, will have a planning desk that sets up coverage of stories in advance, and compiles the daily prospects sheet. These items are never set in stone. As new stories break, reporters may be diverted from one to another. So when the news editor says the managing director of a local company is available for interview in half an hour about a round of redundancies, the reporter will be expected to know that job losses were expected and what the company does.

Whatever the newsroom, ideas for stories and features and ways of covering them must be in synch with the programme or station's understanding of its target audience. It would be pointless suggesting a story on young people's voting habits to a station targeting an audience of over fifties. The more original the idea, the better. No news editor likes to think they are following up stories that have appeared in newspapers or on rival stations or programmes. Find a new approach, a new angle; or, better still, unearth your own story from your own contacts.

Contacts are the lifeblood of journalism and every journalist will keep an address book – electronic or paper – full of the names, home phone numbers and mobile numbers of practically everyone they have ever met. Every person you interview, and every story you cover, will yield someone you might want to talk to again. Calling round your contacts regularly, particularly on slow news days when not much is happening, just might turn up a great story.

Finding interviewees

It can be the most time-consuming and frustrating aspect of the job, but setting up interviews in advance is usually essential. Most organisations have press offices, which can be useful for background information, but press officers are last resorts as interviewees. They have their own interests at heart, not yours. It's far better to start as high in the organisation as you can and to settle for the press office only if there is absolutely no alternative. There usually is.

Chase more than one angle and never rely on anyone to phone you back. You could be waiting for days. For example, you are covering a story about train delays: engineering works have overrun, leaving thousands of commuters delayed or stranded. You decide to call the company responsible for the work to find out why, but the managing director is on another call. Say you will hold on. Or you are told he is out. Ask for his mobile phone number. If your request is refused, despite your best efforts and politest manner, ask if there's someone else you can talk to. If you are still stuck, try another angle. In this case, you could try the train operators for their reaction and a rail passengers' lobby group. If all of this fails and you are staring at the phone in despair, do not waste time but explain your situation to the news editor, who will decide whether you should continue trying or cut your losses.

Leaving the newsroom

Do not leave the newsroom without doing some basic research into the story you are covering, and arrange as much as you can beforehand. Read the newspapers and any briefing material, check the Internet and your news archive. If you are responsible for your own equipment, make sure it all works and that you have spare batteries. There is nothing more embarrassing and unprofessional than returning from a story without the material you thought you had. It happens, but do not let it happen to you.

You should also make sure you know what the newsroom wants. Is it a twenty-second clip of audio for the next bulletin? A three-minute interview for the drive-time programme? A two-minute package for the breakfast show? Or all three? There is no point in getting back to the newsroom with enough material for a lengthy documentary and even less point if it all arrives too late. However, there will be times – for example on breaking stories – when details are scarce. You may know only that there's been a fire at the local hospital or a pile-up on the motorway. Do not hang about – check your kit and go, then establish the facts when you get there and file as quickly as you can. And it may sound simple, but check the map, even if you have a satellite navigation device. Many a reporter has been caught out by assuming they know where, say, Regent Street is, only to discover they should have gone to Regent Road.

Getting permission

Filming or recording on a public highway is rarely a problem, unless you are causing an obstruction, but for almost anywhere else you will need permission. You do not have the authority to enter private premises without permission, and this includes schools, hospitals and other public buildings, railway stations and shopping centres. For example, if you are considering reporting from a shopping mall, you must have permission from the centre management, usually in writing or via email. In the case of railway stations, it's usually the station manager; for hospitals, the chief executive or press office.

You should take particular care when reporting on stories that involve children. Usually, the permission of the headteacher is enough to allow you to record or film on school premises, but you may also have to obtain the permission of individual parents, depending on the story. This is often impractical and you may have to agree that individual children will not be identifiable. Both the BBC's editorial guidelines and the Ofcom code have detailed sections about how to handle stories that involve children.

Health and safety

Journalists sent abroad to war zones are required to undergo hazardous-environment training, while training in health and safety for general field reporting is a legal requirement for all journalists. Cables snaking across a pavement could be a risk to the public if someone trips over them. A radio car or satellite truck parked in the wrong place might cause an obstruction. You might bump into someone while walking backwards trying to grab an interview. In all these cases the broadcaster might be liable if someone decides to sue.

Some situations are more obviously hazardous than others – covering a violent demonstration, terrorist attack, firearms incidents, sieges or bomb threats – and best practice is to find a place of safety from which to film or commentate. Your employer also has a duty of care to you.

Before you leave the newsroom, you must assess the safety of a location and update the assessment as circumstances change. All well-organised newsrooms will have a generic risk-assessment form, usually a combination of boxes to tick identifying the hazard and a brief explanation of any action you will take to minimise the risk. While the Health and Safety at Work Act (1974) does not require that all risk is eliminated, every effort should be made to reduce it 'so far as is reasonably practicable'.

On location

Radio

The beauty of radio may be its relative technical simplicity and intimacy, but the art of radio is sound. The best radio journalism is vibrant, descriptive and takes the listener into the story. It has strong interviews from eyewitnesses and people at the centre of the story, whether that's a party political conference or a murder. Most importantly, it has atmosphere and creates a sense of location. A story about school meals, for example, would include the chatter of children's voices, the clatter of plates and cutlery, the sizzle of the kitchen.

So, on the way to a story, consider what sounds you need to record (wildtrack) to convey the atmosphere, as well as thinking about who you will be interviewing. Never be tempted to add sound effects later – it does not work and always sounds stilted. It's also fakery. If you are at an airport, make sure you record announcements and the hum of the check-in. If you are covering a terrorist alert, record police sirens and traffic noise. Even in what appears to be a quiet location there'll be something – birdsong in a park, distant traffic, footsteps (see Chapter 11 for more on this).

Technological advances have put paid to the days when material was recorded on location and edited back in the newsroom. There are more 'lives' from the radio car and material sent back via wireless links. BBC local radio reporters now use a pocket computer phone which can record broadcast-quality audio, edit a simple package and send it back to the studio without the need for lines or even a radio car. It will also take still pictures and video for the website.

Television

If radio reporters think in terms of audio, then television reporters think in pictures: not individual shots, but sequences. If there are no pictures, nine times out of ten there is no story. Whether you are working alone or with a camera crew, an understanding of visual grammar – how moving pictures are integrated and juxtaposed to tell a story – is crucial. It is your job to make sure the camera captures the essential action, be it a noisy protest march, a celebrity visit to your patch or thinking up clever ways of explaining a pay deal.

Say you are filming in a school which has just introduced a new healthy menu. You should have an idea of all the elements you want to film – children eating in the canteen, kitchen staff serving, interviews with staff and children. Then work out how you are going to break down each of these chunks into editable sequences and how you will structure the final piece to tell the whole story (see Chapter 11 for more on this).

On pre-planned stories you'll sometimes get a chance to 'recce' (short for 'reconnaissance') the location beforehand. This means you can have a good look around and work out the best place for the camera and pick a good position for a piece-to-camera (PTC) or stand-up. Usually, though, you'll have to think on your feet and grasp opportunities as they arise.

If you are going to include a PTC (and it is not compulsory, despite what you might think from watching most news programmes!), then it needs to be there for a reason other than personal vanity. They work well when placing the reporter at the heart of the action – the viewer can see you were there. They can be used to explain parts of the story which have no pictures: for example, when you have a statement but no interview. However, putting PTCs at either the start or the end of an item has become a cliché and is probably best avoided. Never record a PTC that is more than approximately twenty seconds and try to ad-lib around particular words or phrases rather than memorise a whole script. And, if possible, introduce movement – walk a few steps or into frame.

News conferences and the scrum

The set-piece news conference, or 'presser', is not particularly broadcast friendly. However, in some cases – for example, police appeals for witnesses – they provide the best opportunity to get actuality from those at the heart of the story. Pictures of a row of people sitting behind a table against a corporate logo do not make good television, but a soundbite from a bereaved mother might well be worth it. On the other hand, every news organisation will get the same soundbite.

Always arrive with plenty of time to set up your equipment and find a good seat. Check with the organisers to see if there will be one-to-one interviews after it – the best way of getting your own interview. But record the conference anyway in case the plan changes. Radio journalists can steal a march on their television rivals by conducting their interviews while the TV people set up their equipment.

While there is an element of organisation with the news conference, that is not the case with the media scrum. Here, it is the person with the sharpest elbows who usually gets the best actuality. Hordes of reporters wielding cameras, microphones, flashguns and notebooks yell questions at someone at the centre of a big story. Often these scrums come after reporters have been staking out an individual, or at the end of a big court case, or outside the home of a scandal-hit celebrity or politician. For ordinary people not used to publicity, they can be intimidating and intrusive, and there are times when it is right to withdraw, as reporters did in the aftermath of the Dunblane massacre in Scotland in 1996, when sixteen primary schoolchildren and their teacher were shot dead in a school gym.

User-generated content

In the days after a tsunami struck large parts of South East Asia on Boxing Day 2004, broadcasters were inundated with video footage of the tragedy filmed by survivors. It was dramatic, eyewitness material and the first big example of how so-called 'citizens' journalism' was finding a place. Earlier the same year, footage of cars being swept through the flooded village of Boscastle in Cornwall was handed to broadcasters by residents, having been filmed on ordinary domestic camcorders.

It was during the terrorist attacks on London in July 2005 that the full possibilities of user-generated content were brought home to news organisations. People caught up in the attacks used mobile phones to capture the aftermath, walking to safety from a bombed tube train.

Now it is commonplace for broadcasters to seek such material in the wake of a big story. They do so by on-air requests and on-screen captions. Reporters also request CCTV footage as part of the raw material of a story. In 2006 a closed-circuit camera recorded pictures of a woman apparently being hit by a police officer at the back of a Sheffield night club, and the pictures were used widely by local and national broadcasters.

While user-generated content of this sort has a place and may be dramatic, it poses questions for journalists in terms of how to use it. Ownership of the copyright resides with the person who shot the film, so permission to use it is needed, and a fee might be demanded.

Videojournalism

The term 'videojournalism' first came to the UK in 1994 with a cable television experiment in London, Channel 1 (Boyd, 2001; Franklin *et al.*, 2005). Its backers, among them Sir David English, immediately realised the financial implications of doing journalism with new, small, lightweight cameras and set out to make 'polished news at low cost' (Boyd, 2001: 383). One-person crews, working with a reporter, were already being used for some jobs in some regional television newsrooms, but they used conventional, large Beta cameras. Channel 1 took this process a step further by removing the specialist camera operator and giving the camera to the journalist.

Reporters in mainstream television watched sceptically as Channel 1 journalists searched London for stories. They simply did not believe that you could do good journalism *and* get good pictures and sound. Sometimes they were undoubtedly proved right, and within the industry the channel was nicknamed 'Wobblyvision'. However, the financial benefits were obvious, and sufficently great for accountants to exert irresistible pressure on editors. Other regional television channels, including Meridian and West Country Television, experimented with videojournalists. A cable channel in Birmingham, Live TV, followed suit. By the time Channel 1 folded in the late nineties, the BBC and ITN were on board too.

Videojournalists represent a new kind of regional television journalist trained in solo camera and editing techniques, which means in theory they can take total control of their news production, from conception to screening. Many have been trained by Michael Rosenblum, an American videojournalism guru. He believes traditional television 'sucks', that it is stilted, predictable, elitist and ill-equipped to portray real life. His mission is to democratise the medium by placing small digital cameras in the hands of anybody who has the drive and enthusiasm to make television themself. He tells them to look for characters with stories to tell, and to film those stories simply and honestly, without the technology getting in the way.

Rosenblum is insistent that we live in a 'video-driven culture'. He describes small cameras, placed in trained hands, as 'the Gutenberg's printing presses of the twenty-first century' (Rosenblum, 2000: 140). There is an ideology here: 'I think television is the most powerful medium in the world today and I think it is an extremely dangerous medium in the hands of the very few . . . The only way to temper the power of this medium is to open it up to millions of people.' Rosenblum also has strong views on the notions of journalistic detachment and impartiality: he does not believe in them. 'When television really starts to work it's not when it only reflects the story that the journalist has captured but in some ways reflects the passion with the feeling of the journalist – the way a painting does.'[1]

BBC videojournalism trainer Mark Egan speaks passionately about the need to devote more time to producing better-quality, more 'real' TV news. He found the time constraints of working as a TV reporter alongside a crew hugely frustrating, and that the pressure of being sent out with a slot to fill in the lunchtime programme led to 'staged' events and artificially choreographed pictures.

> If they're not going to be building the ship in the morning, then you don't want them to fake building the ship in the morning. You'd rather wait until the afternoon and film it for real . . . You are trying to get reality, and reality doesn't happen when it's convenient for us.[2]

Former head of the BBC Nations and Regions Training Centre in Newcastle, Lisa Lambden, says that more opportunities are created for much younger reporters and technical staff:

> The technology is opening this to the masses and in newsrooms what you're seeing is lots of people who previously wouldn't have had the opportunity to get involved in being on screen, not in pieces to camera but actually to be out reporting. They've seen enormous opportunities for themselves to get into the front line of television reporting.[3]

Between March 2003 and May 2005, the BBC trained nearly 600 staff in Rosenblum's videojournalism techniques, in an atmosphere of some scepticism and concern that professional craft skills of filming and editing would be lost or diluted. A survey conducted by the authors among fifty of those attending the three-week courses showed that the training had changed attitudes to some extent. Ninety per cent of respondents agreed that stories appropriate to videojournalism were more personal, tended to tackle human interest topics and were more dramatic. But nearly half still had reservations about the professional 'look' of such items. And more than half did not think the stories were well shot or edited. Taken together, these responses seem to suggest that videojournalism does indeed have the potential to tell the sorts of stories that may be difficult for a conventional crew to shoot, but there are serious reservations about how polished they can be. One staffer said:

'I like the idea of spending a little longer on a story and delving a little deeper, but I suspect that in the end I will just be churning out on-the-day stuff.' Another admitted that it's frustrating waiting around for traditional crews and liked the thought of more technical control, 'but I'm conscious that however good I get to be I can't compete with experienced specialist cameramen and editors'. A third recognised videojournalism's potential: 'I do feel that people open up more with this style of filming. This is partly because we are able to spend longer with interviewees and partly because of the loss of paraphernalia.'

A tangle of wires and tubing spews from her tiny body as the toddler lies comatose on a life-support machine. Jemma had been suffering fits for two days before she was sedated. The medics at Southampton General Hospital have been worried about her chances of survival. They talk us through their strategy as our screen is filled with images of her unconscious face, and her tummy rising and falling ever so gently as a ventilator controls her breathing. They decide to wake her by stopping the feed of morphine and other sleep-inducing drugs. As she surfaces, we see waves of neural activity blip before us on an EEG screen. Only now will Jemma's anxious parents learn whether she has permanent brain damage.

This is powerful, moving television; the stuff of which award-winning documentaries are made. Yet it was shot not by a meticulously produced documentary team, but by a news reporter who happened to be at the paediatric intensive-care unit on another assignment when the drama began. David Fenton's four-minute film for BBC's *South Today* was shot by him single-handed as events unfolded. His lightweight, unobtrusive camera allows him to take us on the ambulance as it speeds up the motorway to collect Jemma from her local hospital in Chichester. We join the Chichester nurse as she prepares Jemma for the journey to the specialist unit in Southampton. We travel with her on that journey, seeing the nurse hold Jemma's drips steady as the ambulance weaves at speed through traffic. Then we share the concerns of the Southampton specialists as they weigh their chances of saving Jemma's life.

Fenton used his camera in much the same way as a print journalist would use a notebook. He recorded a series of events without allowing his technology or production requirements to intrude and to manipulate what was shot. Such candid, spontaneous filming might not have been possible with the traditional television crew, whose heavyweight gear and demanding sound and lighting requirements would have slowed things down and required a more stilted, 'choreographed' approach to the filming.

Conclusion

Newsgathering is at the heart of all journalism and in the context of broadcast journalism requires sound and pictures as well as words. Working practices have changed dramatically in recent years with the demise of the traditional television crew and the advent of still-controversial videojournalism. Technological advances have made it easier than ever to edit material in the field and send it back to base. Broadcast journalists are now not the only suppliers of material: user-generated content has found a place in the newsgathering pantheon. Planning and preparation remain essential, regardless of the pressure of deadlines. But there will never be any substitute for going there: getting out on location, talking to the people who matter and collecting the sights and sounds of the story.

Notes

1 Interview with the authors, 29 November 2004.
2 Interview with the authors, 11 November 2005.
3 Interview with the authors, 11 November 2005.

References

Boyd, A. (2001) *Broadcast Journalism: Techniques of Radio and Television News*, Oxford: Focal Press
Chantler, P. and Stewart, P. (2003) *Basic Radio Journalism*, Oxford: Focal Press
Franklin, B. *et al.* (2005) *Key Concepts in Journalism Studies*, London: Sage
Hudson, G. and Rowlands, S. (2007) *The Broadcast Journalism Handbook*, Harlow: Pearson Longman
Ray, V. (2003) *The Television News Handbook*, London: Macmillan
Rosenblum, M. (2000) 'Videojournalism: the birth of a new medium', *International Journal on Grey Literature* 1(3): 139–42

Asking questions

Interviewing for broadcast news

Jim Beaman and Anne Dawson

Introduction

To the viewer and listener, an interview might look spontaneous and even relaxed, but it is a highly structured conversation between two people, often with contradictory agendas: the Hollywood star who wants to promote his new film but not discuss his drug problem; the politician trying to play down the latest high inflation figures; or the flood victim who would rather not speak to the press at all.

It is worth remembering that anyone can refuse to participate in an interview and may instead issue a statement if they think you will not give them a fair hearing, fear they may be humiliated by you or do not want to risk performing badly. Suggesting that the interview is founded on a 'triangle of trust' between the interviewer, interviewee and listener, McLeish (2003: 64) asserts that if just one side of the triangle is damaged, then 'we have lost something of genuine value'. This opinion is supported by industry guidelines advising fair dealing during interviews, and anticipates the controversy over the transparency of news storytelling techniques.

A large amount of radio and television output is generated from interview material, used for clips in news bulletins, in packaged reports for programmes and helping to inform the content of links and commentary by reporters. So it's important to examine what goes into producing the best broadcast interviews: from finding the right person to talk to and asking the right questions to deciding which sections to use in the final broadcast. You need to be aware of the different skills and techniques in live and pre-recorded interviews, face to face and on the telephone, for radio and television, in breaking news stories and background features. You should also explore the different tensions that come into play when questioning highly polished, experienced interviewees and 'ordinary' people who might have found themselves in front of the camera or microphone because they are unexpectedly in the media spotlight.

Choosing the right interviewee

If you are reporting on a natural disaster, it will be obvious to whom you need to talk: in most cases you will need to hear from a victim (someone whose house is flooded), someone in authority (the fire brigade or water company) and, if appropriate, a campaigner or lobbyist (an environmentalist). If your story is political or about any sort of dispute, there will be two factions and you will need to speak to a representative from each side. If you are putting together a more complex, in-depth feature, you will have a variety of interviewees contributing their own unique viewpoints, so a piece about the standard of secondary school education might include children, parents, teachers, educational researchers, politicians and employers. It is always essential that you get the best possible interviewees: if you need to hear from a chocolate manufacturer about a salmonella scare, you should interview the managing director or marketing manager; do not let the company fob you off with its press officer. If you are in a flooded village, your audience want to hear from the person who has been most badly hit, not from a neighbour whose house is a bit damp but who is happy to tell you stories about other people she's 'heard of' who have had a worse time. To get right to the heart of the story, you need to find the person with the most powerful story to tell, or you need to challenge the politician or health authority chief about why patients are waiting weeks to be seen by a specialist doctor. Many potential interviewees will jump at the chance to appear on air because they see it as an opportunity to raise awareness of their plight or problem, their organisation, product or activity. Others may want to set the record straight by explaining the issue from their point of view or to put a positive spin on a potentially damaging story. Even those who are victims of a tragedy may welcome the experience and find it cathartic just to talk to anyone who will listen. But you need to be sensitive to the fact that they may be confused and unaware that their words and image will be broadcast, so double-check that they give consent for the interview to be aired to a wider audience than yourself.

All interviewees will need to know how you plan to use them if they are to agree and participate fully. They must be told why they have been invited to take part, which topic is being discussed, who will be questioning them, who else may be taking part in the piece, whether it is live or recorded and will take place in the studio, down the line or on location, whether there will be a public phone-in element, and how long it will take. Knowing all this, they may decide that they are not really the right person to interview. You may need to persuade them otherwise. If they insist on pulling out, ask them if they can suggest a suitable replacement. There are any number of reasons why inexperienced potential interviewees prefer not to be interviewed: from not liking how they look on screen or the sound of their voice to worrying about how friends will judge their contribution.

Choosing the right location

Having done your research thoroughly, used all your skills of persuasion and had luck on your side, you have managed to secure all the interviews you need for your report. Now it is essential that you choose your locations well and do not underestimate the power of the background sound or shot to enhance the message. If you are examining the behaviour of football fans at Premiership games, you should record your interviews at a football ground: while taking a group of fans to a quiet room will give you a nice clear recording, there will be no atmosphere to illustrate what the interviewees are saying. Equally, waiting until after the match and doing your interviews in a pub will provide background atmosphere – or 'atmos', as radio reporters call it – but it will be the wrong atmos. You must talk to your interviewees in the place that is *most* appropriate to the story. There are dangers, though, if you record a radio interview while a commentary or announcement is being broadcast over the PA system or while loud music is playing: in addition to your interviewee fighting to be heard above the noise, you will find it very hard to edit because you will have to edit the backgound noise, too. If you are in a location where the background noise can be reduced – for example, by switching off noisy air conditioning in an office, or the TV or stereo in an interviewee's house – you should not be afraid to ask. If not, you will have to wait until the announcement has finished or the band stops playing before you can start.

When you are recording an interview for television, you must also think about what the viewer will see in the background. An image is more powerful than words, and while an interviewee can try to describe her feelings or her situation, the message will be far more powerful if it is properly illustrated. A reporter describing the aftermath of a bomb attack may catch only short snatches of interviews with people who are in great distress and speak little English, but if these are recorded among the rubble of those people's collapsed homes or as the bodies of their neighbours are carried out on stretchers, the story will have been told powerfully. Even in a less dramatic, domestic situation it is important to have the official from the Environment Agency talking about pollution while standing (or crouching) by a river rather than sitting in his office in a shirt and tie. He may need some persuasion to leave his desk and meet you on location, so it is up to you to explain that his warning or advice will be much more effective if he does just that.

If you are conducting a live interview for radio or TV, the same rules apply: you must be in the most effective and appropriate location. But in this case you have the added problem of having to 'manage' the location as well as conduct the interview. You will not have the chance to do the interview again if someone walks through the shot, if a bus parks right in front of the court building you wanted in the background or if someone starts digging up the road where you have parked the radio car, so you must try to make sure your location is 'broadcast friendly' as well as being visually and aurally powerful. Now that radio reporters go out on their own in the radio car and satellite trucks are driven by the camera operator, there is no longer a 'spare pair of hands' to manage the location. It is still safer to take a helper to a busy location, though, and the resulting interview is likely to be of better quality, so do not be afraid to insist on it.

Asking the right questions

While the intention is often to create the impression among viewers or listeners that an interview is simply a recorded conversation, in reality it is often meticulously prepared. As an interviewer, you will generally try to ask direct, relevant questions, and on occasion you must challenge the interviewee's answers. It is important that you pursue with persistent but polite questioning if you feel you are not being given a satisfactory answer. Starting your repeated question with such expressions as 'So, what you're saying is . . .' or 'Can we get this absolutely clear . . .' may help elicit a more satisfactory reply.

During a breaking news story a talented reporter, in the right place at the right time, might record an extraordinary interview 'on the hoof' with no planning. When you are sent to report on a breaking story the best advice is to remember what Rudyard Kipling called his 'five friends good and true', the five Ws: if you remember to ask 'who, what, where, when, why' (and possibly 'how'), you will cover the main points. In a more considered piece you will have time to plan your questions in advance. When planning what you are going to ask you must always remember your audience; part of your job is to act on their behalf and ask the questions they would ask if they had the chance. The increasingly interactive nature of both radio and TV news means that the public does have more opportunities to ask questions, on phone-ins, by email and text, but if you are interviewing the Prime Minister about the country's role in an international conflict you should remember that it is the voters who gave the government its mandate and they have a right to challenge that government via the media.

When planning your questions you need to think about how the interview or interview clips will fit into your finished package so that you can ensure you cover all the required areas. If you want short soundbites you will need to ask the questions in a way that suggests that is what you want. It is worth remembering that a soundbite can be a memorably clear and concise summation of an answer or seem like a contrived or rehearsed statement without any real substance. If, on the other hand, you want a longer explanation for a background feature, you will need to ask a more 'open' question.

Consider the different responses you might get from these two questions to a police chief about teenage gun crime in South London:

● Question 1: 'This is the fourth death this week. Have the police lost control of these streets?'
● Question 2: 'Four teenagers have been shot this week. Is this a crimewave that the police no longer have the resources or expertise to deal with, one that is inevitably going to increase?'

Question 1 is likely to elicit a short defence of the police's position. Question 2 will bring a more considered and detailed response.

It is good practice to prepare extra questions, particularly for a live interview, in case your interviewee gives very brief answers, but do not feel that you must ask all the questions on your list or in your head. Interviewees (particularly experienced ones) get very impatient with new reporters who carry out very long interviews just to try to cover every possible angle but then discover when it is broadcast that all but a few seconds have ended up on the cutting-room floor. A reporter may be asked to go out and cover the same story for both TV and radio. Does this mean they will have to conduct two interviews with the same person? In an ideal world the answer would be 'yes', because the interviewing technique will be different and they have different production techniques and technical requirements. In reality the reporter will choose to conduct the TV interview on camera and simply submit the soundtrack for use as audio for the radio piece. The interviewee will probably be very grateful, as this means they do not have to go through the ordeal twice.

If you want to get a reputation as a good interviewer who has authority but can also demonstrate empathy, listen to what your interviewee is saying and respond, if appropriate. Believe that everyone you invite to be interviewed is entitled to their point of view and should be given an opportunity to put their case. Do not just try to see both sides of an argument; develop a strategy to enable you to challenge both viewpoints. Give an interviewee the opportunity to reply to a question but do not carelessly hand over control to them; think before you speak; get your facts right; and do not be afraid to ask the obvious.

One of the main complaints from interviewees and audiences about interviewing techniques employed by broadcasters is that the interviewer interrupts as the interviewee is answering the question. The BBC's editorial guidelines advise that interruptions, provided they can be justified and explained to both the interviewee and the listener or viewer, should be 'well timed and not too frequent'. Interviewers have a duty to challenge interviewees if they feel that they are evading an issue.

Multiple questions are another bugbear and are best avoided. They confuse the interviewee, who will usually answer only the latter part because they have forgotten (or have chosen to forget) the first part. Leading questions – 'Your department has got this wrong, hasn't it?' – will perhaps generate a more direct answer when calling someone to account.

Another useful tool to help focus, shape and even close an interview is to summarise what has been said by the interviewee and add a final question that will hopefully generate a strong finale: 'You say that the plans now in place will help these families and that the increase in funding will solve the immediate problem, but how can you be sure that you won't be facing the same issues again next year?'

Live interviews

There are particular skills involved in conducting live interviews, and the more planning that goes into them, the better they will be. The clock governs both radio and television output: when you go on air, when you come off air and how much time you have to conduct an interview. You must find out from the producer how long they will have for the interview and then be realistic about how many questions you will fit into that time. You must also think about how you will get the best out of your interviewee. Is it best to woo a politician with a 'soft' question and then hit them with the killer blow halfway through, or to go in straight away with a tough challenge? The nature of the story will probably dictate this. Given the choice, politicians seem to favour the live interview option because they feel they have more control: they can try to get in the last word and what they say cannot be affected by any editing (Jones, 1995: 20). If you are interviewing a member of the public who is nervous and has never been interviewed before, spend time preparing them, building a rapport with them, giving them an idea of what sort of questions you plan to ask and helping them relax. Do not be tempted to give them the exact questions in advance or to rehearse the interview with them as they may try to learn their answers and this will sound very unnatural.

All-news radio channels and twenty-four-hour television news have meant that presenters now conduct more 'live' interviews than they did in the past. There is more of a demand to react to breaking stories and to fill hours of airtime, and less structured interviews play an important role in the way information is disseminated.

Coping with difficulties

As an interviewer, it may be incumbent on you to coax a response out of an interviewee. Someone describing a tragedy or emotional event may stop speaking mid-sentence because they are welling up with tears, so allow them to pause and take a breath by saying something like 'take your time'. Some interviewees will simply be nervous about talking on mike or camera, so encourage them by asking more follow-up questions like 'That's interesting, can you explain how you coped with it?' or perhaps precede your question with a summary of information gleaned from your research or previous responses that will give them a base for their answer: for example, 'So, you were saying that once you arrived in this country you started work and then you met your partner. When did you realise things were starting to go wrong?' If you feel that your interviewee is being deliberately vague when answering your questions, you could try waiting in silent anticipation for more from them. Simply stay quiet and maintain eye contact. You may find they feel obliged to fill that awkward silence and eventually the interview will return to a more fluid pattern. One technique used by experienced interviewees is to try to move the discussion away from your current line of questioning. If you sense this happening, interject with 'That's an interesting point, but isn't it more important for our listeners to know . . .' or 'Can we return to the protests? You were saying that . . .' Hopefully, they will know they have been rumbled and will refocus.

Press conferences can be problematic for the broadcast journalist. They are, after all, stages principally for print journalists *en masse*. Broadcast journalism editors need to decide if the story is worth the time and financial investment demanded to send a reporter and crew. Will the journalist come back with a story worth telling and will they get an opportunity to pose the questions they want to ask during such a contrived and controlled event? TV and radio reporters will usually have to make special arrangements in advance to secure separate interviews with the main players, preferably before the conference gets under way. Although the organisers will want to achieve their PR agenda goals, you should not be afraid to establish your own needs and ask the questions you want answered. Unlike cameras, microphones do not have zoom functions, so if you are collecting audio at the conference make sure you are as close to the speakers as possible so that you return to the newsroom with usable material. Simply leaving the microphone on the table where the speakers are set up or holding a microphone in front of the room's loudspeakers will not give satisfactory results for broadcast. Do not be shy in coming forward to position microphones – after all, both you and the interviewee want their voice to be heard as clearly as possible.

After the event

'Live' interviews are playing an increasingly important role in certain types of radio and television news. For most reporters, however, there will be at least some basic editing involved in every interview they do, and the post-production process is almost as important as the interview itself. While good editing cannot hide the fact that a reporter has not asked the right questions or has allowed the interviewee to ramble or wander off the subject, it does give them an opportunity to separate the strongest, most relevant clips from the rest. Editing is essential to remove fluffs and mistakes, to fit a time slot, remove any legal pitfalls and tell a story efficiently and effectively.

Do not let your interviewee go until you are completely satisfied you have something recorded that you can use on air. Play back a little of the interview to check, but do not offer to play it all back because they may ask you to make changes or insist you do the whole thing again. Once it is in the can, an interview becomes your property. It is your editorial decision, not theirs, to choose to use the material or not. If the interview is conducted live, do not let the interviewee leave until you are cleared by the studio, just in case they want to come back to you later in the programme for further information or more chat. Certainly make sure you have the interviewee's contact details before they leave, for future reference.

Current debates

There has been a lively debate in television for some time about the ethics of editing that has forced all journalists to re-examine the way they set up, shoot and edit pre-recorded interviews. This was underlined in the summer of 2007 when the BBC was criticised for a trailer that was edited to make it look as though the Queen had stormed out of a photoshoot. Traditionally all reporters would film a series of 'editing' shots or 'cutaways' with every interview to give them a variety of ways of cutting it down. While in radio it is possible for a reporter to take two sections of interview and splice them together without the listener being aware of the edit, if you do this with a television interview you will make a 'jump cut', where the interviewee's face literally 'jumps' in the frame. The usual way round this is to shoot a 'two-shot' of the interviewee and reporter sitting together; or a 'noddy', which is a shot of the reporter listening or nodding in response to the interviewee. If the interviewee is talking, for example, about a relative who has been killed in action in Iraq, another technique is to cut away to a still photograph of that person. Until very recently it was not considered acceptable for the video edit to be seen.

However, in the summer of 2007 Channel Five's news editor David Kermode banned a number of techniques at Five News, to help 'rebuild viewers' trust in television' and avoid charges of manipulation. Among the methods to go were the 'noddy', 'contrived cutaways' and 'contrived walking shots'. Kermode argued:

> These are tired old techniques that belong in a different era. Viewers – many of whom create and upload their own content – have a pretty good grasp of what an 'edit' is, so I think the time has come to be honest about signposting when we edit our interviews. Modern digital editing technology means that edits can be made by 'dissolving' from one shot into another, something that wasn't achievable in the days of tape-to-tape editing. It's about being honest, but I also see this as a creative challenge.
>
> (*Media Guardian*, 2007)

So the 'dissolve' has entered the visual vocabulary of television news. Five News has been followed by the BBC in this practice, while other channels continue to use traditional editing devices. For a new reporter, there is no 'right' or 'wrong', but it is vital to be aware of which news organisations use which techniques, because these have become as much a part of the process of matching the target audience as writing style and bulletin content.

Questions will inevitably be raised about the methods used for radio. The use of recorded atmosphere (or wild-track) to enhance illustrative background or mask untidy edits in the final mix is common. Reporters may also re-record a badly worded question post-interview to be inserted during the editing process. The creative use of editing and mixing used to produce wraps, packages, features and documentaries offers a variety of listening experiences through a range of storytelling techniques. For the interviewee, construction techniques ensure a coherent interview that will assist them to get their message across.

Most interviewees and listeners accept that if an interview has been recorded, then the chances are that it has also been subject to the editing process. The use of the 'bleep' to cover bad language on air, for instance, not only masks the offence but draws it to the attention of the listener. Recording an interview and then broadcasting it 'as live' is another technique used extensively on radio when it may be impractical to conduct it live. However, it should be remembered that the method and wording used to introduce the piece via the cue and back announcement should not undermine the integrity of the interview by giving the impression that it is being conducted live. Are radio journalists still trusted by the other two sides of the 'triangle' to conduct, record, edit and set an interview in context without changing meaning?

The future of the broadcast interview

The role and purpose of the broadcast interview continue to develop and change. Interviewers have moved from deferential questioning of those in power and a patronising attitude to the man-in-the-street (when media awareness was at a lower level than it is today) to what many believe is a hectoring style for serious interviews and a public-relations-collaborative approach to celebrity interviews. Now and in the future it seems that nothing less than incisive and straightforward questioning by informed and impartial interviewers is acceptable.

Audiences can hear and watch short-form interviews on radio and television, are offered longer versions on a programme's website and are encouraged to raise questions of their own via message boards, email and phone-ins. With interaction with audience members a priority, programme-makers may give them interviewing opportunities or at least allow them to influence or shape the line of questioning. Potential interviewees, like politicians and others in the firing line, may in future choose to abandon conventional media and offer their views unchallenged via blogs and podcasts. Perhaps they are finally learning a lesson from Huckleberry Finn, who famously said that if he was not asked any questions, he would not have to tell any lies.

References

BBC (2005) *Editorial Guidelines: The BBC's Values and Standards*, London BBC

Jones, N. (1995) *Soundbites and Spin Doctors*, London: Cassell

McLeish, R. (2003) *Radio Production*, 4th edn, Oxford: Focal Press

Media Guardian (2007) 'Five News to ban staged shots', at www.guardian. co.uk/media/2007/aug/30/tvnews.channelfive (accessed 2 April 2008)

Painting pictures 1

Writing, editing and packaging for television

Jeremy Orlebar

10

Introduction

Visual imperatives dominate television journalism, and not just in news. Making factual programmes requires the broadcast journalist to capture pictures that drive the narrative, deliver content and provide contextual amplification. Some of these pictures may be startling, some dramatic, some beautiful. Some may tell a horrifying or harrowing story – prisoners being beaten by soldiers or a dramatic rescue at sea. Many programmes explore ideas and subjects that do not provide exotic locations or dramatic pictures but can tell a journalistically interesting story. Somehow the programme-maker must cajole, seduce and entice the audience into the programme's story and then encourage them to stay with it. The quality, variety, juxtaposition and composition of the pictures are the keys.

Creating pictures with narrative thrust and discursive content is a challenge but one which can result from lateral thinking, constructive creative research and careful observation. Programme briefs in the factual area tend to be ideas-driven, based within genres such as science, current affairs, arts, sport, history, travel or events, and it is most important to be able to treat ideas in a visually distinctive way.

Visualising formats

The audience might think that visualising a programme begins when the camera starts recording; in fact, the production team have been very busy well before then, when the idea is gestating as a brief. For a brief to translate into effective television, the concepts need to be visualised in a way the audience will find absorbing and which deliver content. There are techniques for doing this, which tend to run in fashionable phases.

Television still has a strong belief in the role of the presenter as elucidator. This was honed perfectly in the early era of the BBC's *Blue Peter*. An intrepid presenter would be a human guinea pig, testing a new invention, flying in a jet plane or visiting an exotic location. The concept of 'being there' has always appealed to television producers. When a young viewer wrote in to ask how they cleaned the pigeon droppings from Nelson's statue at the top of his column in Trafalgar Square, *Blue Peter* sent along a presenter and a cameraperson. They climbed to the top of the column and helped with the cleaning process – and made sure the vertigo-inducing views were cleverly shown as well. This is the 'I was there and I did it for you' school of reality television, which undoubtedly has impact and is memorable. This format has now been adapted to extreme situations with a serious explorer-presenter such as Bear Grylls, who demonstrates toe-curling survival techniques in a dangerous environment.

One of the most successful geographical programmes of recent years was the BBC's *Coast*. Memorable helicopter shots of the coastline around Britain are entertainingly intercut with interviews on the ground about the archaeology, people and history of the area. One or two presenters are used to fill in the historical content, conduct interviews and link the impressive pictures. It works extremely well in both a generally interesting and educationally informative way. This is a tried and tested model of intelligent and genuinely educational television, which appeals to a wide audience. The visual imperatives complement the journalistic criteria. This is the key to keeping the audience interested: what is happening, where, to whom and by whom, and why it is important.

Visualising ideas

To turn an idea into a factual, 'televisual' sequence suitable for broadcasting involves choosing a visual style suitable for the programme format, as well as the content. Visual style covers everything from the selection of the presenter (and if there is to be one) to the way the items are filmed and the pace and rhythm of the editing, as well as the choice of music and the delivery of the narrative. This is dependent on a number of factors, including the duration of the programme, or of each segment, and how and when it will be broadcast. Property programmes, for example, may be sequenced for four twelve-minute sections, separated by advertisements, over a sixty-minute transmission time. At the beginning of each section there is an update on the story so far: for example, 'Anna and Chris are looking for a three-bed property on the Algarve and have seen these four properties.' This can be annoying for the audience but programme-makers have found that it brings in new viewers as well as keeping up the narrative for the original audience.

Truthful television

Factual and reality programmes came under intense scrutiny in 2007, with Ofcom examining BBC and ITV programme content and in particular how some scenes in factual programmes had been 'economical with the truth'. It is the visual truth that is at the heart of this ethics debate. When a presenter holds up a catch of large fish we are led to believe he caught all of them himself, although he may not have done so. In the twenty-first century, viewers' rights to the visual truth are considered to be paramount.

However, television is a constructed medium. Truth in a televisual context is very difficult to define and even harder to capture on video. Just take the example of the replay in sport. Often multi-camera angles cannot show whether a batsman has been caught out or a football is over the goal-line. Truth is at best a movable feast. The consideration of ethics is relevant because the viewer particularly relies on pictures to contribute to the truthful understanding of a scene.

Television interviews

Many programme stories derive from interviews. Current affairs depend on them. When it comes to visualisation, the director/producer's job is to find pictures that make sense, are relevant to the story and deliver more information to complement that given in the interview. We need to see shots of things referred to in the interview; pictures need to be active, not just wallpaper, in order to retain an audience. Programme-makers are trained to take many more cutaways than they think they need, so that the interview will not just be talking heads. The sound edits can be covered by pictures and so avoid jump cuts. Is this compromising the truth of the interview? I believe it is not, because the essential truth of what the interviewee is saying is not contradicted, changed or altered by these shots. The editor must have pictures to work with, and if these pictures are relevant they will add context and meaning to the interview. Audiences know this and accept it as part of the televisual experience.

The best television interview will explore the look of the contributor, employing a range of shot sizes that bring the content narrative to the attention of the viewer. Relevant contextual pictures will fill in the detail, and explore the content that the words leave out or that need further explanation.

Technical visuals

Technically and as a way of conveying visual comprehension, an interview nearly always looks better when it is shot on a tripod: steady pictures are easier to watch than 'wobblyscope'. The current fad for shooting interviews with a hand-held camera in a quasi-documentary way tries to achieve a more realistic or authentic feel to the interview, but it does not deceive anyone. I think it creates a visual barrier between the interviewee, the content and the viewer. It may be cheaper and quicker to do hand-held interviews, but production values diminish and meaning is lost as style takes precedence over substance.

Many factual television programmes are made on very limited budgets. The production team may be just one or two people. The cameraperson is likely to be the producer/director who sets up the shots, asks the questions off camera, writes the commentary and does a lot of the research and setting up.

One of the biggest differences between a professional-looking, well-shot interview and something just cobbled together is the framing of the shots from a camera set up on a tripod. Generally that professional look is obtained by using shot sizes that conform to the standard framing for each size of shot. A selection of shot sizes has been developed that fit the TV frame naturally and can be edited together in a way that makes sense visually. This helps the viewer deconstruct the image and pick up on content. Shooting on the 16:9 widescreen format that broadcast television requires means that the interview location and the shot size must be in harmony as there is more screen space to convey meaning.

Shot size

It is normal to have three prearranged shot sizes for an interview: a *close-up* (CU), a *medium close-up* (MCU) and a *medium shot* or *mid-shot* (MS). A typical interview starts with an MS and changes to an MCU during the first or second question; it then goes to the CU for question three. If the interview is getting interesting or the contributor is revealing something very personal or particularly relevant, the camera can zoom in, in-vision, to the CU. This needs practice. The interviewee should look only at the person asking the questions behind the camera, or towards the presenter, and answer the questioner directly. This means the contributor will look just to the left or right of the camera lens, depending on which side the questioner is sitting. This is the ideal position in the frame for an interview, as it shows a full face without the interviewee looking directly at camera. Other standard shot sizes include *very big close-up* (VBCU) or *extreme close up* (ECU), which shows a part of the face, such as the mouth, the eyes or even just one eye. This is popular with music video directors, and for postmodern-looking documentaries. A *wide shot* (WS) is a wide angle of the interview set-up or the scene being filmed.

Shooting cutaways

Cutaways are pictures that can be edited into an interview so that the final piece is not just one long talking head. They allow the editor to cut away from the con-tributor to a relevant picture at the point where there is an edit for content or to condense time. They are preferably shots of what the contributor is talking about, and should always be of something relevant. Well-chosen cutaways not only make the interview more interesting but go some way to creating television with impact that fulfils the audience's expectations. Some of the most useful cutaways are constructed in visual sequences incorporating a variety of shot sizes for each sequence, to provide plenty of options at the editing stage.

Faces

When filming the action shots of someone at work or making something, it helps in the editing to shoot close-ups of the contributor's face concentrating on what he or she is doing. This will make it possible in the edit to condense time. Someone making a cake or driving a car might take several minutes or more in real time, but by cutting to the face this real time can be reduced considerably. Experienced directors try to film the interview first, then shoot related action. This provides a much better idea of what to film for cutaways because the director has heard what the contributor has to say in the interview.

Words on the screen with graphics

Programmes or news items that aim to make sense of complex topics often need to introduce graphics to illustrate ideas, relate statistics or explain concepts. A programme about environmental concerns might be looking at what happens to the waste from a large city. The programme-makers have researched statistics about waste in London:

- London produces 17 million tonnes of waste each year.
- 3.4 million tonnes are household rubbish.
- On average, every Londoner generates 518 kilograms of waste each year.
- 60 per cent of that could be recycled.

The programme looks at ways of reducing and recycling waste. The researchers found that one way to reduce the waste mountain would be to switch to double-sided A4 printing: if this were done, it is estimated that 17.5 billion sheets of A4 paper could be saved every year in London alone.

The programme-makers' challenge is to involve the audience in a popular programme by making visual sense of such statistics. The audience does not want to be intimidated with an overload of information that it cannot remember and perhaps does not really consider important.

A journalist is adept at making statistics come alive for the audience by creating analogies. A written analogy to show the impact of printing on both sides of A4 paper is to say that the amount of paper saved could be wrapped around the earth four times. This could also be a striking televisual analogy by using animated computer graphics to show a revolving globe shrink-wrapped in sheets of paper. This visual could bring home the waste message, but it may be an expensive graphic, and it takes up very little screen time. It therefore may not be good value in television terms, and it may have only limited impact, which is not a producer's recipe for economical use of resources and value up there on the screen. The animated graphic could be allied with live-action filming using other techniques, such as a presenter who could do a piece to camera, an interview, a vox-pop or even a music sequence. An analogy for the amount of waste produced each year by Londoners is that it would fill the Canary Wharf Tower every ten days. Graphics used with real pictures of the well-known tower would make a striking illustration for this statistic.

Computer-generated graphics can sometimes get in the way of the story and may not be as memorable as they seem. Just how many of those animated graphics so popular with news producers do you remember after the bulletin? Audience feedback suggests that they have much less impact than live-action pictures. For example, if the topic is climate change, pictures of polar bears trying to find a solid ice floe in the melting Arctic are memorable and bring home a message. However, live-action pictures do not always have more impact and carry greater 'stickability' than words or graphics on the screen. In fact, many television graphic designers would say a *combination* of words on the screen and live pictures creates most impact and lasts longer in the mind of the audience.

The visually alert journalist knows that pictures tend to simplify, and sometimes exaggerate, political events, especially within a news situation. Energy issues are often illustrated with library stock of queues at petrol pumps, and food shortages with lines of unhappy shoppers at supermarket checkouts. These visual short cuts offer limited explanation and very little meaning in a closed and limited way. Broadcast journalists have to be aware of the political manipulation of photo opportunities created by politicians. But sometimes they create iconic moments that cannot be ignored and go down in history as images of the Zeitgeist. Who can forget Margaret Thatcher looking out of the gun turret of a tank, or Tony Blair's apparently off-the-cuff speech after the death of Diana, Princess of Wales?

Post-production

Creative painting with pictures mostly happens in the post-production process. Editing gives a director a wide variety of visual effects to enhance the programme.

One of the most useful and effective visual effects is the ability to speed up and slow down the picture in-vision. This can compress time within, for example, a long walking shot by starting in real time, speeding up the middle of the walk, then returning to real time for, say, the final arrival at a doorway or meeting with another person. This effect also adds drama and creates pace and energy in a sequence.

Another effect that provides movement and can deliver a painterly colour composition is the 'time slip locked-off shot'. A camera is set up on a wide shot looking at, say, a busy road intersection. The fixed camera is time controlled to shoot five minutes of pictures every hour for twenty-four hours. Edited together and speeded up, this set-up can create a fascinating shot of moving people and traffic with trailing colours at night. This type of shot may have limited meaning in itself, but when matched with a presenter in front of the shot via bluescreen[1] the composite picture can deliver content, impact and narrative with its own visual imperative.

During pre-production the director has to line up the gallery of shots and effects that will create the visual style for the programme, and make arrangements while shooting to allow for visual effects. No matter how sophisticated the digital effects available in post-production, the editor still needs an adequate number of well-composed pictures to work with. Repeated images induce audience fatigue and make the show look lazy. The process of creative editing selects the best shots and scenes, and adds the most informative words. It also structures and shapes the visual material, creating narrative. The journalist's job is to make sure strong visuals add meaning, drive the narrative, bring the audience into the story and above all do not become a wallpaper of stereotyped images.

Creative commentary

> Dawn – and as the sun breaks through the piercing chill of night on the plain outside Korem it lights up a biblical famine, now, in the twentieth century.
> (Michael Buerk, BBC Television)

With these words, Michael Buerk alerted UK television viewers to the tragedy of famine in Ethiopia in 1984. It still stands as one of the most evocative openings to a television news package, spoken over pictures of a blood-red sun and thousands of starving, distressed people.

Commentary, or voiceover, is a crucial part of many journalistic items and productions. It has two main functions: to fill in information that the pictures do not convey; and to contribute extra material to add value to the programme. The function of commentary is to complement the visuals and drive the narrative. Some directors like to write a first version of the commentary during the filming of the programme or very soon after seeing the rushes. The director typically writes the commentary after a first (or rough) cut and before the fine cut of the edit. It is important to write to the pictures that have been shot, rather than make the pictures fit words that have been written in advance. Some tips include: write in short sentences and avoid complex clauses.

The main difficulty is in getting the timing right so that the words fit the pace and rhythm of the editing. The number of words often needs to be cut down to fit the screen time available. In terms of how many words need to be written, a good rule of thumb is: three spoken words equal one second of screen time. Commentary should be brief and to the point, and should not state the obvious or describe what can be seen in the pictures; it should *add* information, comment or, in certain cases, opinion. Any complicated information can be broken down into easily digestible, bite-size chunks: state what, when, where and why.

Commentary is usually in the present tense. If the writing is in the past tense, then the pictures should support it – for example, using archive film or filling in background information about something or someone. Statistics are always hard for the audience to take in, especially if there is no visual clue in the pictures, so they should be made as user-friendly as possible. Instead of 'one-fifth' or '20 per cent', use 'one in five', a statistic the audience is more likely to understand.

The final decision is who should voice the commentary. It is tempting to employ a well-known actor or celebrity to give the programme clout, but the main consideration should be which type of voice is the most relevant and the most suitable for the particular programme. Some actors specialise in voiceover work and seem able to convey a great deal of information through intonation, pace and technique. Some director/producers prefer to speak their own written commentary, arguing that they are in the best position to convey the mood, tone and feeling of the programme.

If commentary is rushed or spoken quickly, it will sound just that – rushed and unprofessional. Short sentences lead to crisp commentary. Dead time, or breathing space, can be built in for the edited original location sound and any added sound, such as music, to do its job, and be complemented by the pictures. Writing commentary is not as straightforward as it might seem, as each word, each sentence and each pause matter. Many programme-makers agonise over writing commentary, but there is a feeling of intense satisfaction when the carefully composed and edited pictures come alive with the added meaning and resonance of a well-modulated voiceover.

Vin Ray (2003) of the BBC College of Journalism advocates what he calls 'The Six Ss'

- Short sentences;
- Sound – use lots of natural sound;
- Script to the pictures – don't write over them as if they weren't there;
- Singularity – tell only one story;
- Simplicity – make it easy to understand;
- Stream – make it flow using lots of transitional words like 'and', 'so', 'now', 'back at', 'but', 'and here's why'.

Conclusion

Modern news broadcasters solicit pictures and content from the audience. This may be cheaper for news producers, and of course in some cases the only pictures available, but these inputs will not replace quality journalism. It is now even more important for the broadcast journalist to create high-quality, creatively organised, genuinely interesting and above all meaningful pictures and content. The broadcast journalist must complement research skills and wordcraft with an ability to transform a conceptual conundrum into a visual imperative with impact, flair and above all meaning. Visualisation skills to create the visual imperatives demanded by modern broadcast television are an increasingly important element in successful broadcast journalism.

Note

1 Bluescreen is the commonly used name for the technique that allowed composite screens using superimpositions of several visuals.

References

Bignell, J. and Orlebar, J. (2005) *The Television Handbook*, 3rd edn, London: Routledge

Orlebar, J. (2002) *Digital Television Production*, London: Arnold

Ray, V. (2003) *The Television News Handbook*, London: Macmillan

Walsh, T. and Greenwood, W. (2007) *McNae's Essential Law for Journalists*, 19th edn, Oxford: Oxford University Press

Painting pictures 2

Writing, editing and packaging for radio

Leslie Mitchell

Introduction

Painting pictures for radio might seem at best optimistic or at worst a contra-
diction in terms. At the heart of this apparent paradox lies the clue concerning what
makes radio such a powerful, engaging and potent means of communication. I
will examine the opportunities as well as the constraints that are involved when
working in a world where sound is the only raw material and the visual image is
unavailable.

Radio has fewer constraints than TV – for one thing, audio equipment is generally
far more portable and lightweight. The skill of the radio journalist lies in harnessing
the power of sound to place the listener at the heart of the story, to give the sense
of being present at the events which are taking place. This skill is the art of blending
recorded words and sounds in such a way as to tell a story clearly and memorably.
However, there is a downside to a medium which is dependent solely on sound –
most of us, for example, listen to radio as a secondary activity; that is to say, we are
nearly always doing something else while the radio is playing in the background. As
radio journalists, we ignore this reality of the radio listening experience at our peril;
an acknowledgement of how the listener actually listens should inform our work at
every step.

The package

A package is a series of interview extracts, linked by a presenter or reporter in order
to present a coherent and interesting story. This is the package at its simplest, and
it is most frequently heard in this form in news bulletins and news magazines. This
is the fundamental way in which the radio journalist's story is presented. (The only
exception is the 'voicer', where, as the term suggests, a story is conveyed simply by
a single voice – reporter or newsreader – reading a prepared script.)

At a more complex level, the package may contain sound from other sources:
actuality recordings, music, film clips and archive material are common examples,
though such material is less common in news packages. Other kinds of factual
programming, such as magazines and features, will tend to make greater use of a
wide range of recorded material. Generally the term 'package' denotes a rather short
item, say between two and five minutes. Although there are no hard and fast rules
or definitions, longer pieces of factual programming tend to be referred to as
'features' or 'documentaries'.

The post-production 'edit' is essentially the process of taking material from a
variety of sources, then combining and sequencing it in order to tell a story in as
interesting and compelling a way as possible. The idea of packaging adds a further
dimension to our understanding of the edit. It conveys the idea of a norm to which
the material should conform. This could be as tightly defined as a 'format', where
the type of material, editorial content and internal timings are all predefined. In
other circumstances packaging might simply consist of adhering to a certain style.

An example of this might be the convention in the newsroom that all packages identify the reporter and station in a certain way: 'John Smith, for Radio City News, at Westminster.'

Packaging is most important for magazine programmes (and in this context the news bulletin can certainly be seen as a magazine). Here, a consistent and identifiable style is an integral part of what defines the programme and makes it unique. Without this kind of packaging, each and every programme within a series would have a different sound and feel and the listener would lose all sense of identification and ownership of the programme, concepts which are of vital concern in a ratings-conscious industry.

If the package lies at the heart of radio journalism, then an appreciation of the importance of its construction is an essential prerequisite of effective production. An understanding of the package will inform every aspect of the gathering, preparation and editing of the material from which it is ultimately constructed.

Writing for the package

This section deals with a number of fundamentals in writing for radio. Here we offer some general suggestions for good radio writing. We will, however, return to the subject of writing in more detail when we come to look specifically at the importance of written links when constructing packages for radio.

In many ways the best scripted radio speech is but an approximation of everyday language; it may sound spontaneous, but it is in fact highly crafted in order to serve the needs of the medium. Compared with everyday speech, scripted radio speech is pared down; the language and sentence structure tend to be simpler, the ideas less complex but detail prioritised. Radio speech and its conventions are best absorbed by careful analytical listening. Our first task, though, is to try to identify a core set of principles which are helpful in getting started with writing for factual radio.

Writing for radio is writing the spoken word

In practice it is impossible to separate writing for radio from reading for radio. The writing is for the spoken word. In an ideal world every word written would be written by the individual who is going to speak the words. In other words you write best if you write for yourself, your own voice, your own individual speech patterns and rhythms. Next best is to write for someone whose broadcast speech is well known to you. While the radio news reporter will invariably write their own links and voice them too, those who are engaged in writing material for longer features, magazines or documentaries may well have to write for another presenter to 'voice'. In this case, if you have never written for this presenter before, it is well worth spending time listening to as much of their broadcast work as possible. In this way you will be able to familiarise yourself with their style and patterns of speech. As you write, it helps if you can hear them speaking your lines 'in your mind's ear'. The guiding principle of writing for radio is to enable the reader to 'lift the script off the page', to make it sound as spontaneous and natural as possible within the conventions of radio speech.

Writing needs to be read out loud

The best possible way to ensure that a piece of script will work well when read aloud is to read it out loud! Even for the experienced individual this is the quickest and most efficient way to discover where the stumbles and repetitions are; where there are moments which do not reflect the natural patterns of speech. Silently reading the written word may find the most obvious errors but it will not draw to your attention constructions which are difficult to read without tripping. There's a simple rule when reading out loud: if you stumble over the same word or phrase twice, rewrite it.

Writing is listener centred

At the start of my career one of the best pieces of advice I was given by a very experienced radio broadcaster was always to try to envisage my audience in my mind's eye whenever I was in front of a microphone. Real or imagined, this audience would consist of a single representative or maybe two, never more. This exercise is a powerful reminder that the radio audience is essentially an intimate one; listening tends to be a solitary activity. An awareness of the audience will inform both the writing of the script and its delivery. Just as the print journalist is highly sensitive to the reader and the newspaper, so the broadcaster will always have an awareness of the audience, the time of day and the network.

On network radio you might have listening figures in millions, yet essentially your audience is a solitary one. This consideration is important because it has a profound impact on the tone of voice of both the script and the way it is delivered. If you are fortunate enough to be able to watch a highly experienced broadcaster at work in a radio studio, you will notice how animated they are when in front of the microphone, whether they are broadcasting live or recording links. Facial expression, hand gestures and even the focus of their attention have all the marks of an intense conversation, so it comes as quite a shock to realise that most of the time no one else is physically present – such is the power of the sense of the audience.

Writing needs to be cliché free

Clichés are well-worn, possibly worn-out adjectives and phrases. Here we are more concerned with common broadcasting clichés. At worst, they are signs of lazy writing and lazy journalism. At best, they demonstrate a lack of imagination.

- 'I've come to see . . .' This is redundant. Why not simply introduce the interviewee?
- 'I caught up with . . .' Was she running away?
- 'We've run out of time' or 'That's all we have time for'. Essentially this is slightly dishonest – it rather coyly suggests the informality of the unexpected in a domain where the planning of time is paramount. This is an example of what one of my early mentors described as 'letting the bones show'.

It is interesting to note that such clichés inevitably place the focus of attention on the reporter rather than on the subject.

Writing needs to be evocative

Good journalistic writing for radio needs to be evocative, yet not overladen with adjectives; it should conjure helpful pictures in the mind of the listener, yet not be cluttered with unnecessary detail. Not far from where I live, the National Grid wants to erect a chain of massive electricity pylons through an area of great natural beauty. The tallest of these pylons is 65 metres. This fact, baldly stated, might not mean a great deal to a radio listener. Technical facts possibly do not help either: 'the equivalent of 65 metres is some 215 feet' is again not very useful when trying to suggest a visual impact. If, on the other hand, the script asserts that these pylons are about three times the size of most of the pylons currently in use around the country, then there will possibly be the dawning of an understanding of their size. Nelson's Column in Trafalgar Square is a good deal shorter than these new pylons. Informing the listener that the height of one of the proposed structures would place it exactly halfway between Nelson's Column and the pinnacle of St Paul's Cathedral is perhaps even more telling!

This is not only an example of using widely understood imagery when writing for radio but a reminder that it is helpful, wherever possible, to use concrete rather than abstract imagery and that simplicity communicates better than complexity. Thus £4,780,000 is far better described as 'nearly five million pounds'.

Writing needs to be active

Good radio writing has energy and vitality, and one of the ways to achieve this is to use active rather than passive language. So the planning committee 'decided' has more force than 'came to a decision' or 'has been considering'. Similarly, use of the present tense wherever possible puts more energy and immediacy into your writing. 'Midtown Rangers are the new League champions!' has more immediacy than 'Last night Midtown Rangers won their match and the League championship.'

Post-script!

For the inexperienced broadcaster it is more or less essential for scripts to be typed. It is difficult enough at the best of times to 'lift the script off the page' and to sound natural. Trying to read handwriting (even your own) simply sets another obstacle in your way. For most readers block capitals are much more difficult to read than regular upper- and lower-case characters. Presenters tend to annotate their scripts with pencilled-in reminders of how they intend to say a particular phrase in order to deliver its meaning as clearly as possible to the listener.

Before the edit

It is only at the point where you begin to assemble all your material that the package truly comes to life. Equally, this might well be the point where the truth dawns that you have not really got a story yet! The fact that many programmes are, as the industry jargon puts it, 'made in the edit' might well lead the inexperienced journalist to think that all problems can be solved in post-production. This might lead to a temptation to plan and research less well on the misapprehension that everything will sort itself out at the edit stage. The result is likely to be a huge waste of time and resources. The joy of the edit is the experience of hearing your ideas come together and take shape as they begin to form a coherent package or feature. There are a number of ways in which to minimise the stress and maximise the creative endeavour of the edit.

Have a detailed grasp of all your material

You will need a clear overview of the material you have gathered; this will consist of written notes and hopefully a log of your recordings. The quick turnaround required of journalists working on a tight news schedule might well preclude any logging of material in a systematic written way. It cannot, however, be overstressed that whenever possible a systematic written log is invaluable, and it is wise to have pre-printed log sheets available for this job. It's a good idea to have a column on this sheet in which you can insert brief comments about the quality of the material. (I usually do this by the expedient of a varying number of asterisks to indicate my initial assessment or enthusiasm.) In this way, there's far less chance that relevant and concise contributions will be overlooked and more rambling and incoherent extracts included in your final package.

Think of the edit while planning and recording

It is always helpful to have the edit and its requirements in mind at every stage of the production process, and perhaps especially when making any kind of recording. There are a number of questions that should be running through the journalist's head during the production:

- Will the answer I'm hearing now edit smoothly or would it be helpful to rephrase the question in order to get a slightly different response?
- Is there a way of asking the question which encourages an answer which makes a preceding question unnecessary? If you have a reasonably confident inter-viewee, you might be able to ask them to give you answers as 'whole sentences'. You are in effect encouraging your subject to answer the question 'How did you find this example of the rare orchid?' by saying, 'I found the orchid when I was out looking for something completely different.'
- Are there good soundbites I can identify? (This is where good logs will help.)
- Does the answer I have just heard contain something which requires a follow-up question even though I have not anticipated it?

- Would any technical explanation be easily understood by a non-expert listener and was the jargon explained?
- Is there some useful atmosphere or sound effects I could record to enliven the package and which would help to paint a soundscape?
- Should I remember to record wild-track (sometimes known as 'buzz-track' or 'room atmosphere') to help me cover possibly awkward edits? In fact, it's always a good idea to spend a minute doing this in every location – you may be thankful you did on many occasions in the editing room.

Editing: interviews, actuality and links

It's helpful to think about the speech content of a package in two ways. First, the interviewee, including vox pops with members of the public. Second, the journalist's own contribution in the form of introduction, links and possibly a conclusion or pay-off at the end of the package. Each of these distinctive contributions requires its own approach, and each will need to be considered in the context of the story to be covered in the package.

Interview

There are three key considerations about the planning and use of interview material that have an important bearing on the package because they relate directly to the journalist's ability to paint an aural picture and so make the story accessible to the listener. These key considerations are motivation, location and audience.

Motivation
We need to remind ourselves of why we bother to interview people at all. After all, most of the information we need in order to tell a story is hardly new; it is probably already out there on the Internet, in clippings, books or magazines, or may even be contained in a press release. Common sense reminds us that one of the most important reasons we have for conducting an interview with a specific person is their particular knowledge or expertise; in other words, they have authority.

At its simplest, this may be the authority of the witness, say to a minor accident or a major incident. Their authority derives from the fact that they were there, they saw or heard. In more complex and technical stories, the authority of the interviewee might well be professional expertise as a scientist, an inventor or the writer of a relevant report. This may seem blindingly obvious, and indeed the experienced journalist will take these issues into consideration almost by reflex, but if there is a clear understanding of the motivation which lies behind the reasons for the selection of a particular individual for interview, then the radio journalist may well be in a position to make more imaginative decisions about the way in which the interview is recorded.

Location
An understanding of the motivation for the interview will not only inform the questions which are to be asked but may well influence the choice of location in which they are asked. A simple illustration will reinforce the point.

If you are putting together a package about a road accident which has recently taken place in a notorious urban black-spot, your motivation for interviewing an eyewitness would strongly suggest that you conduct the interview outdoors, as near to the scene as possible. Lack of control over traffic noise may well produce a recording with a higher background level than would be desirable (but there are usually ways of minimising the distraction: by close mic-ing, for instance), yet the soundscape will paint a picture for the listener far more vividly than were the interview conducted in the comfort and silence of the subject's sitting room.

There are, however, more subtle benefits to be gained from this approach. Most importantly, you might well be assisting an interviewee to be more fluent than they might otherwise be. By taking them back to the scene of the accident they witnessed, you are placing them in the physical environment about which you want to question them. This location will trigger recollections and may well reawaken memories and emotions which would be more difficult to recall elsewhere. An interviewee speaking of an event which takes place 'over there, on that corner by the post-box' is likely to be far more vivid when they can actually see what they are talking about.

The point here is that the questions to be asked can also be subtly different when asked *in situ*. A simple question such as 'Could you describe what happened here?' might well provide an answer that is hesitant. But it could also be raw, colourful and descriptive, and in consequence evocative – exactly what the intelligent interviewer is after because this communicates directly to the listener. The onus is squarely on the journalist to ask the right questions: that is, questions which not only elicit the required information in purely factual terms but encourage the interviewee to use language which is descriptive and colourful, and so can paint those pictures in the mind of the listener.

Audience

An understanding of the needs of the listener will inform the choice and selection of interview material, its tone of voice and complexity. If, for example, the programme deals with technical or scientific matters, great care needs to be exercised to pitch the information at the right level. Too much detail will defeat the listener; oversimplification will patronise and bore.

Actuality

I use the term 'actuality' to refer to the recording of events or situations as they happen. I hesitate to use the more usual expression – 'sound effects' (or 'fx') – as this term may imply the use of artificially constructed or pre-recorded effects, such as those used in drama productions. I would suggest great caution in the use of such 'off-the-shelf' material in any factual programming.

Recordings of actuality may range from detailed coverage of specific events to more general background atmosphere. For example, a city-centre political march and rally might be recorded and include the sound of the crowd, the chanting of slogans and extracts from various speeches. At the other end of the scale, at its simplest, actuality might simply comprise what is generally referred to as atmosphere (or 'atmos'), like the background sounds of a fishing port or factory equipment or even the 'silence' of a particular room. Obviously, recordings of actuality make a major contribution to the sense of place which needs to be achieved in many packages.

Links

The writing of links, including introductions and conclusions, is a skill whose value cannot be overestimated. Links give a package an internal logic, make sense of all the various elements and can direct the attention of the listener to an important point. Badly or carelessly written and delivered links can rob contributions of their potency and vitality and confuse the listener if they fail to provide a logical framework in order to understand the package.

Links are structuring devices

Finding an appropriate structure for your package is ultimately the key to the effectiveness of your storytelling. It is certainly possible to have high-quality interview material, well written links and relevant actuality and still not tell the story vividly enough to engage the listener. The key to good structuring is simplicity accompanied by an informed understanding of the needs of your audience.

It might help to think of the package as a tennis match with arguments – or ideas or points of view – batted back and forth across the net. A tennis match is a good analogy because the game consists of short bursts of activity with the action going quickly from one player to the other. In many ways a good package should be like this, presenting the listener with exciting points and counterpoints rather than long, indigestible interview extracts whose arguments are hard to follow. Your understanding of the audience is vital here. Remember that few of us concentrate exclusively on what we hear on the radio: we often listen while engaged on other tasks. If a vital piece of information escapes us, then we may lose the thread completely. Here the structure of the package can help enormously and the potential of the reporter's links becomes clear.

Links provide information

Links not only take the argument forward but can, where helpful, provide a recap of a point which has just been made. So, for example,

> (Short interview extract from Councillor John Smith, a member of the Police Authority, outlining his objections to a new policing initiative.)
>
> Reporter's link: 'John Smith clearly has serious reservations about the value of community policing, but Inspector Clive Johnston of Everytown Constabulary is confident that this strategy will bring immediate advantages at the local level.'
>
> (Extract from police representative, who puts the case for change.)

In this example, the link is used not simply to introduce the next speaker but to provide some structural 'scaffolding' for the unfolding story. It refers back to the previous speaker and then takes the debate a step further by placing the next contributor in the context of the debate. In addition, the link identifies him as well as establishing the authority he has to underpin his point of view – he is a senior police officer.

It would be a great mistake to assume that the whole policing debate could or should be compressed into these two contributions, one from each of two opposing positions. It might be helpful to revisit each protagonist as the argument develops. Again the links will make an important contribution to helping the (possibly inattentive) listener follow the unfolding story. Such links can be very simple and might consist of little more than a name check: 'Inspector Johnston, again.' Note that the addition of 'again' reminds the audience that this is a contributor from whom we have heard earlier.

By this stage in the package or feature, we have established a clear context for further contributions, so introductions can be kept relatively simple – the reason for inclusion will, by now, be quite obvious. A local resident who is about to describe the experience of having her windows broken by vandals twice in a month might be introduced very briefly: 'Barbara Macintosh has lived on the Brownfield Estate for eighteen years.' (Barbara briefly recounts her experiences and her anxiety about the future of the estate.) At this point you might well wish to return to the local councillor, especially if your notes and your interview log remind you that he has referred to hearing many sad stories during his weekly surgeries. So a further link might reinforce this point: 'And, as Councillor Smith points out, Mrs Macintosh is far from alone in feeling unable to venture out of her house after dark.' (John Smith gives further examples of his constituents' problems.)

In a longer programme, the listener will require more 'recap' by way of a subtle reference to 'the story so far'. This recapitulation also allows those who tune in after the start of the programme to catch up with information they might have missed. 'Signposting', giving structural hints and directions, can be an important way to avoid confusion by preparing the listener for what lies ahead. This might be a direct reference in a link or alternatively might be achieved by the introduction of some actuality sound or atmos which will signal a change of location, mood or speed.

Cue material

It is often forgotten that it is the role of the reporter (or the producer of longer programmes) to provide 'cue material': that is, a suggested script for what might be said before, and possibly after, the package or programme. Again this is a link, but instead of being within the package it links the package (or programme) to what has come before it. This is a very good way to avoid repetition, where the studio presenter virtually speaks the first few seconds of the package before the package officially starts. A good piece of cue material provides an imaginative and factually accurate script which can be adapted by the announcer to introduce the package.

Issues for consideration

- Think about the editing of interviews. Review some of the problems which might occur when interview extracts have to be chosen and shortened to fit into a news package. How do you think such problems might be avoided or at least minimised?
- Discuss the use of sound effects in news packages, factual magazines and documentary features. Taking each of these genres in turn, do you think there is a case to be made for the use of library sound effects to illustrate a story? Give reasons for your opinions.
- How do you think a regular radio magazine programme can encourage audience loyalty?

Conclusion

Writing, interviewing and the recording of actuality sound each makes a contribution to the final package and the pictures it paints for radio. The impact of these contributions will be fully and efficiently realised only if the vital roles of editing and packaging are understood and borne in mind not only throughout the production but at its very conception.

References

Beaman, J. (2000) *Interviewing for Radio*, London: Routledge

Boyd, A., Stewart, P. and Alexander, R. (2008) *Broadcast Journalism: Techniques of Radio and Television News*, 6th edn, Oxford: Focal Press

Douglas, L. and Kinsey, M. (eds) (1998) *A Guide to Commercial Radio Jurnalism*, 2nd edn, Oxford: Focal Press

Hicks, W. (1999) *Writing for Journalists*, London: Routledge

McLeish, R. (2005) *Radio Production*, 5th edn, Oxford: Focal Press

Painting pictures 3

Broadcast and the Web

Mike Ward

Introduction

For a number of years, it was relatively easy to separate online journalism from that practised in television, radio and newspapers. However, with newspapers now publishing video, and broadcasters supplementing their output with Web content, the picture has become somewhat confusing. Much of what follows in this chapter could apply equally to broadcast or online journalism, because it centres on the fundamental changes occurring in the relationship between journalists and those people 'formerly known as the audience' (Rosen, 2006).

However, the purpose here is to focus on online journalism, defined as that which primarily uses the Internet and the Web to communicate and carry content. This is an appropriate choice, because it is within the online environment that the dynamics and roles in this new relationship are currently being defined and tested.

What's changing?

Online, as has been stated frequently in the past, is a user-driven medium. Put ten people in front of a news website and each will embark on a different journey through the content. In an environment where users decide what, when and how they consume news, and can reach alternative providers in seconds, it's critical to provide news and information that leverage the strength of this medium by being timely, accessible and flexible in format.

This much has been known for some time and is now being practised, with varying degrees of success, by some news websites. The other distinct element of online is the readers' ability to publish as well as consume information – and, perhaps more fundamentally, to *communicate* in new and powerful ways. Blogs, social networks, multimedia sharing platforms – the opportunities for people to commune with each other have multiplied rapidly, powered by inexorable advances in digital technology. Again, mainstream media has tried to acknowledge this, expanding their sites to include blogs, forums and polls. Some have also encouraged the submission of what's become known as 'user-generated content' (UGC).

However, this model – the accommodation of individual voices within a mass media setting – is under increasing strain. First, it raises practical problems. When the Buncefield oil depot blew up in December 2005, the BBC received over 6,500 emails containing pictures and video from the public. The BBC News website has since established a unit dedicated to receiving and selecting UGC for publication. But few news organisations have sufficient resources to do this, and even the BBC cannot deal with a flood of material such as at Buncefield. Second, such a centralised approach, with mainstream news organisations seeing themselves as the dominant publishers, even of UGC, ignores a stark reality: mature self-publishing and communication platforms such as YouTube, Flickr and Facebook are now the preferred choice for many individuals because these services also bring with them a valuable sense of organic community that the mainstream news organisation cannot offer.

On the publication of his book *Here Comes Everybody: The Power of Organizing without Organizations* in early 2008, author Clay Shirky was invited as guest blogger on the Penguin website:

> A good deal of user-generated content isn't actually 'content' at all, at least not in the sense of material designed for an audience. Instead, a lot of it is just part of a conversation. Mainstream media has often missed this, because they are used to thinking of any group of people as an audience. Audience, though, is just one pattern a group can exist in; another is community. Most amateur media unfolds in a community setting, and a community isn't just a small audience; it has a social density, a pattern of users talking to one another that audiences lack. An audience isn't just a big community either; it's more anonymous, with many fewer ties between users. Now, though, the technological distinction between media made for an audience and media made for a community is evaporating; instead of having one kind of media come in through the TV and another kind come in through the phone, it all comes in over the internet. As a result, some tools support both publication and conversation. Weblogs aren't only like newspapers and they aren't only like coffeeshops and they aren't only like diaries – their meaning changes depending on how they are used, running the gamut from reaching the world to gossiping with your friends.
>
> (Shirky, 2008b)

Clearly, online journalists now operate in a shared and flexible media space. How well they both adapt to this and harness it will be critical to their future success. Central to this will be the journalist's realisation that, within this shared space, everyone and everything is connected in myriad overlapping networks. Professor Jane Singer, Johnston Press Chair of Digital Journalism at the University of Central Lancashire, states: 'The journalist has far less control over information than in the past – less control over what until now has been an inherently industrial process of producing or making news.' Journalists no longer control:

- Either what is published – anyone can be a publisher – or what people learn about their own communities, as other people in those communities will be putting out information too.
- How people access the information journalists provide – it can be via a news home page, or a search engine, or a link on someone's blog – or what is included in/appended to the journalists' own stories, including comments and views on what they have written.
- All those boundaries that journalists in traditional media environments could easily patrol and enforce. They simply do not exist in a networked environment that is open to anyone who chooses to jump in.[1]

If that sounds daunting, look for the silver lining. If all good journalists should know their audience (or perhaps 'community' is a more appropriate term in this context), being immersed in a networked media space presents unprecedented opportunities to achieve this. The trick is learning to think, and act, in a networked way.

The new tools

If communication is key to journalism, then the twenty-first century so far has been a halcyon age for journalists, if they could only see it. Almost every month, an off-the-shelf application is launched to enhance people's power of communication. Much of what is then communicated (family conversations or exhaustive accounts of people's social lives) obscures the real value of these new tools. Each one is a gift to journalism, because they enable everyone – including journalists – to communicate and engage in completely new ways.

What follows is a list of just a few.

Blogs

Particularly important blogs are those written by people with knowledge in a specific field. Because the information in these blogs is valued by others, they spawn networks of like-minded bloggers. Journalists can see this either as a threat – a rival published source of valued information – or as an opportunity to tap into an important community, both to understand it better and to find story ideas and contacts. A good example of a constructive approach is the BBC's weekly *iPM* radio programme. Instead of attaching a blog to the programme, the producers have built a programme around a blog. During the week before the programme, they ask readers for story ideas, post draft running orders online, invite help with story development and explain why some ideas or stories are dropped.

Micro-blogs

For example, Twitter. If journalists can reach beyond their instinctive dislike of the name, they might find value in Twitter. Twitterers post and view brief updates (up to 140 characters) of their news and activities via their mobile phone, Web browser or instant messaging. Some news organisations and journalists are now using Twitter as a publishing and production resource, finding story ideas and publishing news alerts, but also communicating with other journalists working with them on stories. Blogger J.D. Lasica (2007) has suggested reporters recruit a group of knowledgeable and committed readers as a 'Twitter posse'. When the reporter is about to embark on a complex story or interview, they round up their mobile posse via Twitter to explore angles and lines of questioning.

Social networking sites

Sites like Facebook and MySpace offer opportunities for journalists to connect with people, establish contacts and help people connect with each other. News organisations such as the BBC and the *Guardian* have Facebook pages. Rupert Murdoch went one step further and bought MySpace. So traditional media players have clearly recognised that there are new forums for information exchange outside mainstream news organisations. As Jeff Jarvis (2007b) puts it, local news is not about content; it's about people. 'Our job is not to deliver content or a product. Our job is to help them make connections with information and each other.'

Multimedia file-sharing sites

Anyone who feels they are being ignored by the mainstream news agenda can broadcast direct to the world through YouTube, which hopes to offer live broadcasts by the end of 2008. In addition, the publishing potential of Flickr, the photo-sharing site, has been explored by news organisations. In 2007, Derek Tedder from Sky News reported on demonstrations at Heathrow Airport equipped only with his BlackBerry. He sent text updates to Twitter and took pictures for Flickr. Both were then fed directly to the main Sky News website.

RSS feeds

RSS stands for Really Simple Syndication, and it's the easiest method of keeping in touch with latest news and information on the Web in your chosen field. If your favourite sites and blogs offer an RSS feed (signified by the distinctive small orange and white icon), you can subscribe and receive regular updates as long as you have a feed reader (also known as a news aggregator). Feed readers are readily available online. Popular readers include Google Reader and Bloglines.

del.icio.us

To a hard-nosed journalist, the name has only marginally more appeal than Twitter, but again appearances can be deceptive. Subscribe to del.icio.us and instantly you can store all your bookmarks on a Web page, access them from any PC and share them with others, while they share theirs with you.

A fresh approach

These new tools allow online journalists to consider a fresh and more decentralised approach – stimulating and enabling conversations on other sites as well as trying to drive user contributions to their own. The message is: do not fight the YouTubes and the Flickrs – join them . . . and use them.

Guardian writer Jeff Jarvis is a strong advocate of such networked journalism. He sees it as an opportunity for journalism at a time of uncertainty over the future role of mainstream news media: 'As news organisations inexorably shrink along with their audiences, revenues and staff, I believe that one way for journalism itself to expand is through collaboration with the communities it covers' (Jarvis, 2007a). Collaboration, of course, does not mean capitulation. An important part of the journalist's role will still be to provide content for their 'home' publication. However, this will be enriched by, and linked to, the conversations they have seeded and contributed to elsewhere.

Some journalists are already experimenting with such integration. In 2007, Ben Hammersley reported for the BBC from Turkey on the run-up to the country's national elections. He filed stories for the usual outlets – television, radio and BBC News' online service. But he also reported on YouTube, Flickr, Twitter and del.icio.us.

The trick when adopting these social networking tools is to make them part and parcel of your daily life, not add-ons. Nevertheless, filing information for an even broader range of outlets, as Hammersley attempted, will be challenging for journalists, particularly when operating under time pressures in the field.

A revised framework

Such an integrated approach to journalism requires a rethink from journalists, both about their role and the way they work. With this in mind, journalism lecturer and blogger Paul Bradshaw (2007b) has recast the traditional 'Five Ws and an H' in a new form for the twenty-first century. His point is that the publishing of a journalist's story should be the beginning, not the end, of the communication and information-sharing process. In the future, journalists should hope that their readers could answer some/all of the following questions after reading one of their stories:

- **Who** can I now connect with? Having read the story, the user should want to engage with other people.
- **What** did the journalist read to write this? Journalists linking to their source material should be a matter of course, facilitated by the journalist's own social bookmarking account being part of their byline.
- **Where** did this happen? Journalists should be mapping all their stories, using geotags to locate them on systems such as Google Maps.
- **When** are events coming up that I need to be aware of? If the story is previewing an event, make it easy for readers to add it to their Outlook/Yahoo/Google calendar.
- **Why** should I care? Use databases and other technologies to personalise stories and demonstrate their importance and relevance to the reader. Explanatory calculators, such as the one used on Budget Day Web coverage, are good examples of this.
- **How** can I make a difference? This question tests the journalist's position and role within this new world order. It offers readers the opportunity to 'make a difference' by linking, when appropriate, to online petitions and automated letters of protest to MPs, Bradshaw (2007b) acknowledges this 'may be uncomfortable for journalists used to the principle of objectivity'.

Online news treatment

The shared media space is a place where journalists publish as well as network and share information. Online is such a flexible medium that it offers a rich range of opportunities for story development and treatments by journalists.

Bradshaw (2007a) identifies two distinctive pervasive qualities within the online medium: speed and depth. Online is the most immediate medium, but through its unlimited pagination, ability to link and user-driven properties, it is also potentially deeper and broader than any other. Bradshaw envisages a seven-stage process for the development of stories that harnesses both speed and depth. You might find all seven employed only in a large news story. Nevertheless, they provide a useful framework for the treatment of online news content.

Speed

- Alert – sent out via phone, email or Twitter as a story breaks.
- Draft – published on the blog, this gives initial details, building on the Alert.
- Article/package – situated on the border of speed and depth, this is the more considered piece, the current staple of much online, newspaper and broadcast coverage.

Depth

- Context – this fourth stage is where online shines, building context to the story through links to archives and external sites.
- Analysis/reflection – after the report comes the analysis, including comment from other blogs and reflection/responses to the analysis from the originating journalist.
- Interactivity – structuring interactive elements within stories can take time but they will give your coverage a longer shelf-life. Techniques include Flash-animated packages and wikis, where people can post experiences and information.
- Customisation – allowing readers to customise their consumption by subscribing to an RSS feed for updates or even finding the original story as part of a broader interrogation of your site's content around topics that interest them.

Bradshaw has evolved this seven-part process into a model for online news production – a 'news diamond'. As he explains: 'this news diamond attempts to illustrate the change from a nineteenth-century *product* . . . to a twenty-first-century process: the iterative journalism of the new media; the story that is forever "unfinished"' (Bradshaw, 2007a).

Online writing and story construction

Online journalists continue to play a central role in the news process, enjoying a wide range of methods for sharing information and telling stories. However, if they have reappraised their role and methods in this shared media space, what of their traditional skills, such as writing and storytelling? This is a media space where many rivals compete for the attention of the reader, where it is more difficult to keep people's attention because it is more tiring and takes longer to read a screen, and where the competition is, as the cliché states, 'just one click away'. It's a media space where people are as likely to find a story through a search engine as through a home page, where they can pick and choose what they want and where they resist being made to read stuff that does not interest them. Yet it's also a space where, if you give readers what they want and how they want it, they will engage more completely than readers in other media.

The Poynter Institute (Adam *et al.*, 2007) has carried out a number of influential studies of Web reading habits, using sophisticated equipment that tracks people's eye movements when reading under test conditions. In the latest, in 2007, they tested 600 people as they read news stories in broadsheet and tabloid newspapers and on news websites. One of the surprising results was that, once those tested decided to read something, online readers read more of the story text (77 per cent) than broadsheet readers (62 per cent) or tabloid readers (57 per cent). The study confirmed the accepted wisdom that many online readers scan websites when they read them. But even though the percentage of scanners was higher for online than print, it still represented only 53 per cent of the online readers. The remaining 47 per cent were classed as 'methodical' readers. And, perhaps most tellingly, there was very little difference between the amount of text read by methodical online readers and scanners, once they had started a story. Thus the style and quality of online writing is important – both to guide people to content (scanners used headlines and story lists to make reading choices) and to satisfy their desire to read in depth when they arrive at their chosen story by whatever means.

Some basic online writing guidelines follow.

Body text

Sentences should be short and direct. Use active, not passive, verbs. Keep it simple, using one-sentence paragraphs. Bullet points within a story are a useful technique for summarising information. You also need to get to the point quickly, which is why the traditional 'inverted pyramid' style of news writing works well on the Web, as it demands that the essence of the story is placed in the introduction.

Summaries

These are a useful tool on the Web, often used to introduce a story on an entry page that then links to the full story on the next level. If possible, craft a couple of fresh, tight sentences that summarise the story and invite the reader to click through, rather than just recycle the story intro. If the same person writes all the summaries for a news home page, this can provide a valuable sense of continuity and identity for the news section.

Headlines

As the Poynter study shows, headlines play an important role for the scanning reader. The number one rule for online headlines is to keep them simple and literal. Avoid puns or any other form of cleverness. Headlines that might prompt high-fives and congratulatory emails on a newspaper's subs' bench have no place on a website, where they just do not work. People scanning are confused by them, particularly when they are separated from the accompanying body text in a story list. And search engines do not get the joke – they take them, like everything else, literally, and come up with some strange results.

So headlines, summaries and story introductions need to contain the keywords that readers will think of when searching for the story – another example of how the online journalist needs to write for, and understand, their readership. Yes, it's a user-driven medium.

Apart from writing, what about story construction? There are a number of different models for online stories.

Single-story treatments

The majority of online news stories fall into this category, with a headline, summary and possibly a picture on an entry page leading to a second-level, single Web page devoted to the entire coverage of the story, with text, audio/video, graphics and links.

'Chunked' stories

In this more complex structure, there are three levels of pages: the entry page with summary, leading to a second-level page which contains an expanded summary and links, each going to a different third-level page which is built around a separate theme or aspect of the story, containing bespoke text, audio/video, graphics and links. 'Chunking' (simply breaking the story into chunks) works best on multi-dimensional stories. This approach acknowledges that some online readers do not want to read everything about a particular story. They prefer to look for angles or themes that interest them. Finely crafted composites, such as television packages, deny them this facility because of their very structure, and do not, in the main, translate well to the Web.

So, in essence, experienced journalists who embark on an online chunked story have to set aside a fundamental craft skill that has defined their previous expertise – their ability to gather information from all quarters and synthesise it into a carefully balanced, tightly packaged single summation. In online, when chunking, there is a summary, but it is usually a brief prelude to the individual themes being reported on separate pages. These still require skilled construction because each chunk should 'stand alone', as many will be accessed directly through search engines and may be read in isolation of the other story content. But it's a different process, and mindset, to storytelling in a producer-driven medium such as television news.

Another example of chunking, utilising the full media richness of online, is the rapidly developing field of interactive, multimedia storytelling. The story is once again divided into self-contained sections, but instead of these being arranged in standard format across multiple news pages, the story can be presented within a self-contained unit that the reader enters within a Web news page. There they are offered a choice of avenues to explore. And, in a break with the mantra of user control, some of these avenues will ask the reader to let go, while they are taken on an animated journey through an orchestrated combination of media.

One of the simplest, and most effective, of these combinations is the use of photographs, presented sequentially through an automated slide show, with accompanying audio. The audio can be a voiceover but more commonly, and effectively, it will be an interview with one of the subjects of the photo montage. Ambient sound, recorded at the scene, can also be used. Other textures, including text, can be added to highlight key points.

Such combinations can be very powerful for the reader and creative for the journalist because they provide space and time for the reader to integrate their own thoughts and mental images within the coverage. In comparison, video on its own is very literal. It *tells* you what to see and hear. Animated storytelling works because it is, in many ways, another example of the journalist facilitating a user experience, not dictating it. It's working *with* the online medium.

Other avenues in a multimedia story can contain links, text-based information, maps and graphics or video. The latter does have an important role to play when used in an integrated manner. It portrays action most effectively and is a powerful tool in event-driven stories. The key to multimedia storytelling, as one of its leading exponents, Jane Stevens, points out, is to choose the right story for this kind of treatment and then use the constituent media elements in a complementary, not repetitive, way. 'The best multimedia stories are multi-dimensional. They include action for video, a process that can be illustrated with a graphic . . . someone who can give some pithy quotes for video or audio, and/or strong emotions for still photos and audio' (Stevens, 2007).

Stevens is an advocate of 'backpack journalism' – the reporter out in the field armed with a video camera and a laptop to edit and produce multimedia stories. As she points out, modern video cameras are extremely versatile, and Stevens uses hers to record both video and audio, grab digital stills and collect information that can be used in text or graphics.

Some of her golden rules for multimedia storytelling include:

- Draw rough storyboards at the outset.
- Consider, if possible, doing video interviews twice – first to capture the action and then, in a quieter area, to describe and comment upon the action.
- Keep talking heads to a minimum on video – the nuances of emotion that make some television head-shot interviews compelling are lost in the smaller viewing screen and poorer frame rate on the Web.
- Audio must be high quality, although simultaneous text can be added for emphasis and explanation.
- Use photos singly as introductory story 'establishers' or to set a mood, as well as in multiple-sequence slide shows
- Do not be afraid to use graphics as the centrepiece to the story or some of its sections, with text taking a secondary role.

Such crafted multimedia stories are currently undertaken by only a minority of journalists out in the field. Others are slowly joining but, in the meantime, audience members are walking around with the power to record and publish in their back pockets. Their mobile phones are becoming more sophisticated and powerful with every passing month. Journalists will ignore this at their peril. Jeff Jarvis (2008) already believes that all journalists – newspaper, broadcast and online – should now regard themselves as mojos (mobile journalists), using the same technology: 'For today, a wired journalist without a camera and connectivity is like a hack without a pencil.'

Note

1   Interview with the author, January 2008.

References

Adam, P.S., Quinn, S. and Edmonds, R. (2007) *Eyetracking the News*, St Petersburg: Poynter Institute

Bradshaw, P. (2007a) 'A model for the twenty-first century newsroom, Part 1: The News Diamond', at http://onlinejournalismblog.com/2007/09/17/a-model-for-the-twenty-first-century-newsroom-pt1-the-news-diamond (accessed 21 March 2008)

Bradshaw, P. (2007b) 'Help make "5W's + H" happen', at http://onlinejournalism blog.com/2007/11/13/help-make-five-ws-and-a-h-happen/ (accessed 21 March 2008)

Jarvis, J. (2007a) 'The pro-am approach to newsgathering,' *Guardian*, 27 October, at http://www.guardian.co.uk/media/2007/oct/22/mondaymediasection.media guardian14 (accessed 25 March 2008)

Jarvis, J. (2007b) 'Towns are hyperlocal with data (people that is)', at http://www. buzzmachine.com/2007/07/11/hyperlocal/ (accessed 24 March 2008)

Jarvis, J. (2008) 'Forget shorthand – a camera phone is the new tool of the journalist's trade', *Media Guardian*, 11 February, p. 7

Lasica, J.D. (2007) 'Twitter posse for reporters', Media Shift Idea Lab, 13 December, at http://www.pbs.org/idealab/2007/12/twitter-possees.html (accessed 24 March 2008)

Rosen, J. (2006) 'The people formerly known as the audience', PressThink, 27 June, at http://journalism.nyu.edu/pubzone/weblogs/pressthink/2006/06/27/ppl_frmr. html (accessed 24 March 2008)

Shirky, C (2008a) *Here Comes Everybody: The Power of Organizing without Organizations*, London: Allen Lane

Shirky, C. (2008b) 'Special guest post – Why user generated content mostly isn't', 23 January, at http://thepenguinblog.typepad.com/the_penguin_blog/2008/01/ special-guest-p.html (accessed 24 March 2008)

Stevens, J. (2007) 'What is a multi-media story?', at http://multimedia.journalism. berkeley.edu/tutorials/reporting/starttofinish/choose (accessed 25 March 2008)

Going live

Writing and presenting for broadcast

Marie Kinsey

13

Introduction

The studio light goes on, the microphone's open and suddenly you are live on the air. To some, it's an unbeatable buzz. But for all broadcast journalists fluency, confidence and accuracy in front of the mike or the camera are essential skills. For some, that confidence and fluency are as natural as breathing. Most have to work a bit harder.

It used to be the case that live presentation was the preserve of the anchor, but anyone wanting a career in broadcast journalism just because they want to read the news or present programmes is misguided. The journalism always comes first, and the best presenters are experienced journalists. In the past, reporters were not called on very often, if at all, for live material, and most were much happier with a script. However, these days broadcast news needs to 'be there' and reporters increasingly (some would argue unnecessarily) report from the scene, or are live in the studio with the presenter to explain a story.

Your voice is a tool and a weapon, and probably the most important in your arsenal. It is unique to you and recognisable. It needs to be strong, clear, warm and authoritative, capable of conveying interest and urgency or measured calm as required. It is your calling card and trademark. It will get you a job, so practising to make it the best it can possibly be is an imperative.

Training your voice

The first time you hear a recording of your voice, or read a news bulletin wearing headphones, the sound of your own voice can come as a shock. That's because we do not hear ourselves as others hear us. As you speak, the bones in your skull act like a baffle, slightly altering the sound that reaches your own ears. Other people hear your voice as it really is. When you play back a recording of your voice, all the individual quirks are much more obvious. You just have to get used to what you sound like, but recognising the strengths and weaknesses of your voice is the first step on the road to improving it – and getting rid of any nasty vocal habits you may possess. This means listening critically to yourself, identifying problems and practising over and over again until you improve.

Can voices be trained? There are those lucky few who naturally seem to have the right pitch, are perfectly modulated, put all the emphases in exactly the right places, never run out of breath and articulate every word with precision. Most beginners are not so fortunate and need a bit of help in getting their voice to its full potential. Former BBC Radio 1 *Newsbeat* presenter Janet Trewin believes, 'Whilst professional training can't cure the *truly* unbroadcastable, it may deliver amazing solutions to a wide range of problems, some of which the presenter is unaware of' (Trewin, 2003: 28).

The point of voice training is not to turn presenters into clones who speak with the 'right' accent or in the 'right' way. There is not a 'right' accent or a 'right' way.

In fact, in early 2008 BBC Director-General Mark Thompson agreed that there should be a broader range of regional accents across the BBC's radio and television output (Martin, 2008). Every voice is different and the task is to make it as strong and flexible as possible. Your voice is the tool that communicates information and as long as the audience can follow what you are saying and is engaged, then you are on the right lines. Problems come with anything that might interfere with the audience's ability to understand you, or when characteristics of your voice distract the audience from what you are saying. A very thick accent, a very high pitch, a nasal drone, glottal stops, breakneck speed and sounding bored are all crimes against broadcast communication. Fortunately, these problems are often curable.

Relax

I remember the first time I read a live radio bulletin. It was two o'clock on a wet Tuesday afternoon on BRMB Radio, the commercial station in Birmingham. I had never before realised that it was possible for your knees to knock when you are sitting down and sheer terror made me sound like a cat being strangled. It was not an auspicious start.

Live presentation is stressful, particularly for newcomers, and under stress people tend to become physically tense. Shoulders hunch, you lean forward, tightening your tummy, breathing quickens and becomes shallow, your hands tremble, the pitch of your voice rises and there may be an urge to gabble. Trying to become physically relaxed in the moments before transmission can help your voice and your performance.

Have a good stretch, particularly your arms, neck and shoulders. Sit firmly in your chair with both feet flat on the ground and your back straight, and drop your shoulders to help open your chest and relax your vocal cords. Take several slow, deep breaths to get oxygen into your lungs. Open your mouth and stretch your lips backwards and forwards to loosen them. All this will help calm you, which will mean you read at a better pace, the pitch of your voice will drop and you'll feel much more confident and in control. *Never* run if you are late for a bulletin. You cannot, under any circumstances, read the news if you are out of breath, your heart is thumping and you are gasping like a stranded fish.

Speak up

If you are relaxed, you'll be better able to push out your voice from your diaphragm (around the bottom of your ribcage) rather than your throat. Actors are able to be heard at the back of an auditorium, and they are not shouting. Broadcasters need to develop the same skill of speaking up and sounding natural – projecting the voice. Faced with a microphone either in front of you or pinned to your lapel, it can be tempting to think the mike will do all the work and just turn up the level. This will invariably make you sound weak and lacking authority. The degree of projection is also influenced by the style of programme or station. Commercial broadcasters usually want punchier bulletins while the BBC tends to adopt a more measured tone.

Speak clearly and with meaning

Muttering words through a half-closed mouth will win you no prizes and could be enough to have your carefully prepared demo tape binned within a few seconds. Diction counts. Open your mouth and allow your lips to frame each syllable, particularly at the end of a word, so that it's not swallowed. Practise with tongue twisters: 'Red lorry, yellow lorry'; 'Peter Piper picked a peck of pickled peppers'. The aim is not to see how fast you can say them, but to pronounce them fluently and accurately, without stumbling over any of the words.

With clarity comes pace. If you speak too fast, the audience will not be able to follow you; too slowly and you'll sound funereal. Most broadcasters speak at three words per second, so try counting the number of words in this paragraph and dividing by three. Then read the paragraph out loud against the second hand of a clock. It should take you about twenty seconds allowing for the breaths with a full stop and some longer words.

All is lost if your voice does not bring out the meaning of the words. You really do have to engage your brain before opening your mouth! If you do not understand the story, you will be unable to write it properly and you certainly will not be able to read it properly. This means being utterly familiar with the script and rehearsing it repeatedly. Broadcast newsrooms are full of people apparently talking to themselves – they are reading what they have written, checking that they can perform it with meaning. And if it does not sound right, they rewrite it. That goes for both radio and television.

Getting emphasis and expression in the right place is crucial. Try reading the following sentence aloud and stress a different word each time. 'The man *said* he would help' does not mean quite the same as 'The man said he *would* help'. And what of 'The *man* said he would help'? Your voice also needs to vary its intonation – go up and down its register so that not every story is read in the same way. Very few people utilise the full capacity of their vocal range. Think what you sound like when you are telling a friend a really good story – your voice is animated and lively with lots of expression. One of the big traps as you gain more experience is becoming formulaic – reading every story with the same pattern of intonation and emphasising every fourth or fifth word. The way to avoid this is always to concentrate on what the story means. If it's a serious story, your voice should sound serious. If it's a light story, smile. Listeners can hear a smile.

Frank Mansfield has been training the voices of young broadcast journalists for more than ten years.[1] He says:

> People worry about their voice probably more than any other aspect of their broadcasting performance. And criticising it is almost more personal than criticising their driving ability or (in male cases) their virility. They also worry about the wrong things. Accent is still one of the key concerns when people start on the nursery slopes of broadcasting. Rarely is it a real issue – broadcasting companies quite like provincial accents these days, as long as they are comprehensible. And the near-universal: 'I don't like the sound of my own voice' is another popular myth. The ones I worry about are

the ones who really do like the sound of their own voice – that road leads to self-obsession.

Few people – perhaps 5 per cent of the population – have voices that genuinely grate. Another 5 per cent at the opposite pole have gorgeous voices. They could read the telephone directory out and it would sound fascinating. The rest of us are in the middle, with broadcast voices that can be trained to be significantly better than you started with.

Think of your favourite newsreader. First of all, they don't sound like anyone else – they sound like themselves. So don't try to clone yourself on what you think a newsreader should sound like. Be yourself. But be a version of yourself that is interesting and interested. At a party you have to try to sparkle a little, to make people listen to you. It's the same with broadcasting. A larger-than-life version of you is always more interesting to listen to.

The crucial point is to think about what you're saying while you're saying it. It's amazing how many tyro newsreaders think about how they are reading, not about the content of what they're saying. If you're not listening to yourself, no one else will either. Think about it.

The two-way

The art of talking live and unscripted is more important than ever and the two-way has become one of the most widely used techniques in broadcast journalism. Even twenty years ago it was relatively rare for a presenter to interview one of the newsroom's own journalists, except perhaps a specialist or foreign correspondent who could explain and analyse a particular story (Franklin *et al.*, 2005: 267). But as output has expanded and the demands of rolling news mean information needs to be aired as soon as possible, the technique has become ubiquitous.

Usually, the reporter will write a cue and brief the presenter on appropriate questions to ask. The wise reporter will ensure that the replies are at least in part scripted, if only to insure against a slip of the tongue or inaccuracy, and particularly if there are legal delicacies to dodge. It must always be presented in a fluent, conversational way.

At 6.07 a.m. on 29 May 2003, the BBC's then defence correspondent, Andrew Gilligan, went live on air on the *Today* programme to be interviewed by presenter John Humphrys about the developing crisis in Iraq. It was something he'd done many times before, but this two-way would have repercussions that are still reverberating through broadcast journalism.

In his brief interview, Gilligan suggested that the government had 'sexed up' a dossier on Iraq to include the claim that the Iraq military had the capacity to deploy chemical or biological weapons within forty-five minutes of an order to use them, when it (the government) probably knew the claim was wrong (Hutton, 2004).

On 9 July, Dr David Kelly, an expert on biological warfare and a senior weapons inspector in Iraq was revealed as the source of Gilligan's information and called to give evidence to the House of Commons' Foreign Affairs and Intelligence and Security committees. Nine days later Dr Kelly was found dead in woods near his home.

An unprecedented storm of controversy broke on the heads of politicians, civil servants, the media and the intelligence services. The government convened a public inquiry into the circumstances surrounding Dr Kelly's death chaired by a former Lord Chief Justice of Northern Ireland, Lord Hutton.

Hutton's report, published in January 2004, shook the BBC to its core and claimed the scalps of then Chairman of Governors Gavyn Davies and Director-General Greg Dyke. Hutton concluded that Dr Kelly had taken his own life, but the real bombshell came from the unexpectedly serious criticism of the BBC's journalism (Franklin *et al.*, 2005: 103), part of which said that the BBC's editorial system was defective in that editors did not see or approve a script for the Gilligan two-way.

As a direct result of Hutton, and after its own internal examination, the BBC updated its editorial guidelines: 'We should not normally use live unscripted two-ways to report allegations' (BBC, 2008). But the two-way remains a useful way of bringing viewers and listeners up to date on a story, or explaining stories and putting them into context when no other authoritative interviewee is available.

Reporting live

Whether on radio or television, going live to a reporter at the scene can lend immediacy and make a story more accessible (McCormack, 2004). It's a technique that's also cheap and quick, although writers like Harrison (2000) query the extent to which it actually does help listeners and viewers understand. There needs to be some editorial justification for it in both radio and television. In the case of a big breaking event such as the London bombings or the floods of summer 2007 the rationale is clear: the audience needs to see and hear what's going on as well as having it put into context for them. But, as *Today* programme presenter and former TV newsreader John Humphrys puts it:

> Television news does too many things because they are possible rather than because they are necessary. I have never understood why we must 'go live' to a reporter on the scene two seconds after we have seen the report. You know the sort of thing.
>
> 'Over now to Kate for the very latest. Kate, what's happening?'
>
> 'I've just told you what's happening in my report, cloth ears, and if you weren't listening properly I'm buggered if I'm going to tell you again.'
>
> Sadly, they never do say that, but I live in hope.
>
> (Humphrys, 1999: 199)

Successful live location reporting, whether for radio or television, needs some planning, particularly if you are a beginner. When the adrenalin flows, it's easy to forget your own name, never mind the name of the person you are interviewing or crucial details of the story. Write it down and make lots of notes. If you are following a package on the same subject, do not repeat information.

Live radio reporting

The best live radio reporting is descriptive and colourful, and the language colloquial and conversational. You are the eyes of the audience – tell them what you are seeing and put it into context. Usually the studio will 'throw' to a reporter at the scene, who will pick up the story, perhaps for just thirty seconds via a mobile phone in the case of a bulletin. At the press of a button in the studio you will be able to hear the station output and your cue, so you know exactly when to start talking.

Some programmes may want something meatier, and send you out with the radio car. Here, more complex elements come into play. Not only can you report from the scene in studio-quality sound, but there is the opportunity to conduct a live interview, or play in actuality and effects.

The trick to live location radio reporting is to make lots of notes. Some people find it easier to script the whole thing and manage to read it quite naturally. Others prefer to jot down key words and phrases and ad-lib around them.

Live television reporting

Technology has made it easier than ever to report live from the scene of events, whether from a remote Welsh hillside, a war zone or the local magistrates' court, hence John Humphrys' concern that it may not always be justified. Rolling news channels use live two-ways to fill time, update a story or even set the scene before a big set-piece event – for example, the climax of a court case. Reporters must speak to camera in ways that call for confidence and fluency, with or without notes and to the exact duration required by the studio. Communication with a location reporter is via an earpiece, in which the reporter can hear the instructions of the studio director, usually saying when they are on and how long they have got to say their piece.

John Sargeant, former political correspondent with the BBC and political editor at ITN, found himself at the centre of one memorable and award-winning piece of television reporting in the final days of Margaret Thatcher's premiership in 1990. Thatcher was at a conference in Paris and in the British Embassy on the day of the result of the first ballot in the Tory leadership contest. She did not win the clear result she'd expected, meaning the contest would go to a second ballot. Sargeant was reporting the result live on the BBC's *Six O'clock News* and telling viewers Thatcher may not be coming out of the Embassy. Then:

> There was an eerie silence, which seemed to go on and on, and then a photographer leapt up into the air, describing a sort of arc in front of my face. At home thirteen million people knew exactly what was happening: they were watching a pantomime. Mrs Thatcher had appeared behind me on the steps of the embassy with her two aides, Bernard Ingham and Peter Bean. They were bearing down on me at speed. The newsreader, Peter Sissons, shouted, 'John,

she's behind you.' I knew nothing. I heard nothing. The magic earpiece had failed . . . Bernard Ingham and Peter Bean pushed me roughly aside and shouted, "Where is the microphone? I could not understand why they thought it mattered where the microphone was; surely if that was anyone's problem it was mine.

(Sargeant, 2001: 11)

Thinking on your feet is part of the skill of reporting live on location, but part of it can be planned as well. Have a couple of points you know you are going to make and take particular care to plan your final few words. What thought or piece of information do you want to leave with the viewer? Do not try to memorise every sentence – you'll sound stilted. Remember, it's a conversation, not a lecture.

In the radio studio

[Radio's] essence is that moment of one to one live communication between two human beings. Its material is the human imagination. Its venue is the mind.

(Wilby and Conroy, 1999: 248)

Radio is an intimate medium, which means establishing a rapport with the audience is crucial. It is good at concepts, ideas and argument. It is not television without pictures. Listening to the radio tends to be a solitary experience, often enjoyed while doing something else – driving, washing up, ironing – which means you talk to one person, not to many. Virtually all good presenters try to imagine talking to someone they know well who is interested in what they are saying – a critical friend.

It is the presenter behind the microphone who sets the tone and style of the programme. Either spontaneously or deliberately you find something that marks you out from the rest, something that is a slightly more sparkly version of your ordinary personality and uses your strengths. If you try to pretend, listeners will spot it. You are *talking* to people, not addressing a public meeting.

News bulletins

Many broadcast journalists will have their first experience of live studio presentation reading short, scripted news bulletins lasting two or three minutes. Usually they have compiled and written the bulletin themselves, particularly in local radio, which makes it much easier to be prepared and turn in a professional performance. You should always read each script aloud beforehand to check for tricky sentence structures or difficult names. If you are not sure how to pronounce a name, ask, then write it on the script phonetically. For example, Morgan Tsvangirai, leader of the Movement for Democratic Change in Zimbabwe, would become Maw-gan Chan-gir-rye.

There is a technical aspect to newsreading in local radio that is just as important as the script – the studio. All news production studios are 'self-op', which means that the bulletin reader also operates the desk and checks the sound levels. They open the microphone channel via a fader, play in all the recorded inserts held on the computer from another channel, and increasingly read the bulletin itself from a computer screen, not pieces of paper. (Although you would be wise to take in paper copies of scripts – computers have been known to crash!) Familiarity with the desk is just as important as familiarity with the script.

Developing a routine can be very helpful. Unless there is a big breaking story, make sure your bulletin is ready with a few minutes to spare and take time to settle yourself in the studio. Put on your headphones, select pre-fade, open the microphone and read a few words while watching the sound meter on the front of the desk to check that your voice is 'peaking' at the correct level. Then play part of your recorded inserts to check that the levels of your voice and the recorded material match. Be prepared to 'ride the levels' during the bulletin if there's an obvious discrepancy – move the fader up or down accordingly when the clip is playing. Make sure you are physically comfortable and do not lean into the microphone – adjust it towards you. It should be close enough not to be intrusive, but not so close that you 'pop' – all the letter 'p's you say sound like small explosions.

Every bulletin reader, indeed every broadcast journalist, always has one eye on the clock and gradually develops an instinctive way of recognising when, say, thirty seconds have elapsed. As you are reading the bulletin you should be checking the clock to make sure you are running to time. Remember to take in a couple of extra stories just in case something goes wrong and you need to fill a bit more time.

Some of the time you will not be reading your own scripts, or may not have time (or may not be allowed) to rewrite them to suit your own style. Usually reporters and producers will not mind if you do rewrite, as long as the meaning is not changed. That makes it even more important that you understand the story, can express the meaning with your voice and read it aloud beforehand to make sure.

Finally, it may sound ridiculous, but write down your own name. Most stations will start a bulletin with a house-style sentence, such as: 'Radio Sparkle News at two o'clock, I'm Edna Cloud.' I guarantee that if you have not written this sentence at the start of your bulletin, you will forget to read it. One newsreader of much experience had written down the first few words but not his name and ended up with the memorable phrase: 'The news at eleven o'clock, I'm . . . an oil tanker . . .'

Speech programmes

Outside the treadmill of hourly bulletins and summaries are speech radio programmes that combine scripted and ad-libbed content with a lot of listener interaction. From BBC local radio breakfast shows to *Today* on BBC Radio 4, BBC 5 Live and commercial stations like LBC, presenters are holding together a complex production that began hours before the on-air time and involves studio interviews, recorded items, outside sources and a stream of input from the audience via text, email or phone. It's not just the presenter, of course. Behind the studio glass, in the control room, are the producer or editor, a technical operator and maybe an assistant producer taking calls and messages and communicating with the presenter via screen and talkback.

Broad general knowledge, curiosity about pretty well everything, attention to detail and quick reactions mark out the best presenters. They ask the questions the listeners would pose and talk *to* the audience, not *at* the audience. They never patronise, can master a brief quickly and have the knack of listening to the answers during an interview so that the next question follows seamlessly. They use their personality, act naturally and enjoy it.

Scripts for speech programmes may be less precise than for bulletins, and experienced presenters will be able to ad-lib around them to stick to time or take advantage of some audience reaction. It comes only with practice, so practise.

Note

1 Interview with the author via email, 11 January 2008.

References

BBC (2008) *Editorial Guidelines*, at http://www.bbc.co.uk/editorialguidelines (accessed 14 February 2008)

Franklin, B., Hamer, M., Hanna, M., Kinsey, M. and Richardson, J. (2005) *Key Concepts in Journalism Studies*, London: Sage

Harrison, J. (2000) *Terrestrial TV News in Britain*, Manchester: Manchester University Press.

Hudson, G. and Rowlands, S. (2007) *The Broadcast Journalism Handbook*, Harlow: Pearson

Humphrys, J. (1999) *Devil's Advocate*, London: Hutchinson

Hutton, J.B.E. (2004) *Report of the Inquiry into the Circumstances surrounding the Death of Dr David Kelly, CMG*, London: The Stationery Office, HC247, at http://www.the-hutton-inquiry.org.uk (accessed 14 February 2008)

McCormack, S. (2004) 'The trouble with two-ways', *UK Press Gazette*, 6 February, p. 13

Martin, N. (2008) 'Thompson calls for more regional accents on BBC', *Daily Telegraph*, 17 January, p. 16

Sargeant, J. (2001) *Give Me Ten Seconds*, London: Macmillan

Trewin, J. (2003) *Presenting on TV and Radio: An Insider's Guide*, Oxford: Focal Press

Wilby, P. and Conroy, P. (1999) *The Radio Handbook*, London and New York: Routledge

Reporting sport

Gary Hudson

14

Introduction

Working as a broadcast journalist in sport should be no different to working as a news journalist. The same principles apply: the commitment to accuracy and balance; the need to tell stories clearly and succinctly; and the importance of making reliable contacts. But in practice there are noticeable differences – not all of them desirable.

Many sports broadcasters began in news and swapped the potential for travelling to the world's trouble-spots, covering war, famine and flood, for the opportunity to visit the leading sports events on the planet and watch them from the best seats in the stadium at no personal expense. Who can blame them? Some sports journalists will openly admit that sports reporting is a soft option: there are no death-knocks or talking to the bereaved.

It is possible to consider sports journalism as a branch of entertainment reporting. Sport, it is argued, is essentially arbitrary and useless. People's hopes and fantasies are projected on to the sports personality, who may not have much personality at all beyond an extraordinary physical prowess in some aspect of a game (Tomlinson, 1999, in Rowe, 2005: 127). But this is to undervalue the importance of sport in people's lives. The response to sport is different to the response to other forms of entertainment. As the *Match of the Day 2* presenter Adrian Chiles (2007: 99) has put it, no one, no matter how good the production was, ever put their arms into the air and leapt about with joy in a theatre. And such is the passion of the committed fan that it is the one area of journalism where the audience is often better informed than the reporter. In news reporting it is good enough to be a 'jack of all trades and master of some'. The regional news reporter will not know the ins-and-outs of every local authority's education policy or strategic planning targets within his area. He might know leading councillors and council press officers reasonably well. He might also be on nodding terms with a few senior police officers. But the sports reporter who does not know the recent playing record of all the teams in his patch and who does not have at least most of the mobile numbers for managers, assistant managers and key players – of course in addition to those of club press officers – is not really on top of his game.

Sport covers a wide range of physical activities: professional and amateur; competitive and purely recreational. But the sports agenda in newspapers and broadcast coverage is dominated by football, so for this reason most of the examples in this chapter are drawn from football coverage. Specialist books deal in greater detail with the coverage of other sports.

The culture

It is clear from the television and radio audiences for live games and the attendance at matches (despite rising admission prices) that there is more interest in football than in any other sport. There is more money for its players in Britain than for other sportsmen and women, much of it from the broadcast companies who pay for the rights to televise football in general and the Premier League in particular. It is only a generation since the only live football on television was the Cup Final (either FA or Scottish, depending on where you lived) and a few internationals. Now live games are spread out over the weekend with different kick-off times to suit the television companies. The changing pattern of the broadcasting of football, due mainly to the influence of satellite television, has changed the social and cultural life of a nation. Once football fans were mostly working-class men for whom Saturday afternoon was an opportunity to escape the home and share the communal experience of cheering on the local side. The rest of the weekend was available for other family activities: shopping, outings with the children and going to church. Now the family routine may be determined by kick-off times, and not just of local teams, but of other key televised matches. Women are more likely to attend games and to be interested in other teams' results, and children are as likely to want a replica Manchester United, Chelsea or Arsenal shirt as that of their local club.

These cultural changes represent a challenge to the broadcast journalist. In his guide to broadcast writing, Rick Thompson (2005) makes the point that it is no longer good enough for a broadcast journalist to profess ignorance of sport. Every journalist needs to understand the basics of sport and its terminology, because they will almost certainly be required to write sports stories as part of their job. This may involve compiling results for a late evening or early morning bulletin when they are the only journalist on shift and there is no sports 'expert' on hand to consult. Thompson says the credibility of a radio station or television channel can be blown away by 'a writer who may have a double first in literature and linguistics, but who doesn't know the difference between a birdie and a bogey, doesn't know the name of the manager of Manchester United, or doesn't know what LBW means'. He proceeds to tell the story of a national newsreader (on the BBC) who said that England's opening batsman was out, 'One-B-W' (Thompson, 2005: 27).

Beware the audience

For the specialist sports broadcast journalist the challenge is even greater. Fans may have an encyclopedic knowledge of their club, borne out of a lifelong passion, and the reporter who is not fully 'statted-up' will be found out by viewers and listeners. An occasional error of fact or the wrong figure on a graphic will probably go unnoticed by the audience for a news report. Yet, in a sports report, they'll prompt a flurry of phone calls and text messages. That is because the audience for sport knows and cares about its subject. Sports editors know that perceptions of bias in a station's coverage will also be seized upon in a way that the spin-doctors of the major political parties have only recently learned to emulate.

The cultural dominance of sport, and football in particular, is not necessarily a good thing for society or for Western liberal democracy. The right-wing commentator Peter Hitchens (2007) rejoiced that England failed to qualify for the finals of football's Euro 2008 competition, writing:

> The people who have made football into a sort of patriotic religion now have to realise something serious folk have grasped for many years. This country is a backward, disorderly dump, sliding down every conceivable league table of merit, living on its past, demoralised and deluding itself about its future.

He argued that people had been refusing to care about anything important and that they 'dismissed as "boring" the central issues of our time' because of their obsession with football (*ibid.*). This anti-football diatribe hit upon an important truth for the sports reporter, and one which might not please Hitchens: people want to know about sport – and football in particular – to an extent that they do not necessarily want to know about news. Frequent surveys have shown that TV news is perceived by the watching public as negative and gloomy. Journalists are often criticised for concentrating on bad news at the expense of good. But sport has the power to lift spirits and excite audiences.

Managing the balance of power

All of this means that sports reporters start from a different position to other journalists. Much of the work of 'serious' journalists involves finding ways of presenting information they consider 'important' – politics, health, education and environmental issues, for example – in a way that is interesting. Sports reporters, on the other hand, are presenting events they already know to be of interest to a large proportion of the audience. Although sport does not greatly affect the way people live their lives or their chances of survival, it does affect the way they feel about themselves and the world around them. For that portion of the audience who are not interested in sport, it is the sports reporter's job to engage them in this particular area of popular culture and explain to them why sport *does* matter to such a large number of their friends, families and associates.

Within sports broadcast journalism there is a professional challenge arising from the often cosy relationship between sports stars and those who engage with them professionally. At a football manager's press conference, there is little of the respect shown between politicians and political correspondents, for example. A politician may not like tough questions but they will usually understand the reporter's reason for asking them. There is a symbiotic relationship between the media and the elite personalities they cover: each needs the other, but their goals are not shared. At the simplest level, a sound working relationship between a soccer boss and the media produces regular stories for the reporter and a channel of communication to the supporters of the club for the manager.

There will always be imbalances which mean the relationship risks turning sour. The two groups rarely socialise these days in a way that would have been common as recently as twenty years ago, so there is little opportunity to discuss the mutual benefits of their roles. There may be suspicion or even jealousy: managers and sports performers at the highest level are paid hugely more than the hacks who report their comments; while the reporters will often be better educated and have greater job security than their subjects. All these differences can lead to friction. A comparatively anonymous reporter has the power to affect the career of a well-known professional by reporting discontent or voicing criticism that can be picked up and acted upon by his employers. Football club chairmen are notoriously fickle, and many professional coaches think they may not even understand the game.

Outside observers might be horrified at the way many sports reporters defer to the most boorish football managers. The print media, in particular, seem resigned to reporting and rarely challenging the most vacuous utterances of the top Premier

League managers. Meanwhile, broadcast journalists are powerless to insist on talking to prominent figures who refuse interviews because of some perceived wrong by the organisation for which the journalist works. Allegations in separate BBC programmes about the role of football agents led to three Premier League managers – Sir Alex Ferguson, Sam Allardyce and Harry Redknapp – all refusing to talk to the BBC. Despite the huge sums paid by broadcast organisations (including the BBC) to televise football, it was easy for fans to conclude who dominated the relationship between the broadcasters and these powerful and charismatic characters within their sport.

A year on from the *Panorama* programme which contained allegations against him, Redknapp was arrested and questioned by the police in connection with alleged transfer irregularities at Portsmouth Football Club. He seemed happy for the BBC to report his release without charge, and was quoted as 'speaking to the BBC' when he protested his innocence and outrage at the nature of his arrest. In a more congenial spirit, Ferguson appeared on the BBC's *Sports Personality of the Year* show to present a lifetime achievement award to Sir Bobby Robson. However, after these exceptional episodes, both Redknapp and Ferguson returned to their habit of shunning post-match interviews with the national broadcaster.

It is not only major personalities and national institutions like the BBC who fall out with each other. Many local reporters have fallen foul of the club they cover. Named individuals and, from time to time, specific newspapers and radio stations have been 'banned from the press box' because they reported something the club did not like. The usual response is for the reporter to attend the game anyway and report from the stand, among the paying customers. Almost invariably this results in a compromise where the club agrees to allow the offending reporter or organisation back in, sometimes with excuses and apologies being released for public consumption.

For a sports organisation, the local media are one of its main forms of communication with its paying public. Football clubs recognise the commercial value of free local publicity and invest in media departments who produce the club's own website and liaise with the press and broadcasters. Most of a sports club's revenue comes from the fans – either directly from gate receipts and sales of merchandising, or indirectly through subscription to TV companies who pay for broadcast rights. But they are not publicly funded organisations in the same way as government departments and local authorities. They are private companies with commercial interests to the fore. The reporter cannot use the Freedom of Information Act to uncover their affairs. Arguments about 'the freedom of the press' and 'the public's right to know' will not wash. The channels of communication laid on by the club are for the transmission of information that is mostly uncontroversial: ticket sales statistics, merchandising and promotion, injury news and, where bigger stories are in the offing, arrangements for press conferences. The media department will organise the regular pre – and post-match 'pressers' and the special events that mark the arrival (but hardly ever the departure) of managers and players. It suits the clubs for this information to be in the public domain. But the fans, with their voracious appetites for gossip, want more. So the sports reporter, particularly the local reporter assigned to a club, has always to walk a fine line between getting the stories the fans desire and upsetting the club.

The conflict between reporters and clubs – at all levels of professional sport – is in part a consequence of the globalisation of sport and the huge sums of money now involved in broadcasting rights. Access to the elite figures in sport is carefully controlled by press officers who themselves are part of a club's wider media information department, where primary sources of sports news are channelled through the club's own outlets – their website and TV channel. With few exceptions, most of the small number of staff in these departments are comparatively inexperienced journalists – usually recent graduates whose allegiance to their paymaster, the club, is arguably greater than their allegiance to any journalistic code. Their role is to maximise the club's revenues from its intellectual property rights. Thus, clubs will sell results services on mobile telephones, commentary on the Internet and goals and highlights packages online or on specialist digital TV channels.

These restrictions make life difficult for the traditional journalist working in sport, particularly those working in organisations that do not have the media rights to the events they cover. The popularity of fan sites, which are not run by the clubs but provide the frankest exchanges of opinion and rumour, suggests there is still a demand from supporters for independent information that is not policed by the club. Nevertheless, the difficulties of gaining access to the information controlled by the clubs has led to a world where one commentator can assert with authority that sports journalism 'seems to oscillate between a rather sycophantic cultivation of key sports sources (such as clubs and players) and a sometimes shrill demonization of those same organisations and individuals through sports scandals and exposés' (Rowe, 2005: 127).

The press office

The implication of this comment is that most sports coverage falls within the realm of sycophancy, and that the scandals and exposés are rarer. This would appear to be true, but on a day-to-day basis the 'oscillation' between the two extremes of journalistic behaviour is more frequent than Rowe's comment implies. There are daily conflicts between the commercial interests of football clubs and the work of reporters. The reporter has to recognise the job club press officers have to do and must appreciate that they are not paid simply to answer media inquiries; they are paid to serve the best interests of the football club. The reporter has to hope too that the press officer will respect the journalist's responsibility to editors and in turn to the public they inform. They will need to form a working relationship with a source that on certain days will be deliberately misleading. This differs from the relationship with contacts in many other areas of journalism, because most journalists will want to deal regularly only with sources who can be trusted. In sport, the reporter may have no choice about the reliability or otherwise of his contacts.

The relationship between reporter and club press officer can be illustrated by an example from late 2007. Steve Bruce, the manager who took Birmingham City into the Premier League, had just left the club to take over at Wigan. His former assistant Eric Black had been left in charge, but was not expected to get the job full time. There was mounting media speculation about who would take over at Saint Andrew's, with the contenders including the Scotland manager Alex McLeish. Sky Sports News wanted the latest on the story, even though no formal announcements had been planned. The channel sent an experienced freelance, Steve Lee, and a camera crew to 'sniff around' the Birmingham City training camp at Wast Hills.

Lee called the Birmingham City press office before setting out – partly as a courtesy but also on the off-chance of any developments in the story. He was told: 'There's nothing happening today. You're wasting your time.' When he arrived at the training ground, Lee saw some of the players getting into their cars to leave the ground and flagged one of them down. The player, Gary McSheffrey (whom Lee had known since his time at Coventry City), was happy to explain what had been going on behind closed doors: Eric Black had just said his farewells to the playing staff because he was leaving to join Steve Bruce as his assistant at Wigan. McSheffrey gave a two-minute interview which ran on Sky Sports News. Lee rang the club press office again to ask about Black leaving and was told he was still with the club. Lee recalls telling the press officer: 'That's not what the players are saying.' It was only then that the press officer confirmed that Black was indeed leaving.

When the BBC saw the Sky Sports News broadcast, they took the story a stage further. They made inquiries to the Scottish Football Association and were advised that Alex McLeish had tendered his resignation as the national coach. By that afternoon, BBC Radio 5 Live was reporting that McLeish was to be the next manager of Birmingham City and that BBC man Pat Murphy had broken the story. Whether Murphy would have been able to break the story without Lee's combination of tenacity and good luck is a moot point. What is clear is that the club press officer's early morning comment that nothing would be happening that day and that Lee was wasting his time proved unfounded. The comment was interpreted by Lee, correctly as it turned out, as meaning that there would be no *official* announcements during the day by the football club. His assessment of what happened is a useful guideline for all journalists dealing with sources with something to hide: 'Once you chip away at the foundation, the whole building comes tumbling down.'[1]

Lawrie Madden, a former professional footballer who now works for Sky Sports (and writes for the *Daily Telegraph* and the *News of the World*), agrees that the way press officers attempt to control information is making the job of the sports reporter increasingly difficult. He says: 'The biggest thing is access and as a result it affects the stories you can get from clubs. I've never known a situation where so many journalists have had to rely on blogs and websites. Some players have their own websites with blogs on them, but who knows who's writing them?' According to Madden, who now lectures in sports journalism, fifteen or twenty years ago most journalists would have managers' telephone numbers and could ring them for a story. It is different today. He says he can get hold of the numbers of most of the English managers in the Premier League, because he played alongside several of them, but not the foreign ones. An England cricket captain told him he had an arrangement with his mobile phone supplier to change his number immediately he started receiving too many calls from people he did not want to hear from – and that included journalists.

It is also true that journalists used to socialise with footballers and other sportsmen far more frequently than they do today. The modern reporter would be unlikely to be able to afford the cost of a round if he went out drinking with a group of Premiership footballers, and most editors in broadcast organisations would be unwilling to sign it off as expenses. Information about transfer moves is unlikely to come from the football clubs, who have a commercial interest in keeping their negotiations secret, but may still come from players. These days it is more likely to be planted by a player's agent, who is himself using the media for personal gain.

Lawrie Madden explains the extent of most reporters' access:

> When you go to a football club for the manager's weekly press conference on a Friday or before a game, the TV and the radio and the national reporters are all in one room. They set up their microphones and the manager comes in and you've got fifteen minutes. At the end of that time a woman from the club's media department will say, 'Last question, please.' Then they'll ask us to leave and then do another fifteen minutes for the Sundays. That's all anyone gets. There might be a few people with one-to-one relationships with managers, but mostly everybody gets the same thing – just what's said at the press conference. It's more stage-managed than ever before. They control what players you get to talk to. If there's a controversial incident and there's one player you were hoping to speak to, they'll pull that player out. Football clubs want to protect their assets and show them in a good light so they protect access to them.[2]

Sports journalism and sports broadcasting – the difference

In this context it is easy to understand why sports journalists have been described as more fan club than Fourth Estate (Rowe, 2005). It is much more difficult to uncover the stories the clubs do not want told than to toe the party line. Raymond Boyle (2006: 1) says that in 'the hierarchy of professional journalism', sports journalism has been 'traditionally viewed as the "toy department", a bastion of easy living, sloppy journalism and "soft" news'.

This criticism, though, cannot be applied fairly to sports journalism within broadcasting. Boyle (*ibid.*: 75) says there remains an 'institutional and cultural distinction' between sports journalism and sports broadcasting. He highlights the differences between sports writing, investigation and analysis (sports journalism) and the act of relaying sports events to the listener or viewer at home (sports broadcasting). To the modern sports broadcast journalist, however, the distinction is largely irrelevant to their practice. The range of professional skills within the specialism includes the ability to commentate on live events. This, the domain of the sports broadcaster, is now required of most broadcast journalists working in sport. It requires research and analytical skills and a fluency on air which most news broadcasters are unlikely to be able to emulate.

Conclusion

Sport is news and news is sport these days. It is as likely to appear on the front pages of newspapers as the back. Coverage of England at the 2006 World Cup was as much about the wags (wives and girlfriends) – what they were wearing and where they were shopping – as about the players. The activities of some Manchester United players at a Christmas party – without their wags – provided tabloid headlines for a week at the end of 2007.

In higher education, the specialism of sports broadcast journalism has only recently been recognised (the first course accredited by the Broadcast Journalism

Training Council began in 2006). But the skills of the sports journalism specialist have never had a wider audience in British broadcasting than they do today.

Notes

1   Steve Lee, interview with the author, 18 December 2007
2   Lawrie Madden, interview with the author, 15 December 2007

References

Boyle, R. (2006) *Sports Journalism: Context and Issues*, London: Sage

Chiles, A. (2007) *We Don't Know What We're Doing*, London: Sphere

Hitchens, P. (2007) 'A diabolical defeat . . . and no, I don't mean the football', *Mail on Sunday*, 25 November, p. 34

Rowe, D. (2005) 'Fourth Estate or fan club? Sports journalism engages the popular', in S. Allan (ed.), *Journalism: Critical Issues*, Maidenhead and New York: Open University Press.

Thompson, R. (2005) *Writing for Broadcast Journalists*, Abingdon: Routledge

Tomlinson, A. (1999) *The Game's up: Essays in the Cultural Analysis of Sport, Leisure and Popular Culture*, Aldershot: Ashgate

Reporting business, finance and the City

Marie Kinsey

15

Introduction

Reporting business, finance and the City is a bit like reporting the weather: not much appears to happen most of the time, then suddenly there are floods and everyone's talking about climate change. In the autumn of 2007 financial journalists found themselves back at the top of news bulletins with the collapse of Northern Rock bank, Britain's fifth-biggest mortgage lender, and everyone was talking about a global economic crisis.

For many listeners and viewers, the story of Northern Rock's collapse was, at first, a tale of ordinary people with money invested in the bank trying to save their personal finances from meltdown. However, behind those headlines was an even bigger and much more complex story about how the global lending system between the big banks, which oils the wheels of the financial markets, was facing a crisis that might ultimately affect the finances of millions.

Money matters. People have jobs, earn money, save and borrow; they may invest in shares, commodities and bonds. They have pensions, own homes (or aspire to), must pay bills, are sometimes in debt and aim for a decent standard of living. Much that happens in the economy, in business and on the financial markets will affect them either directly or indirectly. Much that happens in the world at large – famine, wars, changes of government, terrorism and myriad less dramatic events – will affect economies, companies and markets. Reporting the health or otherwise of the economy, the business climate, the state of the markets and whether these markets are working properly is at the heart of financial journalism. In another way it is all about people.

Often it is the characters in the world of finance that are at the heart of the story. Everyone loves a good scandal, and there have been financial scandals aplenty, going all the way back to the South Sea Bubble of 1720. More recently we have had the Guinness affair, the collapse of the Bank of Credit and Commerce International, Robert Maxwell's fleecing of the Mirror Group's pension fund and Nick Leeson, whose high-risk trading caused the collapse of Barings Bank, to name but a few. Hugh Pym, the BBC's economics editor, admits that such stories are the ones he enjoys most, having covered several of them, including Guinness, which ended with the jailing of its former chief executive Ernest Saunders in 1990 for false accounting, conspiracy and theft. '[It's] the characters involved, the sums of money, the City establishment and suddenly all of them are in the dock. It was just a wonderful combination of personalities, power, money, big names like Guinness. It was a cracker.'[1]

The broadcasters

In the UK, financial journalism goes back nearly as far as the earliest share trading, which began in the coffee houses of London in the late seventeenth century. By 1850, London had a well-established, regulated stock exchange, a physical place in

Capel Court in the City of London where members met to buy and sell company stocks and shares and a part of the capital where many investment banks, dealers and financial corporations have their headquarters to this day (London Stock Exchange, 2008).

In 1850, Paul Julius Reuter began using the fastest technology available to send news and stock prices between Aachen, Germany and Brussels – a fleet of forty-five pigeons, which beat the railway by six hours. A year later he opened an office in London that transmitted stock-market quotations between London and Paris via a new undersea cable that had been laid between Dover and Calais. As overland telegraph systems and undersea cable facilities spread, so did the new Reuters agency. In 1865 it broke the news to Europe of President Lincoln's assassination in the United States, a story that took twelve days to cross the Atlantic and threw European markets into turmoil. By 1872 it was sending news and financial material to the Far East and by 1874 to South America. Owned since March 2008 by the Thomson Corporation, Reuters is now one of the world's biggest news, financial information and services companies, with headquarters in London's Canary Wharf. Most other broadcasters subscribe to its diet of news and financial information (Reuters, 2008).

BBC Radio ran a stock-market report as far back as the 1920s but its regular financial coverage did not really take off until the establishment of the long-running *Financial World Tonight* on Radio 4 in the early 1970s, followed by the creation of the Financial Unit (now the Economics and Business Centre) and the launch of the personal finance programme *Money Box* in 1977. As Peter Day, who joined the BBC in 1974, recalls: 'In 1976 the pound went down below two [US] dollars for the first time and the Financial Unit phone didn't stop ringing until the end of the decade, as the newsdesks woke up to one of the great running stories: the economy, inflation and the pound.'[2] On BBC Television, *The Money Programme* was first aired in 1966.

Commercial radio, through Independent Radio News (IRN) and its then sister London speech station LBC, invested in financial journalism through the highly influential financial editor Douglas Moffitt in 1974, a year after independent radio launched in the UK. IRN provided a daily market preview and end-of-day report for its client stations, along with bulletin coverage of financial stories. LBC carried market and company reports at regular points throughout the day and the innovative hourly *Top Twenty Sharecheck*, while Moffitt also presented the weekly personal finance programme *Family Money*.

The big explosion in financial broadcast journalism began during the 1980s when the markets started to deregulate, culminating in the so-called Big Bang of 1986, when the London Stock Exchange revolutionised the way it did business, making it easier to buy and sell shares. Out went face-to-face dealing on the floor of the Exchange and in came electronic trading via computers and telephones. By then, the Thatcher government of the 1980s had already begun its programme of privatisation – the first taste of share ownership for many people. Building societies were turning themselves into banks and banks were offering mortgages. Unsurprisingly, public interest in the world of business and finance was increasing.

The broadcasters responded by expanding the amount of programming devoted to business and finance. Channel 4 launched the lunchtime *Business Daily* in 1987 and it ran until the early 1990s. In the same year, Thames Television, which then held the weekday franchise for London, launched the weekly *City Programme*, which continued until Thames lost the franchise in 1992. The BBC began the early morning *Wake up to Money* and *Weekend Business* on Radio 5 Live and *In Business*, *Nice Work* and *The Bottom Line* on Radio 4, while LBC had *Dawn Traders*.

In the early twenty-first century, the landscape of financial broadcasting is more cluttered. Sky News covered business and finance right from its launch in 1989. In 1993, Reuters bought the television news agency Visnews, renaming it Reuters Television, and a year later started a television service specifically for dealers. CNBC Europe, an alliance between NBC and Dow Jones, aired for the first time in 1998, nine years after it had begun broadcasting in America. BBC Television has added *Working Lunch* to its stable of financial and business programmes. Outside the 'specialist' programmes, mainstream news programmes on the BBC, Channel 4 and ITV devote plenty of time and resources to covering economics, business and money.

Lost in translation?

General journalists are often wary of financial journalism because they think it is about numbers, full of complicated ideas, hard to understand and a turn-off for audiences. Veteran BBC business journalist Peter Day, presenter of Radio 4's *In Business*, argues that such worries are misplaced: 'If people looked to tell stories about business, finance and the economy in the same way they would tell a story about a murder or something, they would lose some of their fear'[3] Hugh Pym echoes the point: 'They've got the sort of narrative that makes a good story in any field, be it entertainment or crime. I suppose that's what makes a really good business story, if it's got the elements that make any good story.'[4]

Telling stories like this – making them accessible without oversimplifying, finding the right pictures and interviewees, and persuading the newsdesk to commission them – is crucial. But financial journalism does call for specialist knowledge and a finely honed ability to turn jargon into plain English. In an interview with the *UK Press Gazette*, the BBC's business editor Robert Peston, who broke the Northern Rock story, said: 'There's no point in whingeing about not getting your story on air if you can't explain why it matters in language that everyone understands' (Smith, 2008).

Financial broadcast journalism also calls for lateral thinking and an ear or eye for a good analogy. Talking to the truck driver while not insulting the professor, as veteran US journalist Ed Murrow put it, is a harder line to walk in financial journalism than in many other specialisms. Financial broadcast journalists are aware of the problem. Hugh Pym says:

> There's a debate about how much you simplify it for people and how much they know already and I think sometimes all financial broadcasters underestimate people's grasp. There's a tendency not to do stories because we think they're too complicated. But equally, taking challenging and difficult stuff and explaining it is part of the job and that's very satisfying when you get it right.[5]

And Peter Day could not be more emphatic: 'Our job is to produce an authentic, coherent narrative voice that a lot of people can understand and participate in.'[6]

Sky News' business editor Michael Wilson says:

> There's a lot of snobbery about rolling news not reflecting a deep analysis of what's going on, but I'm expected to go and talk almost instantly about things and I think I more or less hit most of the main targets that a think-piece might elicit a couple of hours later.[7]

Part of the difficulty, particularly with financial news in television, is illustrating concepts in ways that bring the story alive. Radio is very good at analysis and argument, but television will always need pictures, which calls for imagination on the part of the journalist. And, as the BBC's economics editor Stephanie Flanders explains, sometimes you need luck:

> My producer, Steven Duke, spots a cluster of 'For Sale' and 'To Let' signs bunched together at the side of the road. This is already good news – you'd be amazed how difficult it is to find lots of property signs in one place for illustrating housing market stories. Then a miracle happens. A man with a truck-full of signs pulls up and lets us film him actually putting up another 'For Sale' sign. In TV economics coverage this is about as close to a Bafta-winning action sequence as you're likely to get.
>
> (Flanders, 2008)

The territory

With all that airtime to fill, what actually constitutes financial journalism? Broadly, financial reporting falls into four categories – economics, markets, business and personal finance – but in practice many of these areas overlap and interlink: events in one area usually impact somewhere else. Northern Rock is a good example: the story began in an obscure sector of the American mortgage market, began to affect wholesale money market interest rates (the rates at which the banks lend money to each other), forcing Northern Rock to ask the Bank of England to bail it out. Now that credit is harder to come by, people may feel less well off. A swathe of companies, not just in the banking sector, may find it harder to do business, which may ultimately contribute to lower economic growth in the UK and elsewhere.

Economics

Economics coverage tends to concentrate on the big picture both nationally and internationally. It draws information from many indicators, including company results, stock and bond markets performance, employment, trade, interest rates, inflation, pay deals, consumer spending, currency exchange rates, commodity prices, debt levels, and assesses their effects on economic activity.

Markets

Market reporting tends to cover the daily movements in the prices of shares, government bonds (gilts), currencies and commodities both nationally and internationally. Movements in share prices in the main world markets of London, New York and Tokyo are monitored by the main market indices: in London, the FTSE 100; in New York, the Dow Jones and the NASDAQ; and in Tokyo, the Nikkei. No market report is complete without reference to the main exchange rates: between sterling and the US dollar, sterling and the euro and the US dollar and the Japanese yen. Prices may also be given for the main commodities – oil, gold and sometimes coffee and copper.

Business

Business reporting has perhaps a broader brief. In the main it encompasses company results and reports and any sort of newsworthy activity by companies large and small.

Personal finance

The personal finance reporter will cover everything from tax and benefits through to mortgages and pensions, but from the point of view of the ordinary person. It is an area of financial journalism that gives information about, for example, where to invest, how to minimise tax and where to find the best mortgage. Personal finance reporters will be able to assess the strengths and weaknesses of new financial products and be able to explain the impact of government policy on individuals.

Northern Rock and the sub-prime markets

It was the biggest business story of the year, if not the decade. From early 2007, there had been rumblings about potential problems in the American 'sub-prime' mortgage market. As the term suggests, this is a high-risk section of the market where banks lend money to buy a home to people with poor credit ratings. A sharp rise in the number of people who could not afford to repay their loans left the banks facing huge losses. Financial institutions became reluctant to lend to each other in the wholesale money markets – the oil that keeps the system running – pushing up the cost of money and causing the money market effectively to seize up (BBC, 2008b).

Nobody was quite sure of the scale of the problem. For years, financial institutions, in their efforts to devise new types of investment, had been bundling up sub-prime mortgages and selling them on in the form of bonds and other mortgage-backed securities. In the early summer of 2007 there was a string of stories about sub-prime lenders warning of losses, and on 23 August a group of American and European banks took the almost unprecedented step of borrowing one billion pounds from the US central bank, the Federal Reserve, to ease concerns about credit. A few days later a German bank was sold to the country's biggest regional bank after coming close to collapse because of its exposure to the sub-prime market. In early September, even the Bank of China admitted nine billion dollars of losses (*ibid.*).

On 13 September, the BBC's business editor Robert Peston broke the story that Northern Rock, Britain's eighth-biggest bank, was about to ask the Bank of England to bail it out with a multi-billion-pound loan. Despite reassurances that Northern Rock was not about to go bust, investors queued up at branches all over Britain to withdraw their money. It was the first run on a British bank since 1866 and was only stopped four days later when Chancellor Alistair Darling said the government would guarantee all deposits held by the bank. Ultimately, it was nationalised in early 2008.

Northern Rock was particularly vulnerable because of the way it had financed itself. Normally banks fund most of their lending from money deposited with them by savers. But Northern Rock had relied on borrowing from the financial markets to fund 60 per cent of its lending, a much higher proportion than its competitors. When the financial markets seized up, so did the bank's main source of finance (BBC, 2008a).

The Budget

Every year, broadcasters clear the decks for the big financial set piece of the year, the Budget, delivered to a usually packed House of Commons by the Chancellor of the Exchequer. Financial editors will usually have a copy of the speech as it is being made and it always comes with a small forest of press releases and other details from the Treasury. Alistair Darling's speech in March 2008 covered twenty pages and took about an hour to deliver, but the accompanying detail contained in the Financial Statement stretched to over two hundred pages of analysis, and twenty-one supplementary documents were issued at the same time (HM Treasury, 2008).

The Budget speech follows the same broad pattern each year. The Chancellor begins by giving his assessment of the economic climate and outlines his economic forecasts – how he thinks the economy will perform over the next few years and how much or little growth there may be. He moves on to a consideration about the prospects for inflation. Then he gives an assessment about the state of the government's finances – predictions for borrowing, the level of debt and spending on public services like health and education. A consideration of benefits payments comes next, followed by the business climate and any changes to the business tax regime. Changes to indirect taxes, such as duty on tobacco and alcohol, tend to come towards the end, with changes to income tax and national insurance usually last – along with any surprises.

Interpreting and explaining all this means a small army of journalists and experts contributing to special programmes, news bulletins and websites. A staple feature of all the coverage is 'What does it mean to you?' and many programmes will recruit regional panels made up of families representing different income brackets. Much of this will be set up in advance. The content of the Budget may change from year to year, but the choreography remains the same.

Finding and covering stories

Some major criticisms of financial journalism are that many stories simply go undiscovered and unreported, ideas are drawn in the main from the flow of economic and corporate news releases – particularly for specialist audiences – and journalists do not do enough to help the public grasp the significance of financial and economic news (Doyle, 2006). For instance, the collapse of energy trading company Enron in 2001, the largest bankruptcy in US history, came as a surprise, even though the warning signs had been present in the detail of the company's annual report for the preceding year (West, 2005). Doyle makes a useful distinction between financial journalists working in a specialist environment, where the audience is likely to comprise professional investors and analysts, and those talking to a more general audience: 'segments devoted to business news within mainstream media, fearful of deterring lay audiences, are generally unable to do penetrating and forensic analysis of economic and financial news events' (Doyle, 2006: 450–1).

The BBC, in one of its periodic reviews of impartiality, found that its own business coverage sometimes fell short of the ideal. In 2007, a panel chaired by the economist Sir Alan Budd concluded that most of the output met the required standards and that the BBC had no systematic bias against business. Furthermore, its audience research showed no lack of trust in the Corporation's business coverage. However, the report criticised some interviews for their sycophancy or aggression and expressed concern that:

> Focusing on the individual consumer angle can distort news values and important perspectives can be lost. The polarisation of views between business and consumer means that much of the ground in between is overlooked. This includes the role of business in society, the international context and the workplace. Audiences are well served in their identity as consumers but they are not that well served in their role as workers or indeed as direct or indirect shareholders.
>
> (BBC, 2007a)

It also identified a long-held concern of many financial broadcast journalists that it is sometimes hard to persuade the mainstream newsdesk to cover a story: 'We believe that a lack of specialist knowledge and perhaps a lack of interest on the part of some mainstream programme editors can result in missed stories or angles' (*ibid.*).

The BBC responded to the report by devising new training programmes for non-specialist programming staff to raise the general level of knowledge about business, creating a new 'workplace' reporting role, expanding the range of interviewees it uses and reviewing its business website (BBC, 2007b).

It is clear that many financial stories – business and personal finance stories in particular – come from press releases, and that this area of journalism is not exempt from the 'churnalism' Nick Davies describes in his book *Flat Earth News* (2008), where little is done beyond recycling the press release; and media manipulation by PR companies is endemic. Doyle's research (2006: 443), found that 'The potential presence of "spin" in the interpretation given to economic events by players in the field is a widely recognised hazard' and he reported concerns from one financial journalist that they do little to challenge prevailing systems and norms:

> In terms of economic development, we write about, say, whether countries have been successful in reducing their debt level, but we don't ask why we have a system whereby countries have debts in the first place. We don't challenge – but I'm afraid that's the deal . . . We are not campaigning but we are working within the constraints of reality.
>
> *(Ibid.*: 447)

There are dilemmas peculiar to financial journalism, particularly with respect to conflict of interest and the responsible reporting of stories which might dramatically influence the public – like Northern Rock. In 2000, two *Mirror* journalists, James Hipwell and Anil Bhoyrul, who wrote the 'City Slickers' column, were sacked for gross misconduct after an investigation into a share-tipping controversy at the paper. Both the BBC and the Press Complaints Commission (PCC) have updated their codes of practice, partly as a result of the scandal and partly in response to the EU Market Abuse Directive of 2004, aimed at tackling insider trading and market manipulation. The PCC Code says journalists must not use for their own profit financial information they receive in advance of its general publication, and that they must not write about shares they own without disclosing their interest (PCC, 2008). The BBC's editorial guidelines include a requirement that all people working in financial programmes should register all their shareholdings and other financial interests or dealings (BBC, 2005).

On occasions, more subtle judgements must be made. The collapse of Northern Rock caused much soul searching at the BBC about the potential effect of showing dramatic pictures of queues outside the bank's branches. Hugh Pym recalls:

> The next morning I remember endless debates: 'We must be responsible here, we musn't show people queuing 'cos if the BBC are saying that . . .' There was an incredible sort of combination of how we approach it as reporters and being responsible with 'This is an astonishing story unfolding' . . . If the BBC were accused of sparking a run on the financial system, there's more than one individual job on the line.

Daniel Dodd, former editor of the BBC's Economics and Business Centre, described the thinking on the *Editors* blog:

> From the moment the story broke . . . we were clear we had to handle [it] carefully. We talked internally about the need to be responsible in our coverage – not to provoke panic but to tell people straight what was happening . . . Should we have carried images of the queues? Of course we should and everybody did. The public needs to know what's going on – but we had a responsibility to do it in a balanced way. So the fears of those interviewed in the queues were set against the reassurances of experts from the financial services industry and the politicians and the regulators.
>
> (Dodd, 2007)

Conclusion

The seductive aspect of financial journalism is that it really is about everything. It involves ordinary people, politics and money, and it operates at every level from the local to the global. You have a ringside seat as big events unfold. The challenge lies in making sense of these events for viewers and listeners, using the language of the layman but understanding the language of the professional. The best financial journalists will be able to break news, predict trends, analyse stories *and* explain them to a general audience.

Notes

1   Interview with the author, 11 January 2008.
2   Email communication with the author, 4 January 2008.
3   Interview with the author, 7 January 2008.
4   Interview with the author, 11 January 2008.
5   *Ibid.*
6   Interview with the author, 7 January 2008.
7   Interview with the author, 10 April 2008.
8   Interview with the author, 11 January 2008.

References

BBC (2005) *Editorial Guidelines*, 27 June, at http://www.bbc.co.uk/guidelines/editorialguidelines/advice/financejournal/ (accessed 11 April 2008)

BBC (2007a) *Report of the Independent Panel for the BBC Trust on the Impartiality of BBC Business Coverage*, 25 May, at http://www.bbc.co.uk/bbctrust/research/business_news_impartiality.html (accessed 7 April 2008)

BBC (2007b) *Report of the Independent Panel for the BBC Trust on the Impartiality of BBC Business Coverage, BBC Management Response*, July, at http://www.bbc.co.uk/bbctrust/research/business_news_impartiality.html (accessed 7 April 2008)

BBC (2008a) Rock Pledges to Repay Taxpayers, 31 March, at http://news.bbc.co.uk/1/hi/business/7321995.stm (accessed 3 April 2008)

BBC (2008b) Timeline: Sub-Prime Losses, 1 April, at http://news.bbc.co.uk/1/hi/business/7096845.stm (accessed 3 April 2008)

Davies, N. (2008) *Flat Earth News*, London: Chatto and Windus

Dodd, D. (2007) Blame the Messenger?, *BBC Editors*, 19 September (accessed 3 April 2008)

Doyle, G. (2006) Financial News Journalism: A Post-Enron Analysis of Approaches towards Economic and Financial News Production in the UK, *Journalism* 7(4): 433–52

Flanders, S. (2008) My Week: Stephanie Flanders, *Observer*, 6 April, p. 21

HM Treasury (2008) *Budget 2008, Stability and Opportunity: Building a Strong, Sustainable Future*, 12 March, London: The Stationery Office, HC388

London Stock Exchange (2008) *Our History*, at http://www.londonstockexchange.com/en-gb/about/cooverview/history.htm (accessed 11 April 2008)

Press Complaints Commission (2008) *Code of Practice*, at http://www.pcc.org.uk/cop/practice.html (accessed 11 April 2008)

Reuters (2008) *History of Reuters*, at http://about.reuters.com/home/aboutus/history/informationandinnovation.aspx (accessed 11 April 2008)

Smith, P. (2008) How Money Matters Made Front-Page News, *UK Press Gazette*, 14 March, p. 14

West, S. (2005) Sceptical Attitude is Vital for Accurate Business Journalism, *UK Press Gazette*, 4 March, p. 9

Reporting politics

Nicholas Jones

16

Introduction

Unlike television, radio and the rest of the electronic news media with their ever-multiplying formats and platforms, political life in Britain tends to be pretty stable. Governments may come and go but the party structure has proved remarkably durable and political debate tends to be conducted along well-rehearsed lines. A Queen's Speech opens each new session of Parliament; an annual Budget determines the levels of taxation; and a weekly session of questions to the Prime Minister provides a regular target for the Opposition. Although the line-up of ministers and Members of Parliament might change as a result of a cabinet reshuffle or general election, many of the arguments which are deployed are not just familiar but downright predictable. Here we begin to see why some journalists love political reporting while many others apparently loathe it: they say they dislike having to spend so much time with politicians and are turned off by the posturing inherent in the adversarial way in which the two Houses of Parliament conduct their business.

Nevertheless, over the years, quite a few political correspondents (myself included) have spent almost a lifetime at Westminster. We get a thrill from being among the first to report the decisions which have been taken in Downing Street and Whitehall; we are fascinated by the highs and lows of political life; we are at ease in the clubbable atmosphere of the Palace of Westminster; and we freely admit we get hooked on the unpredictability of general election campaigns when political fortunes can be won or lost.

Two tribes?

Just as there is a deep divide between the journalists who love or loathe politics, so there is an equally clear split among the political correspondents of Westminster. Broadcasters and newspaper journalists tend to belong to two quite separate tribes: we work to different sets of standards and sometimes to widely diverging news values. Whereas the press has a self-imposed responsibility to try to be accurate and ethical, television and radio are regulated by the state and are also required to be fair, balanced and politically impartial. These distinctions are increasingly being blurred by the expansion of the Internet and the growth of newspaper websites which offer not just text but a full range of audio-visual material complete with online radio and television news bulletins. Despite the growing convergence between press and broadcasting, though, a fundamental divide remains.

Newspapers – and now their websites – are self-regulated and make a virtue of being politically partisan, often blatantly favouring one party over another, depending on the political climate at the time or perhaps the whim of their proprietor or editor. Because television and radio services have to be licensed, and are subject to the conditions which are imposed either by the BBC charter or by the regulator Ofcom, broadcasters do not have the same editorial freedom as their colleagues in the press and cannot be politically biased. On the other hand, reporters for national daily and Sunday newspapers cannot avoid the political sympathies of their papers; often they have to write stories in a way which has to take account of a predetermined agenda. Indeed, a free press, unhindered in what it can report and say about the politics of the country, is one of the great strengths of British democracy.

However, an equally formidable safeguard is the importance of ensuring that television and radio output is not captured by one political persuasion or another. Our airwaves have not become a platform for uncontrolled party propaganda; we do not have, for example, the television attack advertisements which dominate – and many observers believe distort – American election campaigns.

Broadcasters in Britain have always defended the need for impartiality, especially during elections. We know that when it comes to deciding who to vote for that most people are probably influenced most of all by what they see or hear on air. Yes, the newspapers may have set the political agenda and influenced the terms of the debate, but a final judgement on who to support might well be determined by the impressions we have formed about the rival political leaders and the way they have presented themselves on television or radio and responded to questions. The need to be balanced and impartial is a responsibility most broadcasters shoulder intuitively, as though it is part of our make-up, almost a way of life, which few of us would wish to change. I would venture to suggest that most, if not all, political correspondents working for established television or radio services – certainly this goes for those I have known – would want their epitaph to say that their broadcasting had been impartial, that viewers and listeners could not detect which, if any, party they supported.

Politics live

In practical terms what really marks out a broadcaster from a newspaper reporter is the ability not just to write a news story or a comment column but the confidence and ability to report on air and to camera. Live broadcasting can be even more demanding. Television and radio correspondents, unlike programme presenters and newsreaders, also have to be technically competent as they will often be required to assist camera crews, sound recordists, videotape editors and so on.

Such is the pace of technological development that the broadcasters of today are becoming increasingly self-sufficient and are often quite capable of operating video cameras, digital recorders and computerised equipment on which to edit their own material. My thirty years as a BBC producer, reporter and correspondent were an era of dramatic change and I have no doubt this will continue to be the case in the years ahead, and perhaps even accelerate. Not only were the broadcasters of my generation constantly having to adapt to new systems for recording and editing but there was a transformation in the way in which we prepared and broadcast our material. New formats required new presentational techniques which began to have a profound effect on the basic structure of political reporting and which I am sure will continue to have an impact.

The lesson which I had to learn, and which again still applies, is that it is essential not to get sidetracked or overburdened by the technical complexities of changing formats. Writing a balanced story, giving fair if not equal access to the rival parties and avoiding any sense of political bias take priority, however difficult it might be to adjust to new equipment or the increasing demands of additional output. Continuous live broadcasting on channels like BBC News 24, Sky News and BBC Radio 5 Live has revolutionised political reporting. Correspondents have to answer questions on the hoof and be able to give what amounts to a running commentary, whether they are reporting on the implications of a statement in the House of Commons or discussing the repercussions of a speech at a party conference.

While live broadcasting has enormous attractions for viewers and listeners – and for journalists – it has led to a fundamental shift in the way political news is presented to the public. When I started broadcasting from Westminster in the early 1970s 90 per cent of what I said on air had been scripted and was pre-recorded; there was very little live broadcasting. I like to think I would have thought carefully about every sentence; chosen any actuality with great care; and checked and checked again to make sure my report was fair and politically balanced. Thirty years later the way in which I was reporting had been turned upside down. I calculated that in 2002, my final year as a BBC political correspondent, 90 per cent of what I said was live and unscripted, and it was usually delivered as part of a two-way conversation with a newsreader or programme presenter.

Therefore, the pressures on the political reporter of today are far different from the 1970s and do get to the heart of the debate about whether political journalism on radio and television is as accurate, fair and reliable as it once was. Conversational journalism is considered to be more accessible for viewers and listeners, who are said to have a greater tendency to switch off, literally or mentally, when it appears they are being 'lectured' to by a political correspondent tied to his or her script. When a presenter puts the journalist on the spot with a difficult question, there is a far greater element of surprise than with a pre-recorded report.

But while programme controllers believe live reporting is what the audience wants – and, of course, it is far cheaper to produce than filmed or pre-recorded material – the correspondent cannot always be as precise as he or she might be if delivering a scripted report. A two-way conversation takes a direction which is determined by the questions and the way in which they are framed, and often the journalist does not get a chance to marshal the facts in the way that would make most sense. A far greater danger is a tendency on the part of the correspondent to oversimplify complex issues and perhaps even exaggerate.

Sources and spin

Political journalism is highly competitive and perhaps understandably some correspondents feel the need to demonstrate they have better contacts than their rivals. On this score I would have to plead guilty and admit that occasionally I took liberties and suggested my sources were probably superior to those of my colleagues. When reporting live from outside Downing Street or the Houses of Parliament it is all too easy to talk up one's own knowledge: 'ministers believe . . .', 'the rebel MPs are saying . . .', 'Downing Street insiders are insisting . . .' and so on. Before making this statement, I might have spoken to no more than a minister's junior aide, a single dissident MP or a Number Ten press officer.

Another downside to the conversational style of political reporting is that it might result in the viewer or listener feeling excluded. If the reporter has been tempted to show off about the strength of his or her contacts, why haven't the audience been let into the secret and told who they are? This touches on what is perhaps an infinitely more worrying repercussion from the failure to identify sources. Interrupting an answer to give detailed attribution for facts or quotations does not always sit easily in a two-way conversation, and the tendency of correspondents to skate over the identity of their sources not only has the potential to undermine the credibility of their reporting but might put them at risk of being manipulated.

Over the years, political journalists have always relied on information given to them on an off-the-record basis, and such is the nature of politics that the practice is bound to continue. Nevertheless, there has been a sea change in the way in which political spin doctors and propagandists seek to exploit the competitive forces which have been unleashed in a 24/7 media environment. Such is the demand for exclusive stories that many journalists think there is no alternative but to go along with the all-too-frequent precondition that their sources must not be revealed. Unfortunately, the trade in unsourced stories has become so commonplace in Whitehall and Westminster that political correspondents are failing to recognise how corrosive this can be in terms of public trust.

In what I think is often a mistaken belief that none of their contacts should ever be identified, and perhaps because they think a hint of secrecy or subterfuge adds a heightened degree of interest, broadcasters as well as newspaper journalists are increasingly attributing statements and remarks to a vast array of unnamed individuals, such as 'cabinet insiders', 'top ministerial aides', 'senior backbenchers', 'close friends' and so on. An alarm bell rings whenever I hear a newsreader say the 'BBC has learned exclusively . . .' and then find that the reporter has based the entire report on quotes from unidentified government or party sources. Was this report really the result of journalistic endeavour or simply yet another story planted by political propagandists who trade information on the condition that their anonymity is preserved?

Given the intense competition at Westminster and the pressure to find exclusives, journalists face a dilemma. Important stories cannot be ignored but audiences deserve to be given at least some indication of how and why the news has emerged. Was it the result of a genuine leak? Did it warrant being called an exclusive? If the motive is merely a spin doctor's desire to trail an announcement, and a reporter is given an advance preview in the hope of gaining favourable publicity, then the bulletin or programme should at least give a health warning or explain how fortuitous the release of the story is for those concerned.

Increasingly, speculation and comment rather than straight reporting of who said what in either the House of Commons or the House of Lords have tended to dominate political coverage in both the press and broadcasting. As the news cycle has speeded up so has the pressure to look ahead, and once an important announcement has been made or a key vote taken place, the focus invariably shifts to the next potential clash or crisis. A rapid turnover of stories has forced political correspondents to go behind the scenes, to search out the sources who can predict what might or might not happen, or alternatively who might reveal the hidden background to a sudden change of plan or an unexpected defeat.

As the 24/7 news environment took hold it was journalists rather than politicians who began having the greatest success in influencing and even dictating the news agenda, putting the government of the day at a distinct disadvantage. While Tony Blair's decade as Prime Minister will always be associated with the word 'spin', he did ensure that his administration transformed the way Downing Street and Whitehall responded to the demands of twenty-four-hour news. Civil service information officers were forced to forsake their nine-to-five mentality. On entering Downing Street as Blair's press secretary, Alastair Campbell's first act was to rewrite the rule book by instructing government press officers to 'grab the agenda' by trailing new policies and decisions even before ministers had made their announcements in Parliament. While there was no doubt that the government's publicity machine developed a faster response rate, the downside was that more often than not control over the flow of information from state to public ended up in the hands of political advisers rather than neutral civil servants.

Encouraging a covert exchange of information with trusted media outlets meant that more formal and regular off-the-record briefings became less important and they are no longer considered as useful as they were in the past. Campbell deserves credit for putting transcripts of Downing Street's lobby guidance on the Number Ten website and also for breaking the closed shop of political correspondents by allowing specialist and foreign journalists to attend briefings. But whereas these twice-daily meetings once served as platforms to explain and promote government policy, now they are little more than Downing Street noticeboards, with the official spokesmen tending to slip into a defensive, 'no comment' mode whenever they are probed too closely.

By instituting his own monthly televised news conferences, Blair (and his successor Gordon Brown) bypassed the lobby and gave the media at large an unprecedented opportunity to challenge the Prime Minister. Even so, these occasional high-profile sessions are no substitute for what I have always argued should be a daily televised briefing, along the lines of those held at the White House, which would force the government to respond to the issues of the day. In addition, in view of the speed and dominance of the Internet, far greater use could be made of emails and websites in order to try to ensure that all sections of the news media receive the same information at the same time.

In my opinion too many stories are still being distributed on a selective basis, usually as exclusives to favoured journalists. But I accept that, whichever party is in power, no government can afford to take its eye off the news agenda. Intense competition between a multitude of news outlets is a fact of life, and no more so than at Westminster, where rivalry is in the blood, whether it be journalist's or politician's. So great is the potential advantage to be gained by either side from exploiting exclusive information, interviews and access that a change in political control is hardly likely to alter the terms of trade. And with little real prospect of there ever being a level playing field, political reporters have to get used to living by their wits and accept that nothing can be taken for granted in the cut-throat world of Westminster.

Reporting Parliament

Parliament itself has become another casualty of the desire of successive governments to create news and become a player in the media market place. No wonder ministerial announcements and follow-up debates attract so little coverage when decisions have so often been trailed comprehensively in advance and when the actual statement contains few, if any, real surprises. Westminster was one of the last legislatures to agree to the televising of its proceedings, and although actuality from the Commons and the Lords was widely used at first, the footage being broadcast has tailed off quite dramatically in recent years. Except for newsy exchanges at Prime Minister's Questions or controversial statements, relatively few speeches or debates are now reported in national news bulletins. However, the daily proceedings are transmitted live on BBC Parliament; extracts can be heard on Radio 4 on *Today in Parliament* or its sister programme *Yesterday in Parliament*; and actuality of local MPs does appear quite frequently in regional programmes.

Remote cameras in the two chambers and committee rooms provide the only pictures and remain under the absolute control of the parliamentary authorities. Access to the reporters' galleries is forbidden to television crews and press photographers. Strict conditions apply to the use of the continuous feed of proceedings: a clip of actuality must not be internally edited between sentences and the footage can be used only in news and current affairs coverage.

Despite what many broadcasters believe are self-defeating rules and regulations – which usually restrict the picture to merely a head-and-shoulders shot of whoever is speaking – the main television news bulletins do very occasionally defy Parliament, most notably if there have been dramatic interruptions. When a protester threw a purple flour bomb at the Prime Minister and campaigners for fox hunting invaded the chamber, the television transmission lasted for no more than a few seconds before the feed was cut. Nevertheless, showing the few images the Corporation had in slow motion prompted the Speaker to rebuke the BBC and other broadcasters for having broken the rules. Political correspondents and producers are told in no uncertain terms that they must not tamper with parliamentary actuality and it would need an editor or controller to authorise any defiance of parliamentary decorum.

Number 4, Millbank

Such has been broadcasters' frustration at the failure to provide more imaginative coverage and a greater variety of cut-away and reaction shots that the radio and television services have established what is essentially an alternative parliament at 4 Millbank, just across the road from the Palace of Westminster. Here, under one roof, are offices and studios for all the leading channels, and it has become the production centre for most political news reports and programmes. Much to the annoyance of traditional parliamentarians, broadcasters would rather conduct face-to-face interviews and prepare their own set-up material than use the often predictable and repetitive point-scoring exchanges which tend to dominate the televised output of the two Houses.

Political interviews need to do more than simply replicate the adversarial cut and thrust of the chamber. Different techniques are required, depending on the storyline and editorial objective. A presenter confronting a politician in a live or pre-recorded programme has to be something of a devil's advocate, ready to ask the challenging question and pounce on any evasion or obfuscation. But many of the interviews conducted in the Millbank studios, or a hundred yards away on College Green, have a different purpose. Their aim is to seek explanatory answers in order to provide reaction clips for news bulletins and feature items. In such situations the interviewer rarely needs to adopt an aggressive or confrontational tone as the intention is simply to obtain the clearest and most persuasive response.

The soundbite

Politicians often arrive primed with a soundbite which they are determined to deliver. Always make sure this answer is properly recorded because, although soundbites are derided, they have often been crafted with great care and are intended to encapsulate the message which a politician is seeking to convey. Such brief, self-contained statements usually emerge at key political moments. Every word was probably chosen for a reason and could have an unexpected meaning or impact, so what on first hearing sounded rather trite might sometimes assume considerable significance.

Occasionally, when correspondents are asked to conduct interviews, they might be unaware or unsure of the precise storyline. Do not be afraid to ask the most basic question: think of it rather like going fishing. Who knows which answers might end up in the net?

General elections and party conferences

General elections and party conferences tend to highlight the dividing line between the adversarial approach taken by a presenter and the firm but fair probing of a news correspondent. Politicians who take part in live or pre-recorded programmes expect to be given a hard time by their opponents and the presenter has to stimulate the liveliest possible discussion. By contrast, the reporter's task is not to be unnecessarily provocative but to get answers which will help to provide an impartial outline and assessment of what has happened. If an election campaign is under way, a correspondent is usually required, or at least expected, to give opposing parties a chance to comment on or describe their alternative policies.

Some broadcasters believe the concept of trying to ensure that each and every election report is balanced between the parties is too formulaic and restrictive and does not always tell the story in the clearest way. They would prefer their output to be judged over a longer period, for example on a weekly basis, which they suggest would demonstrate that their coverage was balanced while at the same time allowed news bulletins and programmes to examine a party's proposals in depth, without the item being cluttered with futile, knee-jerk criticism.

In line with long-standing conventions rather than the regulations which apply during election campaigns, broadcasters accept that their reporting of annual conferences should allow competing political parties an opportunity to put their case. Editors believe they are duty bound to apply a fair degree of balance and ensure conference coverage is not overshadowed by the opportunist criticism of an opponent. Therefore, when reporting at a conference on new proposals or policy differences, the customary practice is to seek out the opinions of opposing factions within the party concerned rather than offer a gratuitous platform to rival parties.

Conclusion

While there is always friction and tempers can sometimes get frayed, politicians and journalists do tend to coexist quite happily in a typical 'love–hate' relationship. We both need each other: political correspondents are forever on the lookout for news about policies and personalities; and the parties need the media to help them communicate with the public. My advice to would-be political reporters is always to try it out for a full twelve months so as to get a real taste of life at Westminster.

A political year has set patterns, rather like winter, spring and summer. The Queen's Speech in November sets out the parliamentary programme for the year ahead; the autumn pre-Budget report precedes the Budget, which is usually delivered early the following year; by spring, the main legislative programme is under way and the various bills are going back and forth between the two Houses; by late summer, the rush is on to complete as much business as possible before the long recess; and then at the autumn conferences the party leaders set out their stalls, heralding the start of another political year.

I joined the House of Commons press gallery in autumn 1968 on becoming a parliamentary reporter for *The Times*. We used to fill two pages a day with verbatim reports of the main debates. My shorthand rate was up to 120 words per minute but some of the more experienced reporters in the team could easily reach 150. Today only sketch writers bother to sit through question time and the opening speeches in debates. The death of the parliamentary page illustrates the way press reporting, like broadcasting, has evolved over the years.

In 1974, on moving to the BBC room at Westminster, I found tucked away in a cupboard a dusty heap of 78 r.p.m. records. They dated from the 1950s – the pre-tape era when BBC correspondents still had to cut a disc in order to record their reports. I have a loft packed with the detritus of my thirty years with the BBC: an old reel-to-reel tape recorder, blocks and china graph pencils for marking, cutting and splicing tape, boxes of used tapes, cassettes and mini-discs. What, you may ask, is the point of keeping reports and interviews of long-forgotten political dramas? I did give a clear warning: life at Westminster can become addictive.

Reporting celebrity

17

Claire Simmons

Celebrities want one thing from you. They want a fawning load of sycophantic drivel and you have to somehow satisfy that celebrity's lust for you telling them how great they are with a really good cutting-edge interview. And that's where you've got to be charming, but lethal.

(Piers Morgan on *Faking It*, Channel 4, 2004)

Introduction

When the final of the first series of *I'm a Celebrity . . . Get Me out of Here!* was aired on ITV (2002a), all the main news channels, including the BBC, carried a bulletin story of DJ Tony Blackburn's success. The news producers knew the audience ratings of ten million could not be ignored and it was a branding coup for ITV that BBC News carried the story. While the phenomenon of stardom is not new, stories about celebrities command growing airtime on broadcast news programmes and the divorce of an ex-Beatle or the drug habits of a supermodel can and do make lead bulletin items.

The exponential rise of celebrity news coverage cannot be reduced to the peripheral so-called 'soft news' agenda; it is now a fundamental part of daily news planning. Despite the numerous images of stars walking along the red carpet for a film premiere and clips from seemingly cosy interviews in the green room, broadcast journalists increasingly find themselves having to negotiate a number of constraints placed upon them by the minders and public relations entourages that accompany celebrities. This not only affects the way journalists gather and produce their news items but can present a distorted image to audiences that interviewing celebrities must be the easiest and most glamorous job in journalism.

This chapter will explore why reporting celebrity is harder than it looks and will examine some of the main concepts that underpin celebrity journalism issues. Further, it will outline practical tools journalists use to cut through the celebrity gloss to get to the facts, and offers advice from experienced broadcasters who work on the celebrity circuit.

The rise of celebrity culture and control

Since the turn of the twentieth century, economic growth has led to increased disposable income and time for leisure pursuits. The film industry, in particular, capitalised on both and in the process created the mediated star. From the 1930s, the Hollywood studios recognised the need to protect celebrities as assets, or products, because it was clear that whoever controlled news about Hollywood could also control public opinion, and this had a direct bearing on making money (Dyer, 1979; Gamson, 1992; Barbas, 2001).

The voracious appetites of fans to learn about the real lives of film stars spawned an industry in itself, and the major film studios set up publicity offices to send photographs, press releases and fabricated studio biographies of their most popular stars to all the media outlets. While the art of spin may be thought of as a relatively recent phenomenon, it was already alive and well in the 1930s, with journalists kept in line by being offered gifts, praise and studio-approved exclusives. Celebrities learned very quickly the worth of maintaining their image to enhance their career. Before long, they employed their own agents, and this has grown into today's thriving PR celebrity industry.

People find meaning through celebrity, according to Turner *et al.* (2000), who suggest the presence of celebrity in everyday life is often about identity and emotional commitment for audiences. It appears that finding one's place and being able to transform oneself with inspiration from role models means celebrities are given a special status almost by default. As Boon and Lomore (2001) state, vicarious relationships with celebrities are likely to play an increasingly important role in people's lives as social networks change and fragment. Even though fame is often fluid and short lived, the public puts celebrities on to pedestals, and this further fuels their mediated status. As BBC entertainment reporter Colin Paterson explains, 'People don't know who their neighbours are any more, yet they think they know celebrities, which is quite worrying. And I think this has a lot to do with why there's such a demand for celebrity stories.'[1]

In the last two decades in particular, with the rise of reality television, fame has become accessible to everyone, and symbiotic relationships between the media and reality television companies have played a major part in making 'fame' achievable. The stars of these shows are usually 'media-made' and are not chosen for any of the discernible accomplishments that used to be the foundation of celebrity.

A familiar phrase of media commentators is: 'If the media can make you, it can also break you.' Contemporary celebrity is arguably more likely to be a media construct, which raises questions about how much celebrity culture is created, or at least maintained, by the media. Without the voracious need for content, there would be no market for media management. Yet, the public relations industry is thriving and gives validation to theories that the level of symbiosis between celebrities and the media is greater than either might admit. For celebrity reporters this brings a different perspective to their role, because the implementation of control strategies has become an inherent part of the celebrity image-building and protection process.

PR agent Max Clifford says his job is similar to that of a middleman, negotiating deals between the media and the celebrity. 'Sometimes I want to build a client up, then at other times keep their activities quiet . . . When I take on a new client the media becomes both my ally and my enemy' (Clifford and Levin, 2005: 190). Colin Paterson says, 'There is a degree of symbiosis, but it depends on how big the celebrity is. While there might be a bit of give and take for an A-list star, I won't put up with some of the daft controls some of the agents try to impose. I'd rather not do the story and the upshot is that they don't get the publicity.' He adds that the problem of PR agents trying to impose controls is increasing: 'They try it on all the time and I've had to do a lot of complaining. The strange thing is that the celebrities themselves are usually okay if you ask them a direct personal question . . . but you have to get past the publicists first and that's part of my job.'[2]

That journalists have always had to negotiate controls and constraints is not in contention, but broadcast journalists need to be aware of the subtleties in celebrity reporting. The following section will examine how news values have changed and how this has affected the agendas of both news and celebrity. Understanding the power plays between the two is a vital part of celebrity reporting because it reveals why control strategies are used and how journalists can counteract them.

News values and celebrity

Many studies consider what criteria are needed for something to become newsworthy. Galtung and Ruge (1973) declare that events involving 'elite' people are more likely to become stories because they serve as objects of general identification. Gans (1979) also recognises that personalities make news, regardless of their actions. Harcup and O'Neill (2001) give 'celebrity' an explicit label when considering whether a story is worth covering. Certainly, running orders in broadcast news prove how news values have evolved to reflect cultural changes in society. News organisations only have to look at the huge circulation figures of *Heat*, *Now* and *Closer* magazines to work out that audiences are interested in celebrity. These sales, combined with the dominance of tabloid newspapers, lead to a debate about how much celebrity coverage is truly due to audience demand or whether the media has created that demand in the first place.

Broadcast news sits uncomfortably within the celebrity mix because it needs to reflect society to secure ratings, yet it must have a good story angle to maintain its editorial integrity. The result is the rise of the specialist correspondent, usually called the 'arts and media reporter' or similar, whose job is not just to cover celebrity stories but to find a sufficiently newsworthy angle to justify coverage.

It is no surprise that celebrity stories are now as likely to make top headlines as a political issue or crime story. The death of comedian Bob Hope was the lead story on BBC1's flagship *Six O'clock News* programme, higher in the running order than the prison release of Tony Martin, who had been convicted of killing a burglar (BBC, 2003). The eviction from the *Celebrity Big Brother* house of the Respect MP George Galloway was third in the running order on the BBC1 *Ten O'clock News* (BBC, 2006), higher than a story about the government's White Paper on education. Even BBC2's weightier news programme *Newsnight* could not ignore the ratings value and anchorman Jeremy Paxman did a short interview with Galloway in the house. Peter Bazalgette, from Endemol, which produces *Big Brother*, relished the request from the *Newsnight* team: 'Here was a chance to make Paxman, Mr Raised Eyebrow himself, he of the Withering Look, determined inhabitant of the Higher Ground, mix with the rest of us' (Bazalgette, 2006: 1).

Some celebrity stories have higher news value than others, particularly where a famous personality is involved in something that is illegal or immoral. Naomi Campbell's assault on a housekeeper and David Beckham's off-pitch antics are both examples of broadcast news stories that now exemplify celebrity reporting. But the higher the status of the celebrity, the more coverage there is likely to be; and, at times, the news 'peg' can be spurious. Woody Allen made the BBC1 *Ten O'clock News* because he was visiting London with his so-called muse, and star of his latest film, Scarlett Johansson (BBC, 2005). When manufactured pop bands Steps and Hear'Say split up, both were carried as news stories on ITV bulletins (ITV, 2001, 2002b). Things that happen to people in everyday life are reflected on the news agenda when celebrities are involved, as was the case when Kylie Minogue was diagnosed with breast cancer, and Sir Paul McCartney sued for divorce.

Many have tried to define the newsworthiness of celebrities using a classification process of A-list through to D-list. Media pundits like to term Hollywood actors such as Tom Cruise and Julia Roberts as A-list stars, while a reality television personality such as Jade Goody may be seen as more of a D-list celebrity. Although the media tends to become more disparaging to celebrities lower down on the list, even the D-list personalities have news value for newspapers and magazines. The difference in broadcast news is that most network programmes are interested only in the big stars, and this correlates directly with their ratings pull and the fact that there is more likely to be a news angle attached to them. It is significant that the power of choice given to audiences via the rise of technology and the plethora of news outlets has a direct bearing on ratings. The raised news value of celebrity is clear and as a result has an impact on both the news and the celebrity agendas. The consequence is an uncomfortable interdependency between the two agendas, and broadcast journalists need to know how to address this if they want to get the best stories.

News agenda versus celebrity agenda

The days of the news presenter sitting austerely behind a desk with a serious demeanour have been replaced with audience-friendly stand-up shots, glossy graphics and a running order that usually offers a glamorous story that appeals to a mass audience. If 'news' can be defined as what people will be talking about down at the pub, then the celebrity news story often fits the bill.

There is a clear agenda for celebrities who know the economic worth of their image. Their publicists like positive stories in the news because they can be perceived as carrying more credibility than simple advertising (Turner, 2004). It is also a good way to maximise publicity, as Nina Nannar, ITV's media and arts correspondent, explains: 'Most celebrities are pretty desperate to get TV news coverage. If they appear in the *Daily Mail* they might get two million readers, but if they get on to our six-thirty news programme, they get six million viewers in one hit. That's pretty compelling for them.'[3]

Celebrity agents will use a number of techniques to get their clients on to the news, the most common being the setting up of 'pseudo-events', as defined by Boorstin (1961). These are planned rather than spontaneous events. Boorstin argues that the authentic news record of what happens increasingly results from the information given out in advance via the pseudo-event. News can be misused and these 'events' are manufactured stories. Politicians have certainly done this for decades. The interesting point is that the psuedo-event is now a major tool to promote the images of celebrities. Whether it is a Spice Girl on tour, Daniel Craig on a red carpet or a platform for George Clooney to air his political views, the celebrity pseudo-event is a key publicity vehicle.

However, there is an intangible consequence of the celebrity agenda and its impact on news agendas concerning the relationships journalists need to forge to succeed in reporting celebrity. In gathering information and producing news stories, there are not just operational influences like deadlines, short durations and technology.

The journalist must also contend with the subtle controls and constraints of the celebrity PR agent. In the next section, these controls will be examined, and practical guidance shall be offered on how to navigate through celebrity spin to get to the real story.

Celebrity control strategies

There are many studies into the role of 'sources' in news, particularly with respect to political reporting. The power of the spin-doctor became a lament of the Blair years and created a media backlash. With celebrity reporting, the 'source' is usually the PR agent, and so far there has been little backlash because celebrity news is about cultural and social messages, rather than issues of public concern. However, problems can occur when journalists used to working in other specialisms or in general news come up against the controlled pseudo-event of a celebrity. At the launch of a new film, book or television programme, for instance, conditions are placed upon the journalist who is sent to report on the event. Objectivity cannot always be achieved, despite a journalist's best efforts. Media management is an acknowledged part of negotiations in the news-making process.

Examples of celebrity controls include:

- **Pre-set questions:** journalists are asked to supply, in advance, a written list of the questions they will ask, and any negative questions are often removed by the agent. The interview can be terminated abruptly if the journalist strays from the approved list.
- **Time-constrained interviews:** one-to-one interviews (known as 'the junket') are often only five minutes in duration, giving the journalist little time to build a rapport and sneak in the 'killer' question (one that reveals something that could create an exclusive story).
- **Press conferences:** often by invitation only and usually with scores of journalists in attendance, which reduces the chance to ask even one question.
- **Exclusives:** while getting an exclusive story is the main aim of broadcast journalists, often these are offered as either a carrot or a stick as a way to play off news organisations against each other and to keep journalists in line by PR agents.
- **Approval before broadcast:** agents will sometimes ask to see or listen to the finished item before it goes on air. This effectively takes editorial control away from the journalist because the agent will want to remove any negative comments before approving the story.
- **Contracts:** agents of A-list stars may ask journalists to sign a pre-interview contract 'promising' not to broadcast any negative coverage. If the 'contract' is breached, the journalist can be sued.
- **Blacklisting:** PR agents can and do threaten to 'blacklist' journalists who are working on a negative story of a celebrity. As agents often have several high-profile clients, being blacklisted means journalists are denied access to many events and interviews, which severely reduces their worth to an editor.
- **Legal threats:** PR agents will try to scare off inexperienced journalists by threatening to sue them for libel.

Not all of these sanctions are imposed all of the time, because the interdependency between the journalist and celebrity is highly contingent. It depends on the popularity of the celebrity at the time and the desire of an agent to garner maximum news coverage. Where the power of the news outlet is greater than the celebrity pseudo-event, the agent may offer an exclusive interview to secure greater exposure to audiences.

If, however, the celebrity tale is highly newsworthy, such as the story of an affair between David Beckham and Rebecca Loos, the news organisations will be in a weaker position and PR agents know they can impose a number of controls. In the case of the Beckham story, Loos employed the publicist Max Clifford. He says he was able to negotiate a £125,000 deal with Sky News (Clifford and Levin, 2005). Sky anchorwoman Kay Burley and a news team were dispatched to Spain to interview Loos, and this made an exclusive news broadcast (Sky News, 2004).

Getting round controls

There are a number of techniques that journalists can use to negate or mitigate controls that agents try to impose. These broadly fall into the following categories:

- **Power of the media news organisation:** the higher the news ratings, the more likely it is the journalist will have the power to refuse celebrity publicity controls. In the news pecking order, a national news outlet will usually have greater power than a local or regional news station.
- **Threaten to drop the story:** because news ratings are so high, celebrities and agents want the publicity and will back down and remove conditions rather than risk not getting any coverage.
- **Charm and diplomacy:** building a good relationship with celebrities and their agents gives journalists better access when a good story breaks. The power of a good contacts book should not be underestimated.
- **Unofficial sources:** when a big story breaks and the celebrity or PR agent is uncooperative, journalists will publish the story anyway, using library footage and interviewing friends, family or acquaintances instead.
- **Knowledge of the law:** PR agents have been known to try scare tactics by threatening legal action to stop a story being broadcast. Knowing the law means that empty threats can be ignored.

Nina Nannar says it is important to counteract any controls: 'Our job is to find a news story and not simply to give celebrities airtime to say whatever they want.' She recalls an incident with an A-list Hollywood star who was so 'belligerent and monosyllabic' that she knew she would not gain anything in the interview. 'I called the news desk and told them the celebrity was being uncooperative and they said, "Fine, drop the story."' It meant that the film was not promoted on the news that night, and for the PR agent, and the film studio, this was counter-productive. Nannar says the power of the news outlet, particularly with a mainstream news programme, is usually enough to stop PR agents trying to impose constraints.[4] Colin Paterson agrees and says that when he has come up against problems he has worked this into his radio two-ways: 'If I've been given the run-around, I tell the listeners what happened. They really like to hear this kind of stuff and it annoys the celebrities because it shows them up.'[5]

Reporting celebrity tips

- **Do your homework:** make sure you know as much about the celebrity as possible before you do an interview. There is little point asking them something that is already well known. Be aware that library footage or cuttings from newspapers and magazines may be incorrect or that facts might have changed.
- **Film premieres and junkets:** premieres are highly constrained events and PR agents usually herd journalists behind a barrier. You will need to jostle with other journalists to get a good position behind the 'rope' and need to shout loudly to get the attention of a celebrity. With junkets (an exhausting round of five-minute one-to-ones for celebrities), ask the obvious questions but try to get in a question that will bring forth something revealing. Bear in mind that the PR agent may be sitting to one side to 'baby-sit' the interviewee.
- **Ask a good question:** make sure your questions are open so that you can elicit as good a response as possible and leave no room for monosyllabic answers. You may get a chance to ask only one question, so ensure you get a response which will make at least a bulletin clip (for radio) or can be wrapped with other images (for television).
- **Listen:** do not interrupt or feel the need to fill any silences. Your job is to get a good recording that you can use in a variety of ways (bulletin clips, package material, straight pre-recorded interview). If you remain quiet when the celebrity gives short answers, they may fill the silence for you and reveal something newsworthy inadvertently. It is best not to work from a list of questions you have written down. Otherwise you may be tempted to stick to the list and will not be listening for opportunities to ask supplementary questions that often bring new information.
- **Be charming:** you may not have much time to chat beforehand or build a rapport, so it is crucial to smile when appropriate, and this also acts as a prompt for the interviewee to keep talking.
- **Keep your cool:** if the celebrity is being uncooperative, do not give up or lose your temper. Maintain your line of questioning, and if the celebrity continually refuses to answer, this can sometimes be turned into a story in itself.

Awards ceremonies

There are hundreds of awards ceremonies involving celebrities, so much so that they have become an industry in themselves. The Oscars, the Baftas and the Brit awards are usually covered by broadcast news networks. With each, the opportunities to interview celebrities are slim during the event, but there is usually a celebration afterwards where many stars gather and can be interviewed. For major events like the Oscars, journalists need to apply for accreditation several weeks in advance and will be issued with special passes. Nina Nannar says:

> The biggest après-award party is the one held after the Oscars by the American magazine *Vanity Fair*. Journalists are restricted to a particular area but you can

interview the major stars as they arrive. You need to shout loud to grab their attention and you have to be really assertive because all the American showbiz networks are there and they're ruthless in pushing you to one side.[6]

Technology plays a significant part and the journalist will do live two-ways via satellite from the scene with the stars in the background walking into the ceremony. The journalist will also send over pre-recorded material via the Internet or satellite for use in later bullets. 'Usually, I'll send material over with holes in it and the news desk will fill those with footage already gathered,' says Nannar, 'like clips from the film that's won the award. But it's always good to get some of the atmosphere across in the piece-to-camera. It shows you're there and viewers like that.'[7]

While the awards ceremonies may seem light-hearted in terms of news story content, Nannar stresses that the networks cover them because they increase ratings:

> The ceremonies, particularly the Oscars and the Brits, are a really big talking point for audiences. People really want to know who won what. There's an increasing interest in the cinema and people want to know which films won. It's akin to wanting to know who won the FA Cup Final. If you put a clip of Clint Eastwood in your headlines it's a ratings draw and people will watch the rest of the news programme.[8]

Conclusion

This chapter has explored some of the concepts that underpin celebrity culture and the role of news. It has examined the controls that celebrities and agents try to impose on journalists to secure positive coverage and has suggested ways in which the celebrity news reporter can get around them.

It is clear that reporting celebrity stories is not a job for the faint-hearted. It may seem to be a glamorous role that gives unprecedented access to the stars, but it requires a great deal of tenacity, charm and strength of character. There will always be symbiotic undertones between celebrities who want publicity and journalists who want stories. Understanding how to negotiate the power plays to secure a great news story is the key to successful and credible celebrity journalism.

Notes

1 Interview with the autthor, 28 December 2007.
2 *Ibid.*
3 Interview with the author, 25 October 2007.
4 *Ibid.*
5 Interview with the author, 28 December 2007.
6 Interview with the author, 25 October 2007.
7 *Ibid.*
8 *Ibid.*

References

Barbas, S. (2001) *Movie Crazy: Fans, Stars and the Cult of Celebrity*, New York: Palgrave

Bazalgette, P. (2006) Brotherly Love, *Media Guardian*, 30 January, p. 1

BBC (2003) *Six O'clock News*, 28 May

BBC1 News, (2005) *Ten O'clock News*, 19 December

BBC1 News, (2006) *Ten O'clock News*, 25 January

Boon, S. and Lomore, C. (2001) Admirer–Celebrity Relationships among Young Adults: Explaining Perceptions of Celebrity Influence on Identity, *Human Communication Research*, 27(3): 432–65

Boorstin, D. (1961) *The Image: A Guide to Pseudo-Events in America*, New York: Harper and Row

Clifford, M. and Levin, A. (2005) *Max Clifford: Read All about It*, London: Virgin

Dyer, R. (1979) *Stars*, London: British Film Institute

Galtung, J. and Ruge, M. (1973) Structuring and Selecting News, in S. Cohen and J. Young (eds), *The Manufacture of News: Social Problems, Deviance and the Mass Media*, London: Sage

Gamson, J. (1992) The Assembly-Line of Greatness: Celebrity in Twentieth Century America, *Critical Studies in Mass Communication*, 9(1): 1–24

Gans, H. (1979) Deciding What's News [excerpt], in H. Tumber (ed.) (1999), *News: A Reader*, Oxford: Oxford University Press

Harcup, T. and O'Neill, D. (2001) What is News? Galtung and Ruge Revisited, *Journalism Studies*, 2(2): 261–80

ITV (2001) *Lunchtime News*, 26 December

ITV (2002a) *I'm a Celebrity . . . Get Me out of Here!*, 8 September

ITV (2002b) *Lunchtime News*, 1 October

Sky News (2004) *News at Ten*, 15 April

Turner, G. (2004) *Understanding Celebrity*, London: Sage

Turner, G., Bonner, F. and Marshall, D. (2000) *Fame Games: The Production of Celebrity in Australia*, London: Cambridge University Press

Part III

Context

Introduction

Jane Chapman and Marie Kinsey

This section moves away from the 'how to' of daily broadcast news to look at broader themes of underpinning knowledge and developing a career. We begin with the field of independent TV production, where six in ten people are freelance and work on a variety of factual formats. This is the uncertain and challenging world that Fiona Chesterton (Chapter 18) describes when she explains some of the realities of the market place outside the newsroom. There *is* a world open to broadcast journalists outside of the news, and survival will be made easier by the many practical tips in this chapter, woven together with a message that correctly identifies journalistic skills as transferable skills.

When it comes to documentary, choices are numerous, for as Jane Chapman points out (Chapter 19) the need to get the production elements right is more focused with a long-form piece. An amateurish approach, such as wobbly camera movements, may seem authentic and endearing at first, but media-savvy audiences soon lose patience when clear sound and visuals are absent.

The importance of your approach to methods of representation is also greater in documentary, although representational issues have a wider and more general application, as Patricia Holland points out in Chapter 20. The first few years of this century have witnessed innovative new styles and formats being developed, but also uncertainty and 'a great deal of anxiety'.

Whether you are grappling with the insecurities of a short-term contract or making a documentary on a tiny budget, knowledge of the law and the ethical environment that underpins journalism are crucial. In Chapter 21 Tim Crook examines the fine line that journalists must walk between obeying the law and preserving free speech. Within television journalism these have particular resonance in the areas of privacy and visual libel – the necessity for pictures creates its own traps for the unwary. Tony Harcup (Chapter 22) poses a key question with the title of his chapter on ethics: 'Fair enough?' He explains how broadcast journalism has developed under an ethical and regulatory framework very different to that of the press and has evolved a different understanding of 'the public interest'. This has produced a rather distinctive culture, even though print and broadcast journalism share a similar philosophy in telling stories and holding the government to account. He also stresses the importance of scrutiny – both internal and external.

This section is brought to a close with an examination of what it takes to be a broadcast journalist: the personal characteristics necessary to get editors to take you seriously and where to go to develop your knowledge and skills. A range of interviews with experienced journalists – and senior programme-makers – graphically illustrates how journalism skills are valued in many other parts of broadcasting, from drama, through entertainment and into management. If you have the desire, the talent and a little bit of luck, that first job in journalism could eventually take you all the way to the top.

Outside the newsroom

18

Selling stories and ideas

Fiona Chesterton

Introduction

One of the key skills you need to make your way in TV and radio production is the ability to tell – and especially *sell* – stories. This chapter provides an introduction to how the broadcast journalist can utilise his or her skills in the broader production market place, focusing on how journalists with good ideas and stories navigate the programme commissioning process.

Beyond the bulletin: the programme landscape

For all its reputation as being a tough environment, in some ways a newsroom has comforts and certainties hardly known within the wider TV and radio worlds. For a start, the majority of jobs in news are on long-term contract, while freelance and short-term contract working is the norm for production. According to the latest workforce census conducted by Skillset nearly six in ten people working in independent TV production were categorised as freelance.[1] To make a living and develop a career there demands resourcefulness, determination and resilience – and most importantly passion. Most people working in the industry become neither rich nor famous and do the job more for love than money.

There are other ways in which the news environment – despite its pressures – offers more certainties than other production areas. There are routines and conventions within even the apparently chaotic daily schedule. For one thing, the output is commissioned and scheduled on a long-term and defined basis; the format is usually fixed and well understood, even if the stories change from hour to hour. And although creativity and ideas-generation can be required, especially on a quiet news day, often the agenda is driven by events. This is not the case with most factual programme production, which operates within a much more complex, fragile and competitive economy.

In the past decade certainly, and arguably ever since the creation of Channel 4 in 1982, which also marked the lift-off point for the independent production sector, programme supply has outstripped the demand from broadcasters. The channel was the first to outsource nearly all of its content creation as a so-called 'publisher-broadcaster', and since then nearly all new broadcasters and distributors of programmes have copied that model. Meanwhile, the traditional 'producer-broadcasters' (ITV and BBC) have reduced their in-house production staff and opened up more of their slots to independent production. In radio, the BBC has until recently been the main producer as well as commissioner of longer-form audio content (built features), but the arrival of Channel 4 Radio should see more out-of-house radio production.

Overall, in recent years there has been huge growth in the independent production sector, and in the number of hours of commissioned factual programming, but increased competition and more choice for the consumer – the viewer and listener – are also posing challenges, especially for more serious factual programming. Given choice, the consumer will often opt for less demanding content – entertainment is the key requirement for the audience most of the time. And the tastes of the audience are the key influence on the commissioners, who are the prime buyers in the broadcast world.

Television, in particular, has an insatiable appetite for the new. This creates uncertainty as well as opportunity. Even the most successful programmes can be axed; only one series at a time is commissioned; there are often delays and indecision; budgets get tighter and tighter. All this can add up to an uncertain life for the average producer, going from one short-term contract to the next. That said – the balance of power between producer and broadcaster is changing in the digital world. In the past few years, the so-called terms of trade with broadcasters have altered in the producers' favour, allowing them to exploit their intellectual property and secondary rights. Now some larger production companies have real value, attracting City investment and making a few company founder-owners (who tend to be their creative heads as well) very rich. In the future, we may see some producers, especially the so-called super-indies, going straight to market, utilising alternative forms of distribution to the traditional middleman, the broadcaster. If that happens, it may change the terms on which the most prized production talent is employed by them. On the other side of the coin, hundreds of smaller companies – especially those who have specialised in documentary and other serious factual programming – have been struggling.

The prospects are potentially still exciting for a new entrant to the industry, but the risks and uncertainties are considerable, too. In this most challenging of market places, then, how should the broadcast journalist graduate with bright ideas and ambition launch their career?

Selling stories: from news to longer-form content

From your training and work experience you will have a grounding in producing news reports and items – so you will be familiar with one-, two- and three-minute productions. But it is a considerable leap to develop ideas that can work as half-hour and hour-long productions. Content and production values need to be of a different order. You will also be familiar with responding to the topical imperative – the story that needs to be told today. But now you have to consider stories that may not be aired for several months, or even a year or two. Will they stand the test of time? If you have done your work experience in local radio, you will have gained some understanding of a pretty small market. But what if your ideas have to work for a national or even a global audience? The bar is raised in every direction.

While you are working in it, news seems like the most important and central of all broadcasting genres. However, in the broader landscape it is actually quite a small, specialised part. Just consider the huge spectrum of factual programmes alone (see Figure 18.1). For several years, *Big Brother* reigned supreme in the audience ratings charts as the most popular factual programme. Yes, reality TV sits within this broad rainbow that also encompasses:

- Current affairs
- Documentary
- Features

- Lifestyle
- Specialist factual (including history, religion, science, natural history, business)
- Factual entertainment
- Talk shows.

Beyond 'factual' proper, there can be a factual and research base to some types of drama and comedy as well.

There are no fixed boundaries between these sub-genres of programming. Often the cleverest and most creative ideas come from cross-fertilisation. Telling a story – the core journalistic skill – is at the heart of all of them.

You may be passionate about just one of these areas. You may have a genuine specialist skill or interest that you want to develop. But if you want to maximise your chances of selling your ideas, then flexibility is the key.

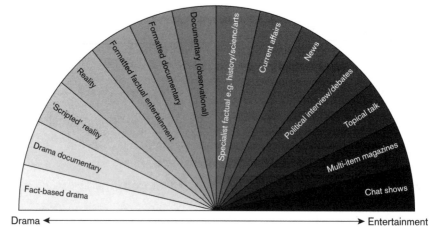

Figure 18.1 The spectrum of factual television

From idea to commission

Ideas for TV and radio programmes sometimes come fully formed from the imagination of a single creative individual, but much more often they are the product of a team – of dialogue between the producer and the commissioner, or the executive producer and his development team.

Independent production companies and producer-broadcasters all put a great premium on good ideas people, but it is a pretty rare event these days for an individual starting out with a good idea for a programme to get a commission single-handedly or even to get a meeting with a commissioning editor, their deputy or even their deputy's assistant. While anyone can access broadcasters' commissioning websites – and in theory there's a level playing field in which the Big New Idea can come shining through – it does not work like that in practice. Indeed, the growth of password-protected e-commissioning may well make the score even clearer: you have to be a bona fide producer before you can get to first base.

In network radio, the barriers to the newcomer are also high. A leading BBC radio commissioner told me that risk-taking on unproven talent is virtually out of the question. The budgets are small and unforgiving and therefore are placed in the hands of experienced producers who can be trusted to deliver. At the time of writing, it was too early to say to what extent the new Channel 4 Radio will be able to support new talent.

If you think you have great ideas, then you are much better advised to find a production company prepared to promote them for you. If it really is a winner, then you should be able to negotiate a place on the production team, and even a small financial share of the production (the production fee). Alternatively, if you have the right sort of idea-generating and creative skills – especially if they are aligned with other production competencies – then you might find yourself a place as a runner or researcher.

One-off ideas have little currency – it's returnable formats that are wanted, and, in the digital world, programmes that can become 'brands', exploitable across channels, platforms and territories. Think big, not small: think global, not local; think multimedia, not just TV. At the same time, the idea must be workable – have ambitious ideas, by all means, but if they cannot be delivered on screen or on air at a price the commissioner is prepared to pay, then they will not be commissioned. Procuring co-production money to supplement a budget is a hard and often unrewarding slog.

The first test for your idea is to be able to define the market for it. Ask yourself: 'Who is this programme for? Who might watch or listen to it? Why will they watch or listen to this in preference to the hundreds of other ways they could spend an hour or half-hour?' These are the questions commissioners ask too, and they attempt to answer them by consulting a mass of audience data, from overnight ratings to sophisticated market analysis. They also have a strong sense of what 'fits' their channel identity/brand, as well as their target audience.

Commissioners will try to express this through their commissioning briefs. These are sometimes rather vague – using current, ill-defined buzzwords such as 'channel-defining', 'edgy' and 'contemporary'. Sometimes, though, they can be very specific – related to a specific time slot and a specific type of programme and highly defined target audience: for example, six thirty-minute programmes in a factual entertainment format to run at 8 p.m. in a midweek slot aimed at twenty-five to forty-four-year-old ABC1 women.

It is vital to understand that the key audiences for commercial TV and radio are young people, the under-thirty-fives or at a stretch the under-forty-fives. The reason for this is twofold. Most broadcasters are still dependent on advertising income, and advertisers will pay more to reach younger people, who are perceived as being more receptive to 'brand' messages. In addition, the newer 'platforms', such as mobile phones, Internet TV and games consoles, are used disproportionately by younger people – so there are more opportunities to maximise revenue from an idea or concept that appeals to them.

Within the UK, this pure commercial logic is certainly in the ascendant, but the public service remits and obligations of the terrestrial broadcasters, notably the BBC and Channel 4, still provide a powerful counterpoint. This provides what you might call the democratic imperative – the idea that there are some stories that the audience has a right to know, stories that raise issues of public concern and debate. This is the heartland of news and current affairs, but given the highly competitive nature of the schedule in which even the most public-service-oriented programmes have to play, there is still a need to demonstrate that the programme will make an impact and can appeal to as large a number of the potential audience as possible.

For mainstream commissioning, your idea – even if it has identified a potential channel or network, slot and audience – still has to have a USP – a unique selling point – to find a buyer. Your USP may consist of:

- **Access:** can you secure an 'in' (the facility to film or record) to people or institutions that others cannot? Can you secure access by your specialist knowledge, by cultivating contacts patiently over time or by getting there first?
- **Talent:** commissioners may be swayed by the on-screen or on-air talent attached to a programme idea. Some of the larger production companies have such star performers on their books; others have an eye to matching the right 'name' to the channel and the idea. The talent must be deliverable, however, not just a wish list. A surprising choice of talent with subject matter can also be attractive, rather than just pinning the current hot name on the proposal. New talent is infinitely more risky, but spotting it – perhaps someone who has made their name in another medium – is a real skill. It's a harder sell, but it can win rewards for both producer and broadcaster.
- **Real people:** people, and not just famous people, are at the heart of most programmes, especially if they have extraordinary stories to tell. Are you offering compelling characters?
- **Treatment:** how do you propose combining the story/concept with the people and access in a production style that is distinctive and fresh? Sometimes new technology can help you here; sometimes it may be working with a particularly inventive director; sometimes it is about combining genres and styles in unusual and innovative ways.
- **Title:** just as a compelling headline can sell newspapers, so a winning title can occasionally sell a programme idea. In the multi-channel broadcasting context, where viewers surf electronic programme guides for something worth watching, a punchy title can stand out. At the very least it might attract a commissioner's eye.
- **Format:** this is televisual gold. The format is a replicable formula that allows the original idea/story/concept to be reduced to elements that can be reproduced repeatedly in different contexts and different countries, attracting viewer loyalty through the 'known' quality of what the audience experience will be. Formats often follow a narrative convention ('arc'): beginning, middle and end.
- **Innovation:** this phrase is often used but can be hard to define. Innovation can be about subject-matter – something new out there on the streets that TV or radio should be capturing. Sometimes it can be about clever reinvention of old ideas. Sometimes it's about treatment and format.

So do we have a sellable idea yet? Well, no. The idea has to be deliverable at a price and to a quality that the commissioner sets. That means you have to have a clear and convincing idea of how the idea is to be delivered, and that you possess the production skills either on your own (if it is radio) or in your team or company to deliver it.

This is another reason why companies and individuals with a proven track record have a clear advantage over newcomers. In a highly competitive environment, commissioners are often risk-averse. They want to be confident of quality and know that programmes will be delivered on time as well as on budget.

The pitch

The process of getting a commissionable idea off the drawing board varies from TV to radio, broadcaster/commissioner and scale of production. However, it is rare indeed for the bright young researcher to be the one to pitch his or her killer idea. The key pitchers are the executive producers and creative directors who have an established relationship with the commissioner. If you are lucky, you might get taken along to help sell your idea, but the pitching skill you may have developed is much more likely to be useful to sell the idea to the exec in the first place!

Sometimes the starting pitch is just an emailed couple of paragraphs to sound out the commissioner. This often precedes the formal business of submitting a proposal, which is increasingly through e-commissioning (a Web-based application). If you are asked to prepare a written proposal for your exec, remember your journalistic training! Write with punch – do not waffle. Lure the reader in with a strong headline and opening sentence. If the programme will be in narrative form, set out the story. If it is a format, explain it clearly and succinctly. Above all, keep it simple. You are not writing a dissertation and if the idea is too complicated to explain in a few sentences, then the commissioner will judge the viewer or listener will not get it either and will switch over.

It may be useful to send a 'taster tape' of your suggested presenter or key contributor, especially if he or she is a new talent as well.

In TV (but not necessarily in radio) at some stage there will be a meeting with the commissioner. This will nearly always be a somewhat unpredictable dialogue where the commissioner will present very firm ideas of his/her own! Occasionally – for the most ambitious proposals – the producer will have 'produced the pitch' with as much attention and flair as putting on a show, but this is still the exception rather than the norm.

Development

In TV, but not in radio, there may then be a 'development' stage, sometimes funded by the broadcaster. Areas for development will be specified by the broadcaster. This may consist of providing further 'taster tapes' of the putative presenter or contributors. It may allow research of the storyline, access and contributors. It could be for developing a particular treatment of the idea. Occasionally, a full-blown pilot programme might be ordered.

It is normal for there to be long periods between the initial pitch and development to the green light. That could mean frustration for the initial researcher – who may have to be 'let go' by the production company after the early work and then find that they are not available to be re-hired by the production when it finally gets commissioned.

Outside the newsroom: selling your skills

The commission is only the start – production and realisation of the programme concept on time, on budget and to the commissioner's satisfaction are what really matter. This is not the place to go into the ups and downs of the production process, but I will conclude by giving some pointers to where your journalistic skills can be deployed effectively in this crucial stage.

- **Working fast and under pressure:** most productions operate under considerable time pressures. Budget restrictions translate frequently into allowing ever less time for the pre-production and production periods. The ability to make judgements under stress is paramount.
- **Working to deadlines:** allied to working fast, this is a key competence. Time really is money, and missing your deadline may have a knock-on effect for the rest of the team and production.
- **Fact-finding and checking:** understanding where to find information – and even more important, in the Google age, knowing how to check information for accuracy and corroboration. It is important to use a wide range of sources – not just one site on the Internet. For example, do not be shy about telephoning experts about topics covered in the programme.
- **Making information fit for programme purpose**: preparing and presenting research briefs that offer key facts and information for others in the team, like the director. You may not be able to attend shoots yourself.
- **Finding programme contributors:** identifying individuals who may make telling contributions. This may involve initiative, resourcefulness, persuasiveness and even cunning. You may be able to assess the suitability of people from telephone conversations (again, not just from the Internet!), but old-fashioned leg-work may also be required.
- **Knowledge of the law:** your knowledge of the basics of law, such as libel, contempt and breach of confidence, is absolutely essential for dealing with people and programmes. Your understanding will give you a vital awareness of the potential 'elephant traps' of programme-making, and avoid expensive trouble later down the line.
- **Technical allied to editorial skills:** your course should have equipped you with camera, sound-recording and editing skills which will be useful in contexts other than news. To be a self-operator is often essential in both radio and television production. But note that long-form production skills require you to understand new disciplines and higher-level skills, such as creating programme sequences, using sound.
- **Writing for broadcast:** writing well is in truth a rare – and declining – skill in productions. Some would even call it an art-form! It is not enough to create visual- or sound-pictures: the commentary can enhance a programme significantly.

You may well be able to add to this list – if you have manned a local radio newsroom on your own, with remote editorial supervision, you have invaluable self-resilience and resourcefulness. Or you may be a great team player. Personal attributes, so-called 'soft skills', and the hard skills of hard news can be combined to make you invaluable. They could help you go far, even to the very top.

Conclusion

Many broadcast journalism graduates will not end up working in TV or radio newsrooms, but the world outside of news offers many opportunities to apply skills and techniques learned as journalists. A lot of top names in the broadcast industry began their careers in journalism – and this chapter gives some pointers as to why that is so. So are you ready for life outside the newsroom? It is certainly challenging, and you may not always endear yourself to your bank manager, but it's still a road worth travelling.

Note

1 Skillset, the Sector Skills Council for the Audio Visual Industries, conducted its Employment Census in 2006. This indicated that overall 27 per cent of the workforce was freelance – on contracts of 364 days or less – with 57 per cent of independent TV production workers freelance. Only 17 per cent of those working for broadcasters in journalism or sport were freelance.

References

http://www.bbc.co.uk/commissioning
http://www.channel4.com/corporate/4producers
http://www.five.tv/aboutfive/producersnotes
http://www.itv.com/about
http://www.skillset.org/tv
http://www.virginmediatv.co.uk/commissioning

Radio and television documentary

Jane Chapman

19

Introduction

What makes a good documentary and how do you go about making one? My emphasis is on production considerations that are specific to the documentary genre. I will discuss radio and TV/video generically, together and individually, by specifying the medium as I refer to it.

Definitions

The difference between news and documentary is not merely one of length. Although basic production techniques are shared, there is nevertheless a profound qualitative difference. A documentary should not simply repeat news reports; it has to provide a more in-depth understanding, or present an inside view of something that an audience would not obtain from the news. A documentary will reveal the maker's personal style and approach. A single theme can be explored with more time for explanation and interpretation, more time to present detailed actuality, more possibilities of marrying words with pictures in the case of film or, if the subject is conceptual, of making good use of 'talking head' interviews. All of these factors make the documentary medium suitable for the presentation of issues rather than just events.

Documentaries always involve real people, not invented characters, in a personalisation of a factual theme with an intimate, domestic feel. Audiences take pleasure in recognising and knowing; although new insights will confer new knowledge, consumers of documentary are as likely to consider this learning process as entertainment as they are education. A good documentary-maker will know how to exploit the pact between education and entertainment. A documentary will aim to extend the experience of the audience and to enlighten them by immersing them in another world or theme: the word itself comes from the Latin *docere*, 'to teach'.

When the father of British documentary, John Grierson, came up with a now classic definition of the genre as 'the creative treatment of actuality', he devised a somewhat problematic wording. 'Creative' and 'actuality' are not easy bedfellows. Furthermore, capturing actuality should not be confused with capturing reality. Documentary is more than this. 'Reality' will only be reassembled fragments of what has been filtered by the eyes and ears of the crew and limited by the available technology.

Many documentaries are presented as expository problem-solving, but the creative influence means that the reality presented is mediated and therefore will present a tendentious treatment of events. Why tendentious? Even a 'fly on the wall' documentary will need to be edited, so it will be selective and therefore open to criticism about subjective choices. The conventions of editing tend to dictate a structure that revolves around narrative suspense – itself a fictional technique, although documentary is non-fiction. When a documentary contains a lot of actuality, it will almost always be held together by a narrative structure, and it will be highly mediated. So, for instance, a wildlife film may be slowed down or speeded up to emphasise the movements of certain creatures, and music will be used to add tension or pathos; in short, production techniques are flaunted in the interests of the viewer seeing, hearing and knowing.

Ideas and research

Not every 'lead' will bear fruit. Some ideas are untenable, for a range of different reasons. Funding may not be possible, market research may reveal that somebody else made exactly the programme that you intended only recently, or that access for recording the 'inside story' is not possible. Thus, most research tends to involve a change of direction or some lateral thinking, when the documentary producer ends up turning to a related field.

The more one knows about a subject, the quicker it can be to gauge the best way forward. The maker needs to conquer the relevant information, whatever the style of the documentary. Knowledge increases choice. It is also worth bearing in mind that even with documentaries which appear to rely on the importance of the moment, there are decisions to be made in pre-production. With a television *cinéma-vérité* ('fly on the wall') approach, the pre-production process of selecting participants and seeking their active cooperation for activities to be filmed is of paramount importance, and the pre-production period will also be used to negotiate specific ground rules for filming with the participants. As documentary-maker Nancy Platt says: 'you can't just walk in. You have to fix things first. You have to obtain the permissions and make the arrangements' (Chapman, 2007: 67).

Finding interviewees and locations

Sometimes the choice of social actors for a documentary is easy – as in the case of a celebrity profile. On other occasions the search for participants is more challenging. If a story is to sustain the interest of viewers and listeners for a whole half-hour, or even an hour, the selection of individuals or family becomes all the more challenging and therefore a critical element in the success of the production. Obviously, potential interviewees need to be able to talk in an engaging way, and, in the case of film, to look presentable. Advance decision-making on content will be easier if you have an idea of what social actors are likely to say during recording.

Equally, social actors need to hear from the makers: what the researcher says to potential interviewees about the project in order to gain their cooperation can have repercussions. If the maker is not honest about intentions, there could well be complaints or legal action later, when the member of the public realises that the completed programme is nothing like what was described in order to obtain their permission to record/film. Content, angle, tone and style are all important: parody or humour at the expense of interviewees can be hurtful to the individual concerned, or libellous if they are a public figure. Documentary makers need to be able to deliver whatever has been promised as a condition of recording. Sometimes the interviewee will need to be convinced that the film-makers are going to be fair and non-judgemental to their case. In documentary you have to stay with the relationship for longer than news – maybe weeks or months – and, as with all relationships, trust is the essence.

Location research

Travelling long distances between places not only takes time but costs money. It will be more cost effective if the various places where shooting is planned are within easy reach of the others. Of course, it will be even cheaper if there is only one location, but then the content may not be so interesting. There are issues to consider when selecting locations for interviews. How will the background contribute to the overall feel of the piece? Is it too busy and therefore distracting from what the person has to say? A radio recording will need background noise to convey atmosphere and authenticity of location, but not to the extent that it intrudes on the interview.

The choice of recording position should enhance the mood. Visually, exteriors can appear more natural than interiors, and exterior cutaways usually make more sense, but factors such as weather and time of day may force you to utilise interiors. It is virtually impossible to remove an intrusive background noise from a recording later if one wants to retain the main part of the recording, which may be an essential interview. The story itself is likely to dictate the needs of recording location. I once interviewed a resident who lived near Gatwick Airport and was leading a campaign against the construction of a new runway because of the noise pollution. Her back garden had planes constantly in motion overhead. For once, this intrusive sound was exactly what we needed to illustrate the point of her message.

Scheduling the recording/shoot

There may be strict deadlines for the completion of research, set dates for the availability of crews and budgetary limitations on the number of days for recording and post-production, so assessments will have to be made in advance about how long specific parts are likely to take. Travel time usually forms a major part of the calculation. If distances between locations are great, or if the requirements at any location are complicated, or if there is likely to be a lot of waiting around for an event to happen that is outside the film-maker's control, then calculations can be thrown to the wind. *Cinéma-vérité* style requires much longer for filming. In addition, time needs to be allowed for the practicalities on site, such as securing entry permits, loading or unloading equipment and parking. Choosing recording positions within a building or big location will take time, as will moving between set-ups, meal breaks, setting up lights for video, briefing participants and numerous other considerations for each location. In short, recording always takes longer than anticipated, and often it turns out to be more complicated than originally envisaged.

When interacting with the real world, makers need to be flexible but to have an overall vision, and a sense of ethics, which extends to integrity in dealing with participants and good faith with the eventual audience. A good documentary-maker will set a high store by quality and constantly take stock of what is needed rather than just record aimlessly, although it is important to ensure that there is plenty of choice when it comes to editing. The documentary-maker has a choice of evidential sound styles: testimony via interviews or testimony via observed conversations.

Actuality sequences and observed conversations

In radio, actuality sequences are good for creating ambience, and they will work if they are announced in some way by a social actor, who may say something like 'Now we're going to have a meeting to discuss . . .' or 'I'm going to visit the manager to find out . . .' There may be gaps in the mental picture that is created by the recording of a particular scene, and these must be filled either by the presenter or by a participant.

With a visual medium, it is better to show, not tell. Visually, every shot matters, so they should be thought about carefully. People who are new to a camera are often beguiled by the power of the zoom: in fact, editors detest zooms, unless they are accompanied by other options (at the beginning or the end). 'Zooms work best when they are motivated by the action in the shot, or combined with another camera movement' (Watts, 2004: 136). They can progressively reveal content in a scene, such as when a shot starts on medium and moves to close-up as a person starts to show anger or sorrow.

Usually, directors film an interviewee doing some activity before or after the interview: walking into their office, fetching a file from a cupboard, entering or leaving a building. This can serve several useful purposes: it provides shots over which voice-over can be used to introduce the person before coming to the first extract from their interview; it also provides cutaways which may be necessary as edit points, enabling a film-making style that shows activity and movement while also conveying a sense of location and context for what the person does. The participant's own interview can be used as voice-over for such shots to 'refocalize' visual portrayal, encouraging viewer empathy.

The importance of sound quality

The purpose of location sound recording is to collect material that will be required in order to build a soundtrack later. When a sound operator arrives at a location, he or she will listen to the ambient noises, then take a level and do a test run before going for the main recording. The reason for such preliminaries is to get it right. Wild-tracks or atmos can be used to fill holes in the tracks that may be created in editing when an unwanted noise is cut out.

If a video image merits enhancement, good sound will bring it alive. Documentary film-makers sometimes neglect sound, realising only after the event that extra neck microphones or radio microphones (for recording two-way conversations) would have helped. Audiences will tolerate the occasional bad shot, but if they cannot hear and therefore understand the sound, they will lose patience with the film. It is often just a question of using headphones so that one hears in the same way as the recording, keeping the microphone near to the interviewee (but still out of shot), and watching that the volume needle on the external mixer does not oscillate too dramatically.

Interviewing for documentary

Documentary-making does not mean putting words into the interviewee's mouth. The best parts of an interview are when clear truths emerge spontaneously. However, an interview may be an intrusion into old wounds and tragic memories: 'In the name of the public good we delve into people's lives, invade their privacy, and expose their souls' (Rosenthal, 1996: 152). The dilemma is that the interviewer will want emotions and drama, anecdotes and colourful stories, as well as facts. Facts can be presented with television graphics or by voice-over narration in radio and TV, but there is no substitute for individual human feeling.

The more a documentary-maker knows about the subject involved, the easier it becomes to conduct successful interviews because the questions will be more focused. Although the interviewer should run through the topics to be covered (if this is a formal interview situation), there is always a danger of over-rehearsal so that the participant burns out in advance. Nevertheless, the interviewer must make the person feel at ease and less suspicious of the process; the eventual performance will benefit from any empathy that has been created. Sometimes, though, interviewers should not be too deferential, because this may inhibit them from asking tough questions, especially if the documentary is an investigative or current affairs adversarial style. In more formal situations, the interviewees sometimes asks to see the questions in advance and may want to adhere only to those questions. However, prepared answers will destroy a normally spontaneous, natural, conversational style. The interviewee may also want to hear or view the recording. This is fine as long as participants do not demand a veto over the final edit.

I only ever ask one question at a time, and it will contain only a single point. If the question consists of several parts, the interviewee will inevitably forget or ignore one of the elements. The 'tell me' gambit ensures usable, self-contained statements. The documentary-maker may have to ask the same question again at the end of the interview, if the first answer needs amplification: 'Tell me again about how you . . .' will result in a more succinct, relaxed, usable answer the second time round, especially if the point is important but the interviewee stumbled during the first take.

Alternatively, there may be a two-way conversation featuring the presenter or reporter as well: this is necessary for a confrontational dialogue. Walking interviews are a good idea if using an on-screen television presenter – they provide both movement and the impression of a natural conversation. Radio mikes will be required. An on-screen presenter (often scripted by the director/producer if they are not a journalist or subject specialist) can personalise the experience, enabling a dialogue with participants. However, with film, international sales distributors prefer documentaries without an on-screen presence as this reduces the need for dubbing or subtitles.

Operating video solo on location

A 'one-person band' video operator who directs, shoots and records will have less time to think about situations on location than a crew will. This means that more, not less, preparation will be required. A solo director can take his or her camera to a recce and shoot preparatory shots as a record, and will find that access is easier.

Being unobtrusive is useful in documentary situations where only one person can get inside the action: several people may stand out and move around more slowly. Certain styles of documentary – such as video diaries, investigative journalism pieces, low budget projects, wildlife programmes that may take a long time to capture subjects, fly-on-the-wall sequences shot in confined spaces like inside cars – lend themselves to one-person recording.

Yet there are practical disadvantages to going solo with video: very few people are equally good at all of the skills required. Experienced specialists work faster, more efficiently and usually produce a higher-quality result. Sound may suffer and it is difficult to do other basics such as changing the focal length of a zoom lens while holding a mike and watching the levels. It can also be useful to have others to carry equipment, park cars or watch out for intrusions while shooting. Equipment can easily be stolen on location.

Using sound and image archives

Documentary helps us to retain historical memory, but the role played by archives in documentary projects, and the way it is used, can vary greatly. It can be visual or sound illustration for the voice-over testimonials of the interviewees, where their comments are more generally relevant, or it can be used for one or more sequences with the original soundtrack. Music and sound archive are often used to create atmosphere and/or emotional impact. There are numerous film libraries, both general and specialist, which hold archives and stock shots. The way that a documentary-maker plans to integrate the selected archive material into the rest of the film may form part of the negotiations over copyright, so it is a critical determinant for the future creative direction of the project.

Edit structure and pace

With good editing, the flow that is created makes the audience unaware of the process of compilation, yet it allows them to interpret while actively viewing. Although some documentaries can be assembled in the order that they are shot, and the diary format tends to dictate this approach, each maker has their own idea of what structuring entails. The order in which information is communicated can be a difficult challenge because of the length of a long-form piece. The main criterion tends to be what works creatively with the available material, usually in the interests of achieving a logical narrative flow. The way subjects are positioned, how long they are allowed to talk and what about, the shots they are juxtaposed next to (in video), and the images their voices are laid over will all influence audience reception.

As the amount of raw material is so much more than in a news item, it will need to be reviewed and everything must be systematically logged and assessed while it is being loaded up for editing. Records are needed for all the raw material, particularly when it is derived from third-party sources, such as archive sound or film, newspapers and stills where copyright clearance will be needed. This exercise in taking stock also enables the maker to assess whether any additional recording will be needed to fill gaps ('pick-up shots' in documentary film parlance). Video must have a time code – if there is none, it must be added. Part of the preparation of materials during post-production usually also involves making transcripts of interviews – a prior paper edit helps in both radio and film as there can be huge amounts of material to review. It is a good idea to make a provisional editing plan.

After logging all the sources, sound and pictures need to be selected, structured and layered. Video editors like to lay a rough sound commentary early on as a 'guide track', along with sync sequences which will have their own soundtrack. For video, there may be such additions as special effects, titles and graphics to create. It is important not to be overdependent on music during post-production: usage will depend on the intentions of the project and the target audience. Even if there was no intended structure, there should have been some form of concept which can act as a guide to editing. With this in mind, it is possible to edit scenes one at a time. Connections from lines of dialogue and meaning should emerge to provide links from one scene to the next. Editing aims to maintain a logical continuity between viewpoints or reactions and conversational exchanges, usually with commentary to help join together the fragments. Video editors normally avoid cuts between one static and another and between the same size shot on the same subject. Cuts on action are smoother and there is no requirement for another shot of the same thing just because it is available; as long as a shot is working, it can be held on screen.

Pace is central to the way that audiences respond to a film, for it can set the mood as well as the energy level. Producers are so conscious of pace that they tend to announce the story up front: 'This is the story of . . .' They demand movement and action. One documentary film-maker, Dermot O'Donovan, says: 'These days, it's no more than a series of vignettes strung together: done and dusted within three minutes, then move on. There's a resistance to picking up a theme and staying with it, for fear of losing the audience.'[1] Television cutting styles usually dictate that the shot has to change every two or three seconds, working on the premise that this will beat the channel zappers. The 'either/or' soundbite approach is also very common in television current affairs documentaries.

However, it can be more interesting to let things go unexplained for a while, as a means of attracting audience attention by intriguing them, then following up later with an explanation. Sometimes a filmic, slower rhythm will allow a documentary to breathe. Otherwise the viewer could find that the concentration of argumentation is too much to take. The best way to check if the flow and pace of information are workable is to sit back and look or listen as the audience would for the first, and probably the only, time, assessing whether they will be able to formulate their own conclusions.

Writing voice-over narration

Voice-over commentary provides a framework for understanding the unfolding story, helping to move the documentary along, providing direction, as well as supplying the viewer and listener with the required five Ws (what, when, where, why and who), if they do not appear naturally. It will act like the spine to a book, helping to 'stick the documentary together', and, if necessary, to flag up the location or time – for instance, to create that same day/same place feeling when required. Commentary is conversation, not literary prose, so verbal padding and erudite phrases should be avoided. In fact, many documentary-makers prefer either not to use narration at all or to try to keep it to a minimum. Conversely, if the documentary has an essay style, commentary will be an important element to contribute to the overall message. Historical, social, political and current affairs films all tend to use commentary.

Some pictures take on meaning only with narration. Yet, the old saying goes, 'a picture is worth a thousand words', and images will become illustration if commentary is used to add information. Ideally, a symbiotic but not repetitive relationship between the words and pictures should emerge. Therefore, editors tend to support writing that will '"focus attention upon or feed significance into" the shots' (Vaughan, 1976: 32). This is best achieved when words are written to pictures, so that they enhance the pace and rhythm of the shots and the flow of the film. An assessment of the need for narration should always be made in conjunction with picture and sound, as they will need to be integrated, for it is the effect of the final combination of all three that really matters, not the narration in isolation.

Successful trailers

Jeremy Orlebar writes:

A programme trailer is often the last thing to do after the programme has been edited. This is a pity. A well-wrought trailer can be an effective tool in the promotional armoury of the programme. It makes sense to build the trailer into your pre-production thinking. It can work for the programme in two ways: a stylish trailer can promote the concept of your programme if it is included in the pitch to a broadcaster; while an adapted version can be promotional, and act as an audience gatherer later. Broadcasting companies tend to look more favourably on a programme proposal if it is pitched with a trailer.

Trailers are genre specific. In broadcast journalism, a documentary will typically be pitched in a particular strand area such as politics, social concerns, arts or science. The driving ideas will stem from interviews, some with well-known or controversial names. The temptation is to try to secure the main 'name' interview before pitching the programme. This high-risk strategy – 'high-risk' because the 'name' may be unhappy to do a long interview that may not be broadcast – can work well. Conversely, the pitch that merely *hopes* to interview a 'name' is unlikely to turn the head of a commissioning editor. However, if a short research interview shows that the 'name' has agreed to talk it gives impetus and energy to the pitch.

For the stunning documentary *In the Shadow of the Moon* about the Apollo missions, co-producer Chris Riley researched at NASA and unearthed extraordinary, previously unseen archive moon footage for a very early one-minute trailer. The movie-length feature documentary is remarkable for its outstanding archive footage, and the way it creates a moving narrative using originally composed music and interviews with the astronauts. A movie trailer was released in cinemas using such codes and conventions of cinema trailers as awe, archive realism and revelation.

Codes and conventions of trailers also include the classic enigma tease – pictures and sounds that make the audience wonder what the film is about. Broadcasting trailer codes tend towards information and content, while the best also have style and surprise. A broadcast trailer must persuade the audience that to miss this journalistic exposé would be to miss out on a life-changing and life-enhancing experience.

Audience and the afterlife

Documentaries should have as much exposure as possible – from the Internet to DVD/CD distribution and special video screenings. Audience discussion and feedback provide learning points for the future, while festivals provide opportunities for promotion and for interaction with the wider production community. Distributors can help to enhance the life of a documentary, which is probably more important than any money that it makes. Most people make documentaries because they are passionate about a subject that merits wider communication. The world is your oyster – use documentary to raise awareness and change it, if only in a small way!

Note

1   Interview with the author, 15 June 2005.

References

Chapman, J. (2007), *Documentary in Practice*, Cambridge, Polity Press
Rosenthal, A. (1996) *Writing, Directing, and Producing Documentary Films and Videos*, rev. edn, Carbondale and Edwardsville: Southern Illinois University Press
Vaughan, D. (1976) *Television Documentary Usage*, British Film Institute Television Monographs 6, London: British Film Institute
Watts, H. (2004) *Instant on Camera: The Fast Track to Programme-Making*, London: Aavo Media

Conflicting pressures

News and representation

Patricia Holland

Introduction

In 1955, the newly launched Independent Television News (ITN) daringly featured visible 'newscasters' instead of the invisible 'newsreaders' favoured by the BBC; in 1975, Angela Rippon became the first woman to read the news on a regular basis; in 1997, Five's Kirsty Young stood in front of a studio desk instead of sitting respectfully behind it; in 1999, ITV shifted its flagship late evening news from ten o'clock where it had been firmly held in place by the 'bongs' of Big Ben for decades. Each of these challenges to the patterned regularity of broadcast news caused a public sensation.

But, as the new millennium approached, the security of a predictable schedule, in which a small change could precipitate an outrage, was rapidly disappearing. As they struggled to adjust, television news and current affairs became the focus of intense and conflicting pressures. Changing technologies were bringing to a head a number of economic, political and ideological pressures which had been simmering for many years. Against this background, the transitional years between the Communications Act of 2003 and the inauguration of an all-digital television service in 2012 have seen unprecedented innovation in news delivery and an explosion of new styles and formats. But they have also brought uncertainty and a great deal of anxiety. Long-established institutions appear to be under threat, and long-established values must be managed and negotiated. There has been an outpouring of policy statements, research reports, 'stakeholder' consultations, innovatory proposals and much agonising over the nature of the media in the new, all-digital environment (see, among many other publications, BBC, 2007; Ofcom, 2005 and 2007; DCMS, 2004 and 2006; CMSC, 2007).

I shall be arguing that questions of representation and portrayal should be placed firmly within this context of the politics, economics and shifting technologies of the contemporary media landscape. Pressures affect the *ways* in which news and current affairs programmes communicate, as well as the substance of the communication; and the style of a broadcast has significant consequences for its content.

Conflicting pressures in the transitional decade

With the technological upheaval of the move to digital, journalist-led programmes have been pulled in several different directions. Most importantly, news and current affairs has become a political pivot point. It is the final stop in the contest between those who argue for the continuation of an inclusive, public service system and an institutional framework secured by regulation and legislation, and those who assert that, in a completely digitised environment, any form of restriction on the broadcasting market will be hopelessly out of date.

On the one hand, it is argued that broadcast news has earned the public's trust through its legal commitment to objectivity and impartiality; this requirement is the source of its authority and should continue to be enforced. On the other, it is claimed, there is no reason why broadcast news, just like the press, should not be free to have an editorial line, to indulge in advocacy or abuse, to follow the whims of its proprietor, and generally to throw off regulatory restrictions. These restrictions, it is argued, made sense only when access to the airwaves was limited. When hundreds of television channels and a wealth of converged digital platforms are equally available, even the sober ITN should be 'freed' to compete with channels like Rupert Murdoch's tub-thumping Fox News, of which it is written: 'Where television news once only presumed to cover political warfare, it now feeds it' (Collins, 2004: 4).

Ofcom, the influential Office of Communications, set up in 2003 to regulate commercial broadcasting and supervise the transition to digital, is itself committed to conflicting, if not positively schizophrenic, aims. In one respect it is a *de*-regulatory body, aiming to 'free the market' and relieve the commercial broadcasters of the 'burden' of regulation. In another it is committed to support public service broadcasting into the digital age and beyond (Harvey, 2006). In an attempt to solve this dilemma, Ofcom has designated the terrestrial channels – the BBC, ITV, Channel 4, S4C and Five – as 'public service broadcasters' (PSBs) with specific purposes and characteristics, and has set out to define and monitor the various levels of 'public service content' they are expected to carry. News is at the heart of this commitment, with its obligation to be reliable and impartial (Ofcom, 2005 and 2007).

The BBC, the powerful, licence-fee-funded chief PSB, has renewed its commitment to traditional news values. Its recent document which explored the nature of impartiality in the new environment says:

> Impartiality is and should remain the hallmark of the BBC as the leading provider of information and entertainment in the United Kingdom and as a pre-eminent broadcaster internationally. It is a legal requirement, but it should also be a source of pride.
>
> (BBC, 2007: 6)

However, at the same time, Ofcom has warned: 'Universal impartiality may become less enforceable in a digital environment, where regulated and unregulated services exist side by side on the same platform' (Ofcom, 2007: 71). For the BBC, its impartiality may become a 'haven – a clearing reachable only through dense, unregulated forest. And clearings can be quickly overtaken by undergrowth if the ground is not staked out' (BBC, 2007: 14). In other words, the reliability of 'the news' may no longer be securely underpinned by public policy, and even its institutional base in the BBC is not safe.

Hence the conflicting pressures in the transitional environment. On the one hand, the BBC may be pressured to retreat into a worthy 'public service' ghetto, with its licence fee drastically reduced or even abolished. On the other, political, technological and economic pressures are pushing all the broadcasters, including the BBC, towards a more populist approach. As the age of television scarcity finally gives way to the age of plenty (Ellis, 1999) competition for audiences is intense and the place of any genre which does not attract a big audience is insecure. News and other journalist-led programmes need to draw attention to themselves within an ever-louder cacophony of competing claims. In the words of *Newsnight* presenter Jeremy Paxman (2007):

the problem is that all news programmes need to make a noise. The need has got worse, the more crowded the market has become. We clamour for the viewers' attention: 'Don't switch over. Watch us! You won't be disappointed!' . . . The problem is that a sort of expectation inflation sets in.

Competition for audiences has brought a further set of contradictory pressures which have changed the ways in which broadcast journalism communicates. The news programmes themselves have moved towards an increasingly informal approach; meanwhile, across the schedules, there has been an explosion of material on the margins of journalism, involving popular formats, light-hearted, innovative styles and an embrace of celebrity. Precisely at the time when 'public service content' is expected to distinguish itself, the boundaries between 'serious' programmes and the rest of the output are becoming ever more blurred.

Even as it is argued that the authority and reliability of journalist-led programmes must be protected, the nature and professional values of journalism are being challenged; its special claims disputed. The figure of the journalist is now demystified and dispersed across the schedules and across the platforms. In myriad new hybrid forms, reporters become celebrities and celebrities become reporters; entertainment, 'reality' shows and social issues converge; ordinary people and 'citizen journalists' demand space on the airwaves; while online bloggers, campaigners and mischief-makers claim their role as a 'bulwark against the one dimensional view of events and the world that characterise Big Media' (Katz, 2001, in Zelizer and Allan, 2002: 136). Broadband websites deliver their own brand of audio-visual news, which may be created by newspapers, political parties, businesses and others for whom impartiality and even accuracy may be an irrelevance. One example is 18 Doughty St Talk TV, established by Conservative Party supporters in 2005.

Several writers have argued that the 1990s and 2000s have brought radical changes which have shaken the security of news programming. There is the expansion of the public relations industry and the increasing 'mediatisation' of news sources themselves (Cottle, 2003; Franklin, 1994; Corner and Pels, 2003; de Zengotita, 2005; Miller and Dinan, 2008); there is the inexorable move towards tabloidisation (Langer, 1998); and there is the heightened global visibility of major international traumas, such as the 11 September attacks. Indeed, it has been argued that following the attacks and the subsequent 'war on terror', journalism can never be the same (Zelizer and Allan, 2002). It is now subject to greater scrutiny and potential control both from governments and from extremist groups with international scope. As low-level wars and local conflicts spread across the globe, reporting is ever more dangerous; and the possibility of impartiality is reduced as numerous journalists are targeted, kidnapped and killed. Meanwhile, broadcast news is scrutinised, monitored, supplemented – and frequently contradicted – by myriad Internet sources. All of these things have shaken a simple expectation of authority and reliability.

Against the background of these multiple pressures, I will be looking first at the structure and form of news programmes, and then at the presentation of journalists themselves. These two factors, structure and mediation, are being seriously challenged; yet, arguably, together with their institutional grounding, they constitute the main guarantors of broadcast journalistic authority.

Changing media, changing structure

The very structure of 'the news' has come under scrutiny during the transitional decade. By '*the* news' I mean a recognised, discrete programme, produced and assembled by a specialist team working under an editor. It is produced by dedicated organisations staffed by producers, reporters, researchers and others who usually work exclusively in the genre and share its culture, its assumptions and its approach (Tunstall, 1993). The authority of 'the news' is guaranteed by them, backed by the authority of the broadcaster and the regulatory regime.

News programmes continue to mark out the day with a measured tread: breakfast, midday, early evening, late evening; dividing the news-rich weekdays from the leisured weekends, when shorter bulletins alternate with lunchtime discussion (*Any Questions* on Radio 4) and political analysis (BBC1's *The Politics Show*). Indeed, ITV thought this pattern so important that, in January 2008, it brought back *News at Ten*, together with Big Ben and the venerable presenter Sir Trevor McDonald. The pattern says much about the expectations of a regular lifestyle among the viewing audience. It underpins the address of 'the news' to the nation as a whole: an *equal* address, assuming in its viewers shared judgements about news values and the relative importance of the reports it contains. At the same time it works to renew and sustain those values.

Since 1989, with the launch of Sky, these discrete programmes have been paralleled by twenty-four-hour rolling news on an increasing number of channels, and from the late 1990s a positive flood of innovations has meant that structured and edited news programmes have been supplemented by 'on demand' viewing on multiple platforms and by millions of sources accessed via the Internet (Allan, 2006). The BBC's iPlayer 'makes the unmissable unmissable', declares its promo. As control over the selection and ordering of information moves from the news editors to the viewers, the authority of the broadcasters seems less secure. Against this background it is worth considering how news broadcasts have traditionally indicated their trustworthiness and authority through their structure and presentation.

Every broadcast genre has its own distinct conventions which establish the audience's expectations (Creeber, 2001): to laugh at comedy, to be absorbed by the narrative in drama, to react to the reality of documentary, to savour the style of a familiar chat-show host, to cheer on the favourites – and, as interactivity demands, to vote them in or out – in a game show.

As news and current affairs genres evolved on television, the style, structure and very 'look' of the programmes needed to underpin their reliability and impartiality. Consequently, on the main terrestrial channels, 'the news' is marked off from the flow of the broadcast schedule. Its introductory fanfares, titles and headlines seek both to entice the audience and to make it immediately clear that the following half-hour or so is not to be treated as fiction, comedy or, unless signalled as such, mere light-hearted chatter; that any shocking material it may contain is not for titillation; that spectacular imagery is for information, not effect. The shape of a news programme is itself a performance, a well-established ritual, with a job of work to do.

A news broadcast is a mélange but its structure is tightly controlled. Each programme is carefully paced and ordered, balancing within its allotted space political and social items, both overseas and domestic, with precedence given to those which will affect viewers directly (cancelled trains may take priority over foreign elections). There are dramatic changes in pace, topic and mood, as well as in degrees of importance. Each item is self-contained, linked to the next by a return to the studio. Only at moments of extreme emergency (terrorist attacks; major ecological disasters) will any one topic dominate. The programme is brought to an end with lighter items (introduced by the much-quoted 'And finally . . .'), sports reports and the weather forecast. The ritual is complete.

'The news' is distinguished by its status as a live broadcast. The presenters in the studio share a co-temporality with the audience as they visibly manage and relay the different inputs. The imagery is global in scope, but it is clear that this is the *national* news, grounded in the secure cocoon of the well-lit studio (even if areas of the studio are actually immaterial, created by computer-generated imagery).

Each of the accessed elements has its own visual style: the hasty, *vérité* movement of the camera at the war front; the figure of a reporter standing in the rain, addressing the audience from the pavement outside a government department; the low-quality blur of the urgent mobile phone footage capturing a disaster, whether a flood or a terrorist bomb. This repertoire of images characterises the genre and has itself been used in trailers and promotions for news broadcasts. As it moves between the different registers, the rich visual drama of 'the news' is no less structured and formal than a costume serial or a hosted game show, delivering what Simon Cottle (2006) has described as its 'communicative architecture' (Cottle with Rai, 2006). This carefully edited, balanced and sequenced format in itself asserts a reliable, knowledgeable, structuring presence, securing the authority and universal address of the format.

But the innovations of the digital era mean that the tight structure of a news programme can no longer claim to be self contained; its surface is no longer impenetrable. Mainstream broadcasts constantly point beyond themselves to other parts of the mediasphere. 'The news' and other factual programmes are now embedded in a network of websites and background information, much of it provided by the broadcasters themselves. Questions of representation are made more complex by this constant reference elsewhere, to material which could potentially flesh out, or even contradict, the information immediately on the screen. Every 'story' is reflected back and forth between an increasing number of different media.

The visuals of a news broadcast have themselves become more complex, no longer delivering a single image. Particularly on the rolling news channels, strap lines with moving text deliver headlines and 'breaking news'; they invite viewers to post their comments on the website and to 'press red' for more information. News broadcasts solicit contributions from the public: *Five News* declares, 'If you've got a story, make us a video,' and creates spaces for 'Your News on Five', including material taken from social networking websites, such as YouTube. Viewers are now accustomed to split screens, multiple actions, text and graphics. Many different messages are displayed within a single screen, which may contain a restless movement between locations, topics and voices. The impression is that so much is happening in so many parts of the world that the medium itself is struggling to keep up – as, of course, it always has. If the medium is the message, the message is multiplicity.

For Stuart Allan, analysing the response to the 11 September attacks, informal material transmitted via the Internet got closer to the 'real story': 'In stretching the boundaries of what counted as journalism "amateur newsies" and their webloggers together threw into sharp relief the reportorial conventions of mainstream journalism' (Zelizer and Allan, 2002: 128). However, despite the myth of authenticity which still surrounds much Internet use, few sources deliver the sort of raw, unmediated material and instantaneous reactions which may blossom at times of war and conflict. Instead, much of what is available has been edited and structured according to its own principles, which are likely to be different from the established regularity of traditional broadcast news. The assemblage of sources escapes the control of traditional editorial structures and of the regulatory system. The authority of 'the news' is shaken. In Ofcom's words, 'consumers [*sic*] who place a high level of importance on impartiality will find it harder to discover channels they can trust' (Ofcom, 2007: 71). At the same time, for the BBC, 'This much greater audience involvement has become a major factor in determining impartiality' (BBC, 2007: 5).

The image of the journalist: blurring the boundaries

Questions of the authority and legitimacy of the journalists who manage the rawness of public events on behalf of the viewing public are linked to questions of the trustworthiness of 'the news'. The figures of reporters and newsreaders are central to news iconography. As its mediators they anchor its reliability. In television and the visual media, there have long been anxieties about the presence of journalists on the screen, and the move to digital has renewed some long-standing questions about the nature of professionalism and the possibility of impartiality (Allan, 2008). Journalists, too, are caught between conflicting pressures.

Reporters and newsreaders have a double presence on the broadcast media. On the one hand, they must express/perform/act out the neutrality and impartiality which underpin the authority of a news broadcast; on the other, they are individuals with their own diverse characters, emotions and opinions. The two aspects may well be in tension. Their physical presence on screen will draw attention to their individuality; the nature of their performance will affect the content of the news they report. On the one hand, they may be accused of insufficient detachment; on the other, their manner and professionalism may be seen as a mask for bias or partiality. Hence the visibility of those who deliver the news has been an issue from the early days of television: 'If a newsreader were seen while giving the news, any change in his [*sic*] visual manner, a smile or a lift of an eyebrow might, however little this was intended, be interpreted as comment', wrote Grace Wyndham Goldie, the influential head of television 'talks' in the 1950s (Goldie, 1977: 194–5).

But changes to the figure of the main newsreader reflect changes in the ways in which news authority has been conceptualised and managed. There have been two compelling trends: a move towards informality and a move towards plurality. These have sometimes developed separately and sometimes together, but both have been influenced by the changing institutional structures of UK television. It was the coming of ITN, promising American-style 'newscasters', that forced the BBC to allow the audience to see its newsreaders. The figure of a woman reading the news seemed to throw the dilemmas into sharp focus. Could authority be combined with femininity? And what kind of authority would it be? When it was finally accepted that women could bear the weight of hosting a news broadcast, it was a step towards both plurality and informality, effectively a recognition that authority could take more than one form (Holland, 1987). The coming of Channel 4 in 1982 marked a decisive step towards plurality. Set up in response to critiques of the narrow social representation which had characterised the BBC and ITV, journalists and presenters across the channel were drawn from a diverse range of backgrounds, races and regions. Channel 4's first current affairs series was produced and presented by women, some from a feminist perspective (Baehr, 1987).

A year later, in 1983, the move to informality was hastened by a different development, the arrival of early morning television with the BBC's *Breakfast Time* and TVam on ITV. Instead of the segmented audiences addressed by Channel 4, breakfast television aimed at a broad 'family' audience. After some uncertain starts, early morning television settled down with a loose mixture of news and celebrity chat. Symbolically, the sofa replaced the formal desk, and the manner of the presenters became more relaxed. Conventional 'news' packages were interleaved with jokes, lifestyle and promotional interviews and low-key chatter. Politicians, redesigned as celebrities, could rub shoulders with comics, actors and pop stars. At this point the codes of familiarity had decisively invaded the space of 'the news'.

From the anonymous voice of authority favoured by the 1950s BBC, news presenters gradually moved towards a celebrity status. When Angela Rippon did a high-kicking dance routine on the *Morecambe and Wise Christmas Show* in 1976 – partly in response to endless tabloid scoffing at a woman in a serious role – there was a real sense of shock. Thirty years later presenters are ever more relaxed, more informal, more prepared to drop the mask of responsibility. They appear across the schedules in events ranging from *Children in Need* to *Strictly Come Dancing*, and sometimes struggle to keep their entertainment personas separate from the authority which must return as they resume their professional role. A continuum of performance has been created, requiring the audience to exercise discrimination and judgement.

Yet mediated news remains a global witness to extreme situations, and the figure of the journalist visibly reporting from a location – whether from the scene of a crime, the Prime Minister's office or a war zone – plays a significant role in securing the status of a news broadcast. The reporter stands in for the eyes of the viewer, observing a situation, seeking out witnesses, adding explanation. The presence of a known reporter, sometimes putting themself at risk ('*our* Africa correspondent', '*our* science editor') anchors a report in the expertise, experience and judgement of the journalist backed by the institution. In John Corner's words, it provides 'an imaging of the *process of reporting itself* . . . linking the viewer to a seen source of information and allowing a personalised investment of a trust in the visible processes of inquiry, the search for truth' (Corner, 1995: 67).

Since the 1980s, non-professional journalists have had an intermittent presence on UK television, with series such as ITV's *Your Shout*, the BBC's *Video Diaries*, and many Channel 4 programmes which gave 'ordinary people' the opportunity to investigate, report and voice their opinions. By the 2000s, the boundaries between journalists and non-professional or celebrity presenters was becoming well and truly blurred. Helped by the easy accessibility of very small cameras and recording equipment, the 'video diary' mode had become standard. The role of the journalist has expanded, mutated and dissipated.

When the journalist Sean Langan took a concealed camera through the fundamentalist Islamic states for *Langan behind the Lines* (BBC2, 2001) – sharing with the audience his horrified fascination for the football stadium in Saudi Arabia where beheadings regularly take place, or snatching a glimpse of Taliban in Afghanistan beating up a woman who was not, according to them, properly dressed – his intimate personal style as he shared thoughts, impressions and feelings with the camera pushed at the boundaries of conventional, detached journalism. Many other programmes have involved the use of covert filming, with the reporter literally acting a role. In the first *MacIntyre Undercover* series (BBC1, 1999) Donal MacIntyre became, among other things, a football hooligan, a fashion photographer and a care worker.

Although reporters are still expected to restrain their emotions and to conceal their political preferences (however, the BBC's Martin Bell made powerful arguments for 'a journalism of attachment' at the time of the Bosnian war), there is increasing space for professional journalists to speak in a variety of different registers, both on the mainstream channels and on blogs and websites. A variety of formats offers greater personal scope. Although these may sometimes exploit the politics of emotion and outrage, they also recognise that the personality of the journalist and their own commitment to a story may add the type of authority valued by those who have long suspected that 'neutrality' is a mask (Holland, 2001a and 2001b).

At the same time, celebrity reporters and new formats have meant the dispersal of news-related material across the television genres. A glance at recent output reveals, among many other formats: veteran political pundit Peter Snow reviewing the state of the nation with his son Dan (e.g., *What Britain Earns*, BBC2, 2008); the eccentric Conservative politician Ann Widdecombe tracking down wayward teenagers ('hoodies' and truants) and pursuing them with a hectoring tone which verges on self-parody (*Anne Widdecombe versus . . .*, ITV, 2007); celebrity chef Jamie Oliver revealing, and setting out to improve, the state of nutrition in schools (*Jamie's School Dinners*, Channel 4, 2006); businessman Gerry Robinson investigating and proposing improvements to a local hospital (*Can Gerry Robinson Fix the NHS?*, BBC2 with the Open University, 2007).

Condemned in the 1990s as 'infotainment' (Brants, 1998) and in the 2000s as 'reality television' (Biressi and Nunn, 2005) these hybrid genres are searching for innovative ways to attract an audience as they face the challenge of a changing political and economic environment. They reveal news and current affairs-related programmes negotiating and managing changes and pressures; balancing demands for populism with traditional journalistic values; seeking, in Stuart Allan's (2004: 77) phrase, 'a cultural politics of legitimacy' with varying degrees of success. These are *cultural* responses to commercial, political and ideological pressures, and they defy a narrow definition of 'public service content'. Arguably, by supplementing mainstream journalism, they could effectively strengthen rather than replace it.

Conclusion

The double challenge to the structure of 'the news' and to the role of journalist as authoritative mediator has shifted broadcast journalism decisively towards a looser, less formal approach. But 'the news' has long been part of a complex web of broadcast output. Even before the coming of the Internet, interested members of the public were able to follow a 'story' across the media – though documentaries, rival news items on various channels, current affairs programmes, archive, biographical and reminiscence programmes, as well as programmes of comment and discussion. 'News' has always involved an interweaving of 'stories' across the days, weeks and years, and across sources.

As this complexity multiplies with the digital media, the commitment to maintain the status and authority of broadcast journalism as the guarantor of public trust and the core of public service broadcasting has become more problematic. However, it is clear that technological changes may be managed and utilised in many different ways. Ultimately the outcomes of the move to digital, as the transitional decade gives way to a fully digitised environment, will be determined by political as much as technological pressures.

References

Allan, S. (2004) *News Culture*, 2nd edn, Maidenhead: Open University Press

Allan, S. (2006) *Online News: Journalism and the Internet*, Maidenhead: Open University Press

Allan, S. (2008) 'Journalism without journalists? Rethinking questions of professionalism', in L. Steiner and C. Christians (eds), *Key Concepts in Critical and Cultural Studies*, Urbana: University of Illinois Press

Baehr, H. (1987) 'Firing a broadside: a feminist intervention into mainstream TV', in H. Baehr and G. Dyer (eds), *Boxed in: Women and Television*, London: Pandora

BBC (2007) *From Seesaw to Wagon Wheel: Safeguarding Impartiality in the Twenty-First Century*, London: BBC Trust

Biressi, A. and Nunn, H. (2005) *Reality TV: Realism and Revelation*, London: Wallflower

Brants, K. (1998) 'Who's afraid of infotainment?', *European Journal of Communication* 13(3): 315–35

Collins, R. (2004) *Crazy Like a Fox: The Inside Story of How Fox News Beat CNN*, New York: Portfolio

Corner, J. (1995) *Television Form and Public Address*, London: Edward Arnold

Corner, J. and Pels, D. (eds) (2003) *Media and the Restyling of Politics*, London: Sage

Cottle, S. (ed.) (2003) *News, Public Relations and Power*, London: Sage

Cottle, S. with Rai, M. (2006) 'Between display and deliberation: analysing TV news as communicative architecture', *Media, Culture and Society* 28(2): 163–89

Creeber, G. (2001) *The Television Genre Book*, London: BFI

Culture Media and Sport Committee (CMSC), House of Commons (2007) *Public Service Content: First Report of Session 2007–8*, London: The Stationery Office, HC36-1

Department of Culture, Media and Sport (DCMS) (2004) *Broadcasting in Transition* London: DCMS, HC380

Department of Culture, Media and Sport (DCMS) (2006) *A Public Service for All: The BBC in the Digital Age*, London: DCMS, Cm6763

Ellis, J. (1999) *Seeing Things*, London: I.B. Tauris

Franklin, B. (1994) *Packaging Politics: Political Communications in Britain's Media Democracy*, London: Edward Arnold

Goldie, G.W. (1977) *Facing the Nation: Television and Politics 1937-1976*, London: Bodley Head

Harvey, S. (2006) 'Ofcom's first year and neoliberal blind spot: attacking the culture of production', *Screen* 47(1): 91-105

Holland, P. (1987) 'When a woman reads the news', in H. Baehr and G. Dyer (eds), *Boxed in: Women and Television*, London: Pandora

Holland, P. (2001a) 'Authority and authenticity: redefining television current affairs', in M. Bromley (ed.), *No News is Bad News*, London: Pearson Education

Holland, P. (2001b) 'Spectacular values: the pleasure of the text and the "contamination" of current affairs television', *Visual Culture in Britain*, 2(2): 33–47

Katz, J. (2001) 'Net: our most serious news medium?', at http://features.slashdot.org/article.pl?sid=01/10/05/1643224 (accessed 2 July 2008)

Langer, J. (1998) *Tabloid Television: Popular Journalism and the 'Other' News*, London: Routledge

Miller, D. and Dinan, W. (2008) *A Century of Spin: How Public Relations Became the Cutting Edge of Corporate Power*, London: Pluto

Ofcom (2005) *Review of Public Service Television Broadcasting: Phase 3 Competition for Quality*, London: Ofcom

Ofcom (2007) *New News, Future News: The Challenges for Television News after Digital Switch-over*, London: Ofcom

Paxman, J. (2007) *Never Mind the Scandals: What's It All For?*, James MacTaggart Memorial Lecture, Edinburgh Television Festival, 24 August

Tunstall, J. (1993) *Television Producers*, London: Routledge

Zelizer, B. and Allan, S. (eds) (2002) *Journalism after September 11*, London: Routledge

Zengotita, A. de (2005) *Mediated: How the Media Shape Your World*, London: Bloomsbury

Freedoms and responsibilities

Law for broadcast journalists

Tim Crook

Introduction

A comprehensive learning guide on UK media law[1] for broadcast journalists can be found in the many well-written books on the subject. This chapter is designed to give you an intense and selective distillation. The purpose of studying the subject at university is to go beyond a kind of brick-laying knowledge about dos and don'ts and apply a critical evaluation of the why as well as the how of media law.

The legal regulation of broadcasting compared to the self-regulation of the press means a different environment for broadcast journalists. At its most obvious, press reporters can take the tools of their trade – a notebook and pen – into a courtroom, while the tools of the broadcaster's trade – cameras and microphones – are banned. And there is the potential for tension between the role of the journalist in holding governments, organisations and individuals to account, while walking the line of legal restrictions.

There was a short-lived experiment to allow cameras and recording in courtrooms in Scotland in the 1990s that faded away when the judges became concerned at what was described as 'a media circus' surrounding the global televising of the murder trial of O.J. Simpson in Los Angeles. There has been closed-circuit televising of the Hutton Inquiry, the inquest into the death of Diana, Princess of Wales and Dodi Fayed and a few murder trials attracting significant media interest. But the English judges continue to restrict the potential merely to cabling into 'overspill' media and public gallery tents and annexes. In fact, the only true broadcasting in England from the Royal Courts of Justice may have been in 1982, when the author negotiated the sound recording and transmission of the valedictory speeches of Master of the Rolls Lord Denning in the Lord Chief Justice's Court.[2]

At university students are encouraged to recontextualise the nature and development of media law and critically appreciate the status and purpose of the journalist within Britain's liberal capitalist society. In trying to understand how the system works, some journalists believe their function in a democratic society is to question the justification for legal decision-making in every case. A debate endures about whether the proper role of the journalist is to be a lapdog or a bloodhound. Knowledge, understanding and a critical appreciation of legal constraints help journalists navigate the grey areas between the public's right to know, the individual's right to privacy, the principles of open government and transparent justice.

The broadcast journalist is faced with three key areas of control: contempt; defamation; and privacy. Crucial to these is the concept of 'public interest'. What constitutes the public interest is not a matter of consistent agreement between judges, politicians and journalists. Some journalists argue that several aspects of UK media law could be against the public interest because they fail the key tests of justice and legal validity. It is argued that punishments and disincentives that include imprisonment and huge amounts in damages and legal costs are disproportionate to the harm that mere broadcasting of information can cause. It is also argued that media law sanctions are negative remedies against journalism in a free and democratic society and there has been very little transparency, publication, notification or consultation with the media during the last thirty years, a period which has seen an exponential rise in primary and secondary media law legislation.

On the other hand, critics of the media argue that the law needs to check the catastrophic damage to the emotional and economic well-being of individuals and companies[3] caused by negligent publication. The incorporation of the European Convention of Human Rights into British statute law[4] means there has to be a balancing exercise between freedom of expression and the rights to life, reputation, privacy and a fair trial. British media law needs to ensure that a fair trial takes place through due process of legal proceedings and not in the media. Vulnerable witnesses need to be protected from vigilante reprisals and intimidation, and state investigators and security forces need to be protected from revenge attacks and damage to national security. The purpose of media law is to ensure that broadcasters exercise their power of communication with responsibility and respect the dignity of the human individual. Public interest is not simply what interests the public in terms of prurience, voyeurism, gossip, curiosity and entertainment.

Consequently, in your study of media law you need to be able to formulate your own opinions about whether journalists are given fair rights of representation in being able to challenge decisions to hold court cases in secret. Has the balancing exercise by judges diminished the right to freedom of expression to the point of subordination against other rights such as national security, privacy, along with the exaggeration of the imperative of such fundamental rights as life and a fair trial? In a democratic society how much moral discretion should be given to journalists when they wield their mighty pens or tap away on their keyboards when editing digitally across multimedia platforms? What follows is a survival guide and a cue for debates around these questions.

This chapter falls into two parts. The first is a discussion of key aspects of the law as it applies to journalism, with the emphasis on broadcasting. The second section is a more detailed explication of the law in tabular form.

Contempt

The law of contempt is designed to protect the right of an individual to a fair hearing. Most media contempt law is determined by an act passed in 1981 that enabled judges to issue specific bans on court reporting. Orders under section 4(2) postpone reports of court proceedings, and orders under section 11 prohibit reports of information withheld from the public before the proceedings. The act was criticised for creating an opportunity for judicial activism but was also welcomed in providing a simple rule that media contempt was a publication that tended to 'create a substantial risk of serious prejudice'. It was clear that the rule should apply when reporting crime or legal stories after an arrest had been made, warrant for arrest had been issued or when a civil case had been 'set down for trial'. It was clear that substantial risk related to the size and timing of publication. Serious prejudice related to the nature of the content and how it could 'seriously' influence jurors or potential jurors. It was common sense that the key risk areas were publishing the previous convictions of accused people, accusing them of more serious offences by mistake, saying they had confessed, publishing details of police evidence or commenting on the honesty of the defendant or witnesses.

However, there has been a discernible shift in the application of media contempt strict liability[5] in Britain. Much more seriously prejudicial content is being tolerated after arrest and before charge on the basis that the 'fade factor' in 'substantial risk' means that jurors do not hold memory of the material that could prejudice their minds.

The contemporary problem of terrorism and the extension of detention limits for terrorist suspects for up to twenty-eight days has meant a longer period between arrest and charge where the media vacuum has been filled with intense speculation and reporting in the 24/7 world of rolling news. In one major inquiry, the Home Secretary and senior Scotland Yard Officers held a press conference after arrest to explain the overall nature of the investigation and outline the main allegations.

It is not clear if the judges are happy about this. The leading UK jurists on contempt law, Sir David Eady (a High Court judge) and Professor A.T.H. Smith (an academic and barrister) have recently written: 'according to some commentators, the strict liability rules have continued to be honoured more in the breach than the observance ... [It] would seem to indicate either a need for more determined enforcement of the existing law or the desirability of introducing reform with a view to bringing practice into line with principle' (Eady and Smith, 2008: vii). In a speech in 2007, the former Attorney-General Lord Goldsmith said there was a perceived need for greater openness in terrorism cases, and a huge public interest in information being available about the progress of police investigations and the steps being taken to protect the public and bring dangerous offenders to justice (*ibid.*). In addition, the Court of Appeal ruled against the Attorney-General over an injunction he had obtained against the BBC, which wished to report a leaked memo concerning the Scotland Yard inquiry into loans for peerages. The court decided that Article 10, Freedom of Expression, trumped an evaluation of the risk of a fair trial being undermined (Article 6). This means that the application of strict liability after arrests was a restriction on the freedom of information guaranteed by the Human Rights Act 1998.[6]

There has also been a move towards '*voir dire*' inquiries into jury panels to exclude the risk of media prejudice. In 2008 the trial judge at Ipswich Crown Court in the case of Steve Wright, who was accused of murdering five women, directed jurors to excuse themselves if they had any involvement and knowledge of the victims and inquiry, and to avoid reading and consuming media about the case or indulging in Internet research. In addition, 'reserve jurors' were empanelled. This was very much in the US style of encouraging jurors to concentrate on the evidence and 'put out of their minds' the influence of prior or contemporary media coverage. It was also an extension of the practice of Old Bailey judges in terrorist trials asking people on jury panels to excuse themselves if they or their relatives had any involvement or experience of terrorist incidents or membership of the security forces.

Defamation

This is probably the biggest risk faced by any journalist – the risk that something broadcast will damage an individual's reputation. It is also a very controversial area with concerns that it overprotects the rich, powerful and wealthy and that the dice are loaded against the journalist. In the UK the practice of uplifting winners' legal costs in conditional fee arrangements[7] means that insurance companies determine the battle lines in defending libel proceedings and their decisions are based on profit rather than truth/justice and freedom of expression. It can also be argued that the UK has been far more oppressive and late in recognising a 'no fault' public interest defence for journalism in *Reynolds v. The Times* (1999) and *Jameel v. Wall Street Journal* (2006).[8] The USA established a much higher protection of freedom of speech in libel long ago through the case of *Sullivan v. New York Times* (1964).[9] There, plaintiff/claimants have to prove actual malice or a reckless disregard for the truth. Two of the Supreme Court judges Justices Black and Douglas, even postulated whether there should be a defamation law at all.

There is a clear disparity in media legal culture between the USA and the UK. It might be argued that the slow move to a no fault defence in Britain has partly come about through an anti-media culture. The phenomenon of libel tourism so that foreign nationals can sue in the English courts even if only a few copies of the magazine, book or newspaper have been sold in the English jurisdiction is hardly favourable to the interests of freedom of expression.

The defence of justification is difficult to apply successfully. When Helen Steel and David Morris challenged McDonald's, it took seven years to bring the case to a conclusion and it ended only when the European Court of Human Rights ruled that the affair was a breach of the right to freedom of expression and the right to a fair trial.[10]

There are many aspects of defamation law that could be reformed. Unlike contempt, there is no standard phrase or sentence of definition. The benchmark maxims that libel is 'lowering a person in the estimation of right-thinking members of society generally', 'exposing somebody to hatred, ridicule or contempt', 'causing somebody to be shunned or avoided', or 'damaging them in their trade, profession, work, or office' appear to belong to an age when the aristocracy and bourgeoisie were anxious about what their servants were reading and the only people travelling on the top deck of the Clapham omnibus were male, middle-aged and heterosexually married. The fact that libel can be by innuendo, depends on the natural meaning of words and might also involve the expression of language that arouses extreme pity means that the author is effectively dead, *à la* Roland Barthes.[11]

In most disputed libel cases the potential libel meaning is decided by judges. They have set out the ideological frame of what should be permitted as 'responsible journalism'. Lord Nicholls, in the Reynolds ruling of 1999 (see above), with good intentions, set out ten criteria.[12] As a result, journalists who made honest mistakes could be protected from libel actions only if they effectively jumped ten hurdles of conduct that included proving they gave a right to reply, reported it fairly, properly evaluated the credibility of their sources, avoided sensationalism, and selected a story in the public interest. By 2006, the senior judges in the Jameel case (see above) tried to create a more liberal climate: judges should not second guess editors who have to make decisions under the pressures of intense deadlines and where the opportunities to investigate, check and verify are limited. It is important to realise that this 'public interest' defence for honest mistakes is granted by judges and not by jury verdict; and by judges who are generally appointed from a very narrow ethnic, gender and class base.

There is a particular pitfall for the television journalist. It is possible to libel someone if the meaning of words and pictures *taken together* damages a reputation.

For example, in a story about dodgy plumbing firms, it might be possible for someone to claim that the broadcaster is alleging that a particular individual, if seen on the screen, is a poor plumber.

Privacy

This has become another minefield for the broadcast journalist. According to the BBC, it is the single biggest area where journalists seek advice from their in-house lawyers. Article 8 of the European Convention of Human Rights states, 'Everyone has the right to respect for his private and family life, his home and his correspondence,' and this became UK statute law in 1998.[13] There had been criminal and civil privacy restrictions directed at journalists for nearly a hundred years. They simply had not been defined as 'privacy'. Examples include the statutory and judicial restrictions on identifying sexual offence complainants, children/youths in criminal proceedings, 'vulnerable witnesses', and the parties involved in divorce and child custody proceedings.

It can also be argued that the Official Secrets Act has been a mechanism of protecting a notion of 'privacy' for the state in relation to politically sensitive information. 'National security' is the key concept, which tends to be defined by the executive and confirmed by judiciary. The media can be persuaded to agree to secrecy where there is a real threat to life, but when this overlaps with political and propagandist sensitivities the ethical and legal position becomes much more ambiguous. The self-censorial media blackout in 2007/8 on Prince Harry's deployment to Afghanistan brokered by the Society of Editors is an example of this.

In 2008 a large proportion of a murder trial at the Central Criminal Court was held in secret because the judge had been persuaded that this should be the case. He made his decision in a secret hearing and for secret reasons. In 1994 the author challenged the reasons for holding an entire drugs trial in secret, but the appeal at the Royal Courts of Justice was held in secret and the ruling was given in secret, and the issue of whether the appeal was successful will have to remain a secret.[14]

There is constant pressure to prosecute and convict people who work for the government and wish to be whistle-blowers on the grounds of conscience. Katharine Gunn and Derek Pasquil had charges against them dropped. Cabinet Office communications officer David Keogh and House of Commons researcher Leo O'Connor were prosecuted, convicted and imprisoned. They went to jail for six and three months, respectively, and when their trial accidentally remained in open court to discuss part of the 'secret' memo they had passed to each other, a gagging order on the media not to report the information was sustained at the Court of Appeal.[15]

There is a risk that the culture of 'national security' is motivating UK judges to issue an almost arbitrary pattern of censorship orders. In 2007 the details of a legal action accusing British soldiers in Iraq of murdering and abusing civilians remained secret for almost a year. However, it could also be argued that these instances of secrecy represent rare and exceptional circumstances and constitute a response by the UK state and judiciary to unprecedented threats to security by international and domestic terrorism and the consequences of the country's military deployment in conflict zones abroad.

To all intents and purposes, the entire operation of the Family Courts system occurs in secret. This can be confirmed by any examination of online listings of Family proceedings at the Royal Courts of Justice in London. Many Family proceedings at the first-tier magistrates' courts should be in open court, but public and press rarely venture into them and most court officials are not sure whether they should be there or not.

Privacy operates as prior restraint on the publication by the media of accurate information, whereas libel is a remedy against publication of untrue allegations and imputations. Generally privacy applies pre-publication and libel post-publication. Both areas of the law trade on human emotions: libel in terms of honour, self-esteem and status; privacy in terms of personal security, dignity and familial duties.

However, Parliament has resisted legislating for an explicit 'privacy law'. Instead, Article 8 of the Human Rights Act 1998 has seeded judicial activism to convert the law of confidentiality as a contract between powerful celebrities and their employees into a privacy duty that also binds the media as a third party. In cases involving public figures such as the model Naomi Campbell, the singer Loreena McKennitt and Prince Charles[16] the jump from confidentiality to privacy was achieved by creating a legal block or remedy against the media for the publication of confidential/private information where public interest was not deemed to be what may simply interest and entertain the public.

Privacy remains a growing area of media law. In 2008 the author J. K. Rowling won an action against a picture agency over the photographing of her one-year-old son in an Edinburgh street (*Murray v Big Pictures*) and rulings by Mr Justice Eady (*X & Y*, 2006, and *Mosley v News Group Newspapers*, 2008) indicate that media exposure of infidelity will not be permitted unless they can demonstrate a 'public watchdog' interest with freedom of expression no longer regarded as the trump card.

The reach of privacy is now expanding into new areas:

- There is an increasing phenomenon of extending the principle of the vulnerable witness into the vulnerable defendant and convicted criminal; for example, the perpetual gagging order on the whereabouts and activities of Maxine Carr.[17]
- There is growing anonymity and partial anonymity for armed services personnel in courts-martial, armed services and police marksmen who kill civilians in security operations,[18] criminals facing vigilante justice, undercover state investigators and all kinds of witnesses to serious crimes. A man extradited from Morocco on charges relating to the £50-million Securitas robbery in Tonbridge appeared at Maidstone Magistrates' Court and was 'not named for legal reasons'.[19]
- There is the increasing phenomenon of terrorist suspect detainees and individuals subject to 'control orders', asylum-seekers and political/economic refugees in the immigration legal process being deracinated in media coverage to the point that they are referred to only as A, B, C, Y or X.
- There is an increasing development of the 'anonymous' concept in communications culture. The notion of the non-person designated as X or Y is spreading throughout many aspects of journalistic coverage of legal issues and legal proceedings. It includes myriad areas of civil litigation, such as the identities of individuals in persistent vegetative state cases, their doctors, relatives and health professionals.

These criticisms are part of an ongoing debate about the relationship between media freedom and legal responsibility. For every criticism of family law secrecy there is a valid argument that such confidentiality is imperative for the interest of children in custody disputes. What justification is there for media exploitation of the private agony and distress experienced in family breakdown? Where this involves any public interest in global celebrity Family Division judges do respond with the public release of their rulings.[20] When the government engaged in a consultation exercise on opening Family proceedings to the public on a no-names basis, a survey of young people involved in such cases revealed opposition to such a move.

It should also be acknowledged that while there has been a tendency to develop and increase media privacy law, this has been counter-balanced by legislation that gives the media (and any person) the power to extract and publish previously private information held by government and public authorities. The Freedom of Information Act 2000, which came into force in January 2005, established the right of access to information in the public interest. The legislation is enforced by an information commissioner with a right of appeal to an information tribunal. Freedom of information requests have resulted in an impressive array of media stories that question the exercise of power by government and authority. These include the abuse of expenses by Members of Parliament and the conduct of police, local authorities and other government bodies.

Conclusion

This chapter has been written for the purpose of being a nutshell introduction to the subject: not only to the law itself but to the debates surrounding the law and its implications for the always fraught relationship between media freedom, the public's right to know, national security and individual privacy. The rest of this chapter is a tabulated guide to the key areas discussed above. It is hoped that your learning can go beyond the mechanics of understanding the basic rights and wrongs of media law to consider the wider contextual ethical background and debates on why media laws are created and developed.

Notes

1 The United Kingdom has three separate legal systems: England and Wales; Scotland; and Northern Ireland. Scottish law is more influenced by continental civil/Roman law. However, UK media law statutes passed by the Westminster Parliament tend to have a similar remit across all three jurisdictions and variations are to be found primarily in judge-made law. There are also separate legal systems operating in the Isle of Man and the Channel Islands that are not subject to UK statute law.

2 My predecessor as IRN Old Bailey correspondent, Ken Dennis of the Press Association, had previously recorded and broadcast the valedictory ceremony on retirement of the Recorder of London in a courtroom of the Central Criminal Court.

3 In the United Kingdom companies have what is known as 'legal personality'.

4   Through the enactment of the Human Rights Act 1998 in October 2000.

5   'Strict liability' in law involves criminal liability for the criminal act: i.e., publication (known as *actus reus*) with a diminishing application of mental intention (known as *mens rea*). Consequently, media contempt in the Contempt of Court Act 1981 excludes a lack of intention to commit contempt as a defence.

6   *Attorney General v. BBC* [2007] EWCA Civ 280.

7   A form of 'no win, no fee' where costs are guaranteed by insurance premiums and 'uplifts' on costs in order for the loser to pay the winner in legal fees and compensation.

8   *Reynolds v. Times Newspapers* [1999] UKHL 45 and *Jameel v. Wall Street Journal* [2006] UKHL 44.

9   *New York Times v. Sullivan* [1964] 376 US 254.

10 *Steel and Morris v. United Kingdom* [2005] ECHR 68416/1.

11 Roland Barthes was a French structuralist/poststructuralist philosopher who argued that the author should not be regarded as the origin of his/her text or the authority for its meaning; hence the title of his seminal essay, 'The Death of the Author'.

12 The Decalogue is the Old Testament Christian ethical code of immutable and universal laws set out in the Ten Commandments collected from Mount Sinai by Moses.

13 The Human Rights Act 1998 came into force in October 2000 and its remit covers England and Wales, Scotland and Northern Ireland.

14 The case is unreported because the ruling by the Court of Appeal was *in camera*.

15 *Times Newspapers Ltd and Others*, Court of Appeal, Criminal Division [31 July 2007].

16 *Campbell v. MGN Ltd* [2004] UKHL 22, *McKennitt v. Ash* [2005] EWHC 3003 (QB), *HRH The Prince of Wales v. Associated Newspapers Ltd (No. 3)* [2006] EWHC 522 (Ch).

17 Maxine Carr's partner Ian Huntley was convicted in 2003 of murdering two eleven-year-old girls in Soham. Carr was convicted of perverting the course of justice by lying to the police after the girls had been killed. She obtained a general injunction against media coverage of her identity and whereabouts after her release from prison. See *Carr (Maxine) v. News Group Newspapers Ltd* [2005] QBD, 24 February.

18 The identity of the police marksman who shot Jean Charles de Menezes at Stockwell underground station in 2005 remains a secret despite the successful prosecution of the Metropolitan Police under health and safety legislation. It is argued that public identification of police firearms specialists would render them vulnerable to reprisal and undermine their effectiveness in future operations.

19 He was identified after making his first UK court appearance, but no explanation was given as to why he had been anonymised during the extradition process.

20 This occurred at the conclusion of the divorce of Paul and Heather McCartney in 2008. It was apparent that many aspects of the dispute had been leaked to the media. The proceedings remained in private. Heather Mills McCartney was not successful in an appeal to prevent the judge from making his ruling public.

References

Banks, D, Greenwood, W. and Welsh, T. (2007) *McNae's Essential Law for Journalists*, 19th edn, Oxford: Oxford University Press

Bloy, D. (2006) *Media Law*, London: Sage

Bloy, D. and Hadwin, S. (2007) *Law and the Media*, London: Sweet and Maxwell

Brook, H. (2007) *Your Right to Know*, London: Pluto Press

Crook, T. (2009) *Media Ethics and Laws: Power with Responsibility*, Essex: Kultura Press

Crook, T. (2009) *Crook's Media Law: Theory, Practice and International Perspectives*, Colchester: Kultura Press

Eady, D. and Smith, A.T.H. (2008) *Arlidge, Eady and Smith on Contempt – First Supplement to the Third Edition*, London: Sweet and Maxwell

Frost, C. (2007) *Journalism Ethics and Regulation*, 2nd edn, London: Pearson Longman

Media Lawyer, ed. Mike Dodd [a bimonthly newsletter/journal published by the Press Association], at http://www.medialawyer.press.net

Quinn, F. (2007) *Law for Journalists*, London: Pearson Longman

Smartt, U. (2006) *Media Law for Journalists*, London: Sage

Court reporting rules for broadcast journalists

Reporting of preliminary magistrates' court hearings for offences tried by jury at the Crown Court or 'either way' offences	Under section 8 of the Magistrates' Court Act 1980 broadcasters should limit their reports to: (a) the identity of the court and the names of the examining justices (b) the names, addresses and occupations of the parties and witnesses and ages of the accused and witnesses (c) the offence(s) or a summary of them with which the accused is charged (d) the names of the legal representatives engaged in the proceedings (e) any decision of the court to commit/transfer the accused or any of them for trial and any decision of the court on disposal of the case of any of the accused not committed (f) the charge(s) on which the accused, or any of them have been committed/transferred and the court to which they have been committed/transferred (g) the date and place to which committal proceedings have been adjourned, if adjourned (h) any arrangements as to bail on committal or adjournment (i) whether a right to representation funded by the Legal Services Commission as part of the Criminal Defence service was granted to the accused or any of the accused (j) whether the court has decided to lift or not to lift these reporting restrictions. These restrictions have been known in many media law textbooks as 'the 10 points'. In practice, the UK media have found that any factual report respecting these criteria will not face prosecution when it includes an element of uncontroversial colour. For example, describing how the accused is dressed and the presence of relatives or newsworthy people in the public gallery is unlikely to create prejudice or attract prosecution. Avoid reporting objections to bail, the previous convictions of the accused and prosecution or defence allegations.
Reporting hearings at the Crown Court prior to or at the beginning of a trial	'Preparatory' hearings are sometimes held at the beginning of long and complex criminal trials to resolve evidential/case management issues and applications by the defence that there is no case to answer. Under the Criminal Procedure and Investigations Act 1996 reports of such hearings are restricted to: 1) name of the court and the judge; 2) names, ages, home addresses and occupations of accused and witnesses; 3) charges or a summary of them; 4) names of lawyers; 5) date and place to which proceedings are adjourned; 6) arrangements as to bail; 7) whether legal aid was granted. The vast majority of pre-trial hearings at the Crown Court are not covered by these restrictions. These include 'plea and direction' hearings.

Court reporting rules for broadcast journalists (cont.)

	Obviously guilty pleas that will be followed by sentence hearings should be reportable. Care should be taken not to report matters that could create a substantial risk of serious prejudice to a future trial in situations where the judge has not made a section 4(2) postponing order under the Contempt of Court Act 1981.
Reporting bail applications	Bail applications at magistrates' courts have always been held in open court, but this was not the case at the Crown Court where they were held 'in chambers', in other words in private. However, in *Malik v. Central Criminal Court* [2006] Mr Justice Gray ruled that such applications should normally be held in public.
Reporting Youth Courts	Nothing should be reported that could lead to identification of the youth or school that an accused youth or witness attends. Only reporters are permitted access to Youth Court proceedings. Breaches of anti-social behaviour orders (ASBOs) are brought before Youth Courts. The blanket anonymity applying to these courts is empowered from section 49 of the Children and Young Persons Act 1933. In 2005 the law was amended so that Youth Court justices have to make an order if they wish ASBO-breaching youths to retain their anonymity.
Reporting Family hearings	On the very rare occasions when these proceedings are in open court you can only report: names, addresses and occupations of the parties and witnesses, a concise statement of the charges, the defence and counter-charges in support of which evidence has been given, submissions on any point of law arising in the course of the case and the decision of the court, the judgement of the court and the observations of the judge. Under section 69(2) of the Magistrates' Court Act 1980, journalists cannot be excluded from family proceedings unless the court is dealing with adoption arrangements or with evidence involving indecency.
In Camera/**In Chambers**	These expressions normally mean that the court hearing has been in private with the press and public excluded, but the Administration of Justice Act 1960 states that publication of a report of a hearing in these circumstances will not be a contempt, unless the case concerns the Children Act 1989, wardship proceedings involving children, proceedings under the Mental Health Act 1959, national security issues relating to the Official Secrets Act 1989, or secret processes and confidential matters, such as disputes involving patents, inventions or the financial viability of banks or building societies. It is unlikely that fair and accurate reports of private hearings will carry qualified privilege unless the information emerges from a press conference held by one of the parties to the hearing.

Contempt law for broadcast journalists

Reporting criminal inquiries	Postponing reports of trials to avoid prejudice	Prohibiting matters withheld from the public before proceedings	Television and radio coverage	Reporting the views of jurors
Strict Liability Rule – a media contempt is a publication which creates a substantial risk of serious prejudice. Television coverage needs to be alert to the use of images of arrested suspects where identification could be an issue at trial.	Courts have the power to order the postponement of information, parts of trials and whole trials under section 4(2) of the Contempt of Court Act 1981 in order to avoid prejudice to the administration of justice.	Courts have the power to prohibit media publication of matters withheld from the public before the proceedings under section 11 of the Contempt of Court Act 1981.	The Administration of Justice Act 1925 prohibits the use of cameras or live sketching during court proceedings in England and Wales. The legislation does not apply in Scotland. Scottish judges, therefore, have a discretion or sketching.	Section 8 of the Contempt of Court Act 1981 makes it an offence for jurors to communicate information about their deliberations on the verdict(s) or for journalists to solicit jurors about their deliberations to permit photography, filming
Applies when a case is active; time of arrest, issuing warrant for arrest, issuing of a summons, oral charging, or when a civil case is set down for trial. (Contempt risk in civil cases relevant only to libel, false imprisonment and malicious prosecution cases sitting with juries.)	Such orders need to state clearly what the media is postponed from reporting (extent) and the exact time when the order ceases to apply (usually return of all verdicts). Section 4(1) of the Contempt of Court Act 1981 states that no person can be guilty	This relates to anonymous witnesses who fear reprisals or complainants of blackmail where the threatened menaces are embarrassing. The orders should be used only where the courts had a previous common law power to conceal the information.	It is also an offence to photograph and film people entering and leaving 'court precincts'. It would be advisable to find out what constitutes the precincts at specific court complexes so that camera/tripod positions are not challenged by the police.	The contempt offence should not prevent jurors being interviewed about their experiences outside the deliberation process or for their opinions about many aspects of the trial, such as the judge, conduct of lawyers, and outcome of the case, such as verdict and/or sentence.

Contempt law for broadcast journalists (cont.)

Reporting criminal inquiries	Postponing reports of trials to avoid prejudice	Prohibiting matters withheld from the public before proceedings	Television and radio coverage	Reporting the views of jurors
There is a defence under Section 5 of the Contempt of Court Act 1981 to protect radio/TV programmes and reports on public interest subjects that are 'merely incidental' to ongoing trials.	of contempt for broadcasting fair, accurate and contemporaneous reports of court proceedings in good faith where no orders have been made.			However, the judiciary is very sensitive to media approaches to and dialogue with jurors.
The twenty-eight-day detention period in terrorist cases lengthening the period between arrest and charge, combined with the intensity of 24/7 media coverage, is shifting observance of the Strict Liability Rule to the time when a charge is made. Campaigning programmes with a partial position could be liable under common law contempt if there is an intention to prejudice a future trial.	These orders are usually issued to cover parts of jury trials heard in the absence of the jury where arguments about inadmissible evidence are ventilated. The freedom of expression Article 10 of the Human Rights Act places a legal obligation on courts to minimise the derogation from the open justice principle.	These orders are occasionally made in relation to information revealed to the public in open court and this is strictly not empowered by the legislation. Orders that prohibit media reporting should be constructed from the legislation providing the power to do so.	Section 9 of the Contempt of Court Act 1981 makes it an offence to use a tape recorder or bring into a court a tape recorder for use without leave of the court. There is also a practice direction from the Lord Chief Justice of England and Wales prohibiting the broadcasting of tape recordings of court hearings.	There is a tendency for judges to create a *cordon sanitaire* around jurors in terms of their identity. Sketching, photographing and filming of jurors could be considered 'impeding' the administration of justice. This is despite the fact that jurors answer to their names when sworn in and are rarely concealed in public proceedings.

Defamation law for broadcast journalists in a nutshell

Libel factors for broadcast journalists	Absolute privilege and qualified privilege	Public interest qualified privilege	Fair comment	Innocent dissemination	Justification
Libel is lowering the estimation of right-thinking members of society generally, exposing somebody to hatred, ridicule or contempt; causing somebody to be shunned or avoided, or damaging them in their trade, profession, work or office. Libel can be by innuendo, depends on the natural meaning of words, and can also involve the expression of language that arouses extreme pity. TV journalists must be careful of soundtrack commentary libelling individuals identifiable in visual footage. This is libel by association.	Court reporting if fair, accurate and contemporaneous (published to nearest deadline) will be absolutely privileged. This defence applies to publications by Parliament and the words of parliamentarians. The point about absolute privilege is that it is a defence to report libels expressed by people in court that they know to be untrue. Malice cannot undermine the defence of absolute privilege.	The Jameel/Reynolds defence arises out of two House of Lords cases: *Albert Reynolds v. Times Newspapers* [1999] and *Jameel v. Wall Street Journal* [2006]. In the first case Lord Nicholls set out a ten-point framework for responsible journalism that could in certain circumstances mean that journalism produced in the public interest that had wrongly defamed individual(s) should not be liable for libel action.	An expression of an honestly held opinion, based on true facts, on a matter of public interest and without malice. The comment should be recognisable as comment based on facts that are true or protected by privilege and the comment should be made by an honest person, however prejudiced he might be, and however exaggerated or obstinate his views.	This is available for live broadcasters and Internet publishers. When a libel comes out of the blue from a guest or radio/TV participant you will have a defence if you took reasonable steps to prevent the publication and did all you could to mitigate the sting of the libel when it was uttered or written.	The story needs to be true in substance and fact. In England and Wales the burden of proof is on the media defendant and not the claimant. You need credible witnesses and evidence to persuade a jury on the balance of probabilities. This is expensive to defend. The current nature of the justification defence does not assist investigative journalism.

Defamation law for broadcast journalists in a nutshell (cont.)

Libel factors for broadcast journalists	Absolute privilege and qualified privilege	Public interest qualified privilege	Fair comment	Innocent dissemination	Justification
Libel has to be published to a third party (an audience of one will do), involve defaming some-body who is alive, not dead, and the person defamed has to be referred to and can be identified by implication. The libel writ must be issued within a year of publication. Groups of defamed people can sue together. It seems the group factor does not exceed twenty-five.	Qualified privilege – 'subject to explanation or contradiction'. This defence applies to fair and accurate reports of public meetings, local authority meetings and statements from government bodies (including the police). It is useful to remember that firefighter, ambulance/paramedic and coast-guard bulletins are not privileged.	The Nicholls pointers on responsible journalism: 1) The seriousness of the allegation. The more serious the charge, the more the public is misinformed and the individual harmed, if the allegation is not true; 2) The nature of the information, and the extent to which the subject is a matter of public concern; 3) The source of the information. Some informants have no direct knowledge of the events. Some have their own axes to grind, or are being paid for their stories; 4) The steps taken to verify the information; 5) The status of the information. The allegation may have already been the subject of an investigation which commands respect; 6) The urgency of the matter. News is often a perishable commodity; 7) Whether comment was sought from the claimant. He may have information others do not possess or have not disclosed. An approach to the claimant will not always be necessary; 8) Whether the article contained the gist of the claimant's side of the story; 9) The tone of the article. A newspaper can raise queries or call for an investigation. It need not adopt allegations as statements of fact; 10) The circumstances of the publication, including the timing. The list is not exhaustive. It is important for broadcast journalists to maintain a neutral and impartial approach to reporting. The *Daily Telegraph* lost the Reynolds defence argument in their libel dispute with the MP George Galloway because the edition carrying reports of allegations based on documents found in Baghdad included editorial comment that appeared to be hostile and biased against Mr Galloway.			
Trade unions, associations, public authorities and govern-ment bodies cannot sue. Private and public companies can. Lifting	'Subject to explanation or contradiction' means that if somebody accused of something wants to put their side of the story you should report it within a	Despite the initial optimism that 'the Reynolds defence' would strengthen freedom of expression as a paradigm in the law of defamation, subsequent cases demonstrated the opposite. High Court judges such as Mr Justice Gray and Mr Justice Eady tended to apply the criteria too strictly or elevated and prioritised criteria such as 'the seriousness of the allegation' to the point where 'the gravity of the allegations "permeates through and affects most, if not all, of the other tests"'. In the Jameel case the Law Lords decided the defence should turn on two issues: whether an article			

or following up libellous stories from one medium to the next means that you are in danger of repeating the libel. If you review or use a libellous story in radio/television from newspapers you are still liable.

reasonable amount of time. Press conferences and the press releases connected to the conferences are covered by this category of qualified privilege.

The qualified privilege defence applies to fair and accurate reports of past court hearings, and parliamentary proceedings. Only the malice of the reporter or publishing organisation can undo this defence.

Judges decide whether words are capable of a defamatory meaning. Juries decide the facts. Sometimes judges sit alone to decide meaning and facts, as in the McDonald's libel case – the longest running in British legal history.

was on a matter of public interest and whether it was the product of responsible journalism. They said Lord Nicholls' ten factors should be useful pointers and not tests to be satisfied or hurdles to be jumped. The Law Lords emphasised the importance of revitalising freedom of expression by ensuring that journalism in the public interest should not be undermined by libel laws. They also warned judges not to second-guess the professional decisions that editors have to make under the pressure of deadlines. As a result of the Jameel ruling, in 2007 investigative journalist Graeme McLagan, who had lost on a Reynolds libel defence over his book on police corruption, *Bent Coppers*, at the High Court, succeeded in his appeal.

'Neutral reportage' is being recognised as a dimension of the Reynolds public interest/qualified privilege defence. In a nutshell it extends a defence to the attributed and neutral reporting of allegations and counter-allegations by parties to a political dispute in which the public has a legitimate interest. In the 2006 case *Roberts v. Searchlight* two members of the British National Party sought to sue the anti-fascist magazine *Searchlight*, its editor and journalist. Mr Justice Eady ruled that the 'neutral reportage' defence could be available even where the journalists had not been neutral. The key test was the manner of reporting. The magazine argued that it had merely reported allegations against the BNP members without adopting or endorsing them. The judge highlighted the importance of reporting both sides in a disinterested way.

Media privacy law for broadcast journalists

Protection for sexual offence complainants

All sexual offence complainants (male and female) have media publication anonymity for all time after they have made a complaint of a sexual offence. This statutory prohibition remains even when they can be seen giving evidence and their names are disclosed in the public courtroom. They can waive their anonymity to help a police inquiry or for some other personal or public interest reason. It is important that their permission is in writing. Broadcasters need to be alert to disguising distinctive voices, dress codes and hairstyles properly when interviewing complainants with anonymity, as identification by anyone who can recognise a complainant would be a criminal offence. In exceptional situations a criminal court can lift the anonymity if it is judged that the restriction presents a substantial block to the reporting of the case. Child sex offence complainants (aged fifteen and under) can never waive their anonymity. Bear in mind that the range of sexual offences for which complainants have anonymity has been considerably expanded.

Protection for children/youths

Youths (aged seventeen and under; in Scotland fifteen and under) can have anonymity if an order is made under the Children and Young Persons' Act 1933 – known as 'Section 39 Orders'. This applies to witnesses and defendants. They should not be made if the child victim is a baby or so young as not to be conscious of the effect of publicity: i.e., under four. They should not be made if the child victim is deceased. Children who are wards of court and in local authority care cannot be identified as the subject of Matrimonial/Children Act proceedings, or any other custody disputes. It may be possible to give publicity to a child who is a ward of court where the event or issue bears no relation to the proceedings.

It is important to avoid the risk of jigsaw identification: e.g., when one media organisation reports the case of a father raping his daughter and another reports it as a named man accused of raping an unnamed young woman. The audience could put 2 and 2 together. Anti-Social Behaviour Orders (ASBOs) are applied for by local authorities with the support of the police. These are technically civil proceedings. Youths being dealt with should be identified in order to comply with the spirit of the legislation, although the courts should take into account the welfare of the youths when balancing privacy with freedom of expression. Publicity supports the principle of 'naming and shaming' and warning people in the community that troublesome youths should not be at large in shopping centres or banned areas. If youths breach ASBOs they are dealt with by 'Youth Courts' in criminal proceedings. There is normally default anonymity for youths in these courts under section 49 of the Children and Young Persons Act 1933, but on 1 July 2005 the law was amended so that Youth Court justices have to make an order if they wish ASBO-breaching youths to retain their anonymity. The situation has been complicated by the fact that Parliament has also given Youth Courts the power to impose ASBOs on young offenders at the same time as they are convicted of criminal offences. In this situation journalists have to use their initiative to persuade the justices to lift the default reporting restrictions to identify the ASBO youths.

Media privacy arising out of Article 8 of the Human Rights Act 1998

In Britain there has been rapid progress in establishing a media privacy law through the decisions of judges using Article 8 as the seed for their judicial activism. In 2004 a slim majority of Law Lords in Britain's supreme court (the Judicial Committee of the House of Lords) affirmed a right to privacy for the model Naomi Campbell in a news article published in the *Daily Mirror* newspaper. Campbell had lied to the general public when she denied taking drugs. The *Mirror* published a photograph of her proving the lie. But Campbell said her privacy had been invaded because she was photographed leaving a Narcotics Anonymous meeting in the affluent Chelsea area of London. The *Daily Mirror* said the photograph was taken in a public street and there was a public interest in publishing it. The Law Lords' decision was by a majority of three to two. The majority of the Law Lords emphasised that the privacy being protected related to Ms Campbell's medical treatment for addiction. In the same year Princess Caroline of Monaco won a case at the European Court of Human Rights on the basis that taking her picture with her children while in a public place was an invasion of her privacy. The Human Rights Act also requires the courts to take into account any relevant privacy codes issued by the PCC, BBC or Ofcom when considering restrictions that prevent broadcasts or print publications occurring. Many lawyers and judges in the UK now concede that the UK has a clear and developing law of privacy. The trend was confirmed in December 2006 with two Appeal Court rulings. In *McKennitt v. Ash* the judges supported the High Court judge Mr Justice Eady who ruled that a book by McKennitt's former friend, *Travels with Loreena McKennitt: My Life as a Friend*, revealed personal and private details that the singer was entitled to keep secret. In *HRH The Prince of Wales v. Associated Newspapers*, the Court of Appeal decided the *Daily Mail* was not entitled to publish substantial extracts from a handwritten journal kept by Prince Charles relating to his visit to Hong Kong in 1993 shortly before the colony was handed over to China. In a balancing exercise the judges decided that it was necessary to restrict freedom of expression in order to prevent disclosure of information received in confidence. The court had to decide whether it was in the public interest that the duty of confidence should be breached.

Protection for 'vulnerable witnesses'

Section 11 of the Contempt of Court Act 1981 and the Youth Justice and Criminal Evidence Act 1999 give protection to 'vulnerable witnesses'. Blackmail victims (where menaces are something embarrassing) are entitled to anonymity irrespective of whether an order has been made. When 'vulnerable witnesses' are giving evidence, the judge can clear the court and leave only one journalist present. It is an offence to report this exclusion before the end of the trial or to report the special measures taken to protect the vulnerable witness. The courts can ban identification of adult witnesses (aged eighteen and over) if satisfied that the quality of the evidence or level of cooperation will be diminished by fear or distress. Under the Serious Organised and Crime and Police Act 2005 it is an offence to disclose new identities of witnesses under police protection because of violence or intimidation, or any details of other arrangements for their protection. Under the right to life provisions of the Human Rights Act, the High Court can make injunctions on media identification of the identity and whereabouts of notorious convicted criminals, such as the child killers Mary Bell, Jon Venables and Robert Thompson, and Ian Huntley's partner Maxine Carr (who was convicted of perverting the course of justice and feared violent reprisals after her release from prison).

Fair enough?

Ethics and regulation in broadcast journalism

Tony Harcup

22

Introduction

Journalism for television and radio manages simultaneously to be just like other forms of journalism and yet totally different. Broadcast, online and print journalists live in the same world and breathe the same air yet frequently appear to operate on different planets. Consider, for a moment, media reaction to UK broadcasting's fakery scandals of 2007: the TV trailer that appeared to show the Queen storming out of a photoshoot in an unregal huff; the phone-in competitions in which winners were apparently selected before lines closed; and the viewers' vote to choose a name for the *Blue Peter* cat when, horror of horrors, the name declared the winner was not actually the one with the most votes.

What happened when these shenanigans were discovered? Indignation was howled, teeth were gnashed, souls were bared, and heads were made to roll – all to the accompaniment of jeers and cheers from the great British national press. Yes, the press. The same press that gave us the faked diaries of Adolf Hitler (Rupert Murdoch's *Sunday Times*), that once fixed a spot-the-ball competition to ensure that nobody won a much-trumpeted million-pound prize (Robert Maxwell's *Daily Mirror*), and which frequently publishes stories claiming that the European Union is outlawing bent bananas (it is not) or that local authorities have banned Christmas (they have not). The same press that, in the wake of Princess Diana's death, promised to stop buying paparazzi pictures; that routinely 'tidies up' people's quotes; that campaigns for or against particular political parties or policies; and that boasts a remarkable tendency to uncover stories that somehow reflect well on the business interests of their respective proprietors – not least among them being stories knocking the BBC. Not all the press do such things, of course, at least not all of the time; but a substantial portion of our national newspapers do, a substantial proportion of the time. So much so that an impartial observer might be forgiven for thinking that members of the UK's newspaper industry have got quite a cheek when they criticise the ethical standards of their broadcasting counterparts.

Not convinced? Try walking into a newsagent on any Sunday morning and looking at the front pages of the most popular newspapers. Then go home and switch on TV or radio news. How many of the redtops' salacious stories are picked up by the BBC, ITV, IRN or Sky? Very, very few, and usually only when the celebrity concerned has decided to speak out, thereby adding fuel to whatever fire may have been sparked. Do broadcast journalists turn their noses up at these stories because their viewers and listeners are uninterested in such low matters as sex and drugs and rock 'n' roll? Hardly. People who buy the papers are largely the same people as consume broadcast news. No, it's because for a range of historical, political and technological reasons the broadcasting industry in the UK has developed under a different form of regulation, with different traditions, coming up with different answers to ethical questions and a different understanding of 'the public interest'.

This is not something inherent in broadcasting itself but is a result of the way the industry has been regulated in the UK, where twentieth-century politicians feared the impact of political propaganda or other forms of indecent material being beamed directly into the living rooms of unsuspecting families. If you want to see the evidence, Andrew Marr suggests you note the difference between Murdoch's relatively straight Sky News channel in the UK and his virulently right-wing Fox News channel in the United States:

> In America, Fox News openly avows Rupert Murdoch's politics: but its British cousin Sky News, constrained and influenced by British television culture, does not. A relatively young tradition of politically impartial news was established here and has taken root. And this came about, let us remember, not because British journalists were more virtuous than journalists anywhere else, but because parliament decided to set up a system which was in deliberate tension – a licence fee for the BBC which kept the politicians relevant, and other constraints for the commercial companies, but day-to-day freedom for broadcasters.
>
> (Marr, 2005: 305–7)

So statutory regulation of broadcasting means that, unlike with the press, transgressors can be fined or have their licence to operate tightened or even removed. Of course, the 'day-to-day freedom' referred to by Marr can lead to severe tensions at certain times, such as when the Thatcher government fell out with those broadcasters who insisted on asking awkward questions at the height of the Northern Ireland 'troubles', or when the Blair government – in the shape of spinmeister Alastair Campbell – attacked the BBC over Andrew Gilligan's reporting of the run-up to the Iraq War. But most of the time it seems to work as a form of regulation that, arguably at least, results in a more ethical form of journalism than can be seen in sections of the press – formalised in the tighter provisions and tougher penalties of the Office of Communications (Ofcom) code for broadcasting and the BBC's editorial guidelines when compared with the Press Complaints Commission's often criticised code of 'self-regulatory' practice.

Little wonder, then, that broadcast journalists tend to snort with derision whenever conversation turns to press self-regulation. The broadcast and print journalism traditions in the UK are certainly different; as different as rugby is from football, argue Tim Gopsill and Greg Neale in their history of the National Union of Journalists (NUJ). However, many journalists move between the two forms of journalism with apparent ease:

> They work to different codes and regulations, yet they cross-fertilise, they work together, they mesh. Perhaps this is why British journalism is as good as any in the world, while football is not . . . Newspapers have for three hundred years been fiercely independent of the state, and even when in decline are so strong that no government can touch them. They can be outspoken, outrageous, irresponsible and generally over-the-top . . . Broadcast journalists, by contrast, are conscious of offering a public service providing reliable and authoritative information . . . Of course, newspaper journalists work hard to get their stories right, and broadcasters to make them lively and entertaining – and this is why British journalism . . . [is] so strong: the secret is in the mix . . . There is a unifying thread to their work.
>
> (Gopsill and Neale, 2007: 231–2)

That unifying thread, they argue, is provided by the ethical code of conduct drawn up by journalists within the NUJ in 1936 and updated periodically since, most recently in 2007. The code lays down essential principles of ethical conduct for journalists, be they working in broadcasting, print or online, as reporters, subs, editors, photographers, producers or doing any other form of editorial work. Even those journalists who are not conscious of the details of the code's provisions, or who have not signed up to it as members of the union, 'will have absorbed its principles from their peers' (*ibid*.: 232); principles such as distinguishing between fact and opinion, protecting confidential sources of information, and upholding the right of citizens to be informed (see the full code at: http://www.nuj.org.uk/inner Pagenuj.html?docid=174).

Stand up, stand up for ethics

It is this principle of the public's right to information that has underpinned some of UK journalism's most high profile ethical battles, which in recent decades have tended to centre on broadcast journalism: the occasion when the police turned up mob-handed at TV studios and seized equipment, for example; something perhaps normally associated with authoritarian states far from the UK. In 1987 Special Branch raided the BBC's studios in Glasgow and took away material relating to a controversial *Secret Society* television documentary concerning a British spy satellite called Project Zircon. Under government pressure, the BBC declined to broadcast the programme – which had been made by investigative journalist Duncan Campbell – prompting thousands of its journalists to stop work for two hours in protest and the NUJ to organise an unofficial public screening (Gopsill and Neale, 2007: 268).

Such a collective expression of ethical concern may be rare but it was not unprecedented. Just two years earlier around 4,000 NUJ members in the broadcasting sector had staged a one-day strike in protest at censorship of a BBC *Real Lives* television documentary about Northern Ireland (*ibid*.: 264–7, Bolton, 1990: 166–7). This ethical walkout was better supported than any BBC strike over bread-and-butter issues such as pay (Curtis, 1996: 279). Rival journalists at ITV even voted to join in to show their support, with just one vote against, and the action became 'the strongest single affirmation of principled, independent journalism in the union's history', forcing BBC governors to screen the programme despite opposition from the government (Gopsill and Neale, 2007: 264). And in 2004 journalists joined other BBC staff in spontaneous protests when, in the wake of the Hutton Report, the Corporation's governors sacked Director-General Greg Dyke, who issued what he later described as 'the most grovelling of apologies' for having stuck by Andrew Gilligan's story that the Blair government had 'sexed-up' its notorious pre-war dossier on Iraq (Dyke, 2004: 22–6).

However, it would be wrong to think that ethical issues arise only during coverage of war, terrorism or spying. Most ethical choices facing broadcast journalists are far less stark than whether to back down in the face of bullying by the government of the day, of whichever party. Ethical issues can arise on the little as well as the big stories, from the smallest local commercial radio newsroom to the biggest global news operation. They include issues such as whether to approach a grieving parent for an interview, how many knocks on the door might constitute harassment, whether to interview or film a child, whether to grant someone anonymity, how to protect such anonymity, whether to film on private property, whether to doorstep someone, what constitutes taste and decency, whether it is ever acceptable to edit the order in which events took place, whether there is a public interest defence for going undercover to investigate a story, and how to edit an interview without being unfair to the interviewee or misleading the audience.

Such issues can crop up when you least expect them, often on what appear at first to be relatively innocuous stories; and when they do, decisions usually need to be taken fast under stressful conditions. To help journalists think through such potential issues in advance there are now an increasing number of books discussing the ethics of journalism (see below) and, most important of all for those working in the industry, regulatory guidelines. However, the BBC's editorial guidelines (in conjunction with the Ofcom code) should not be seen as an imposition from on high, according to Hudson and Rowlands (2007: 184–5):

> These guidelines are the result of years of experience and case studies, drawn up by senior editorial figures, many of whom have had to make critical and controversial decisions in their own careers . . . Just as there is no such thing as a truly new story, there should be no contentious issue that isn't covered by the guidelines. If one arises, be assured there will soon be a policy about it. In short, there is no greater reservoir of experience to draw upon. The guidelines . . . are a one-stop shop for any reporter worried about the appropriate way to cover a delicate story.

Far from being divorced from the realities of journalism on the ground, such guidelines are, they say, 'a working tool, consulted by broadcasters every day' (*ibid*.: 184). They are also a reminder to broadcast journalists to think about the implications of what they are doing – that means every story, every day.

The impartial imperative

A goodly proportion of both the BBC and Ofcom guidelines explains what the broadcast journalist's statutory requirement to be impartial means in practice. According to the BBC, impartiality entails 'a mixture of accuracy, balance, context, distance, evenhandedness, fairness, objectivity, open-mindedness, rigour, self-awareness, transparency and truth'. As if that was an insufficiently potent brew, it adds that impartiality also requires 'breadth of view and completeness' (BBC Trust, 2007a: 5–6). One way of helping to achieve this is for journalists not to be content with looking at 'both sides' of a story but 'to get out more, and devote more time to exploring the undercurrents of opinion through broader reading and listening, and broader personal contacts' (*ibid*.: 34). The BBC argues that its public service framework sets it apart from more opinionated forms of journalism: 'Although many newspapers maintain a strong commitment to accuracy and fairness, none of them particularly espouses impartiality as a virtue. Fairness within a partisan context is not the same as impartiality' (*ibid*.: 16).

However, BBC journalists do not always deliver the high standards of impartiality demanded by the Corporation, according to a study – commissioned by the BBC itself in a characteristic piece of self-reflection – of the ways in which business stories were covered. The study found that the BBC's business coverage could be 'unconsciously partial and unbalanced', sometimes by being too sympathetic and 'sycophantic' towards businesspeople and at other times by adopting a 'hostile and aggressive approach' (BBC Trust, 2007b: 3 and 18). Furthermore, there was a tendency for business stories to be framed from a consumer perspective rather than from other possible perspectives, such as those of workers: 'Around 29 million people work for a living in the UK and spend a large proportion of their waking hours in the workplace. However, little of this important part of UK life is reflected in the BBC's business coverage' (*ibid.*: 19).

After analysing the evidence, an independent panel commissioned by the BBC Trust concluded that, although 'most of the BBC's business output meets the required standards of impartiality', problems included a preoccupation with consumers which resulted in some partial coverage (see also Chapter 15):

> Focusing on the individual consumer angle can distort news values and important perspectives can be lost. The polarisation of views between business and consumer means that much of the ground in between is overlooked. This includes the role of business in society, the international context and the workplace. Audiences are well served in their identity as consumers but they are not that well served in their role as workers or indeed as direct or indirect shareholders.
>
> (*Ibid.*: 3)

Clearly, then, the BBC agonises over its impartial imperative; as it agonises over much of what it does. Media commentator Brian Cathcart (2007) notes: 'No other British organisation of any size that engages in journalism puts half as much effort into considering the ethics and the propriety of what it does.' As a result of this, 'by and large the British public trusts it more than any other source of news'. Such trust depends in part on the commitment to impartiality that is central to broadcast journalism – commercial as well as that funded by the licence fee – and which appears to be important to the audience, a.k.a. citizens.

A survey of 2,000 people in the UK found 84 per cent of them agreeing – half of them strongly – with the statement 'Impartiality is difficult to achieve, but broadcasters must try very hard to do so'; only 3 per cent disagreed. However, this view was itself a partial one, because there was 'noticeably' less support for impartiality among those younger than twenty-four and among black and/or working-class people (BBC Trust, 2007a: 19). This changing social, political and media landscape has led the BBC to conclude that 'impartiality today requires a greater subtlety in covering and counterpointing the varied shades of opinion – and arguably always should have done' (*ibid.*: 36).

Impartiality is a problematic concept. It is defined by media theorist Denis McQuail (2000: 321) as 'balance in the choice and use of sources, so as to reflect different points of view, and also neutrality in the presentation of news – separating facts from opinion, avoiding value judgements or emotive language or pictures'. Yet these very notions of balance and neutrality have themselves been challenged by some broadcast journalists who advocate their abandonment in situations where to be impartial would mean standing 'neutrally between good and evil, right and wrong, the victim and the oppressor' (Bell, 1998: 16). Former BBC correspondent Martin Bell called for 'a journalism of attachment' that, while accepting that 'the facts are sacred', would see journalists who were covering conflicts accept the 'moral responsibility' that they have the power to influence events, not merely to report on them (quoted in McLaughlin, 2002: 178). Christiane Amanpour of CNN has argued along similar lines:

> I have come to believe that objectivity means giving all sides a fair hearing, but not treating all sides equally. Once you treat all sides the same in a case such as Bosnia, you are drawing a moral equivalence between victim and aggressor. And from there it is a short step toward being neutral. And from there it's an even shorter step to becoming an accessory to all manners of evil; in Bosnia's case, genocide. So objectivity must go hand in hand with morality.
>
> (Quoted in Seib, 2002: 53)

The most important thing, argues Jon Snow of *Channel 4 News*, is to strive to be fair: 'I'm against neutrality. But I'm for fairness at the same time. Complete fairness. You've got to recognise what your dispositions are, and balance them by allowing other points of view' (quoted in Roy, 2002: 38)

In the end, it comes down to trying to be truthful and fair, no matter what obstacles are put in your way and no matter what your own feelings are:

> Broadcast journalists have an ethical responsibility to report impartially, independent of external pressures, and a legal responsibility to be politically neutral. That is difficult to do and harder to maintain . . . [I]nevitably, opinions come into play when journalists select which facts to report and which sources to quote . . . Challenging facts, and their sources, and separating them from propaganda and spin are among the first duties of any journalist. Establishing the 'truth' of any situation is a near-impossible goal. Truth is almost always subjective. But striving for an accurate and balanced account is fundamental to the job.
>
> (Hudson and Rowlands, 2007: 271)

It is the striving for accuracy that is key here. Such a goal might not always be reached, but if it's not even the aim then surely it can *never* be achieved.

This commitment to accuracy – and fairness – is arguably of increasing importance in an age in which broadcast journalists without an ethical grounding might be tempted to use some of the hardware and software now at their disposal to 'improve' reality for the sake of a better story. With current broadcasting and editing technology, for example, it is increasingly possible to edit selectively, with little risk of detection, to alter what appears to have happened or to change the sense of what someone has said. 'As soon as you misrepresent the truth or distort the facts as you understand them, what you are engaged in is not journalism,' insist Hudson and Rowlands. 'It is trickery or fraud, and completely unethical' (*ibid.*: 317). You have been warned.

Taking ethics seriously

In essence, then, a concern for journalistic ethics is a concern for distinguishing between right and wrong; it is also a concern for journalism in the public interest, not merely journalism that interests the public. It should never be about doing what you think people will put up with or that you can get away with. Yet ethical journalism has been laughed off as an oxymoron for as long as there have been journalists. Seventeenth-century hacks were described by one commentator as a 'moth-eating crew of news-mongers' whose job was to 'gather up the excrements of the kingdom' (in Clarke, 2004: 24). And in 1930 the poet Humbert Wolfe articulated the continuing feeling that journalists were not to be trusted, when he wrote in his verse novel *The Uncelestial City*:

> You cannot hope to bribe or twist,
> thank God! the British journalist.
> But, seeing what the man will do
> unbribed, there's no occasion to.
>
> (Quoted in BBC, 2001)

In many ways not a lot has changed since then and journalists still tend to be represented in popular culture as lying, pushy sleazebags who would sell their own grandmother for a good story. Sadly, some journalists do their best – or their worst – to live down to such an image.

Yet, in other ways, much has changed since Wolfe damned us in verse, not the least of which has been the development of a broadcasting industry with a strict regulatory system, as discussed in this chapter. Something else that has changed, albeit more recently, is that ethical issues now receive far more attention – not least on journalism training courses, as Chris Frost (2007: 2) observes:

> Journalistic ethics have only very recently become a seriously regarded subject for study by practitioners and journalism academics in the UK. A two-hour session on a wet weekday afternoon halfway through a one-year course was very much the standard teaching for would-be journalists until towards the end of the 1980s and early 1990s.

Today, not only is the teaching of ethics taken more seriously on most under-graduate and postgraduate journalism courses but ever more organisations are taking an active interest. One such organisation is Mediawise, a charity concerned with raising the ethical standard of journalism. Its director is former journalist Mike Jempson, now also a visiting professor of media ethics at the University of Lincoln, who observes:

> Journalism is under scrutiny as never before. The field of media ethics is being picked over by a veritable land army of quasi-academic and professional institutions churning over the issues that have dogged journalists for genera-tions, and chewing over how we can do our job better . . . Journalists and the public now have a veritable farmers' market from which to select their ethics.
>
> (Jempson, 2007: n.p.)

Among the organisations that have set out their stalls in this ethical market place, in addition to Mediawise itself (www.mediawise.org.uk), Jempson lists the following:

- the Institute of Communication Ethics (www.communication-ethics.org.uk);
- the International Communications Forum (www.icforum.org);
- the Institute for Global Ethics UK Trust (www.globalethics.org);
- the Media Corporate Social Responsibility Forum (www.mediacsrforum.org);
- the Media Ethics Institute (http://ncfmedia.blogspot.com);
- the Media Standards Trust (www.mediastandardstrust.org);
- Polis (www.lse.ac.uk/collections/polis); and
- the Reuters Institute for the Study of Journalism (http://reutersinstitute. politics.ox.ac.uk).

By the time you read this, more will undoubtedly have sprung up. And then there are the discussions that take place when journalists speak ethics unto other journalists, through the NUJ or the BBC College of Journalism, for example.

Conclusion

Far from being worthy but dull, ethical journalism is actually better journalism because it treats people as citizens rather than merely as consumers (Harcup, 2007). Yet, being put under the ethical microscope can be an uncomfortable experience for journalists. As the BBC's Andrew Marr noted of the way in which some of his colleagues' note-taking and other working methods were dissected during the Hutton Inquiry: 'Many of the reporters slouched at the back of the courtroom . . . wondered how their own practices would stand up to that kind of examination' (Marr, 2005: xv). However, of all people, surely journalists should welcome the scrutiny of our fellow citizens even when it means we have to wash our dirty linen in public. After all, don't we tell everyone else that it is in the public interest for them to be scrutinised by us?

Further reading

Absolutely essential reading for anyone wishing to work in – or study – broadcast journalism within the UK are the Ofcom Broadcasting Code (www.ofcom. org.uk/tv/ifi/codes/bcode) and the BBC's editorial guidelines (www.bbc.co.uk/ guidelines/editorialguidelines), along with the *Ofcom Broadcast Bulletin*, which details its rulings on alleged breaches (www.ofcom.org.uk). The evidence presented to the Hutton Inquiry into the death of Dr David Kelly (www.the-hutton-inquiry.org.uk) and the BBC's subsequent Neil Report (www.bbc.co.uk/info/policies/pdf/ neil_report.pdf) also illustrate in unprecedented detail how a series of ethical issues around relations with sources, note-taking, scripting and live two-ways played out in practice. An interview with Andrew Gilligan, the radio journalist at the heart of the Hutton Inquiry, is featured in Harcup (2007).

Recent books that present a guide to a range of ethical issues facing journalists in the UK in particular include those by Frost (2007), Harcup (2007) and, although slightly dated now, Keeble (2001). Sanders (2003) takes a more philosophical approach to the subject. Ethical issues pepper the memoirs of Marr (2005), Snow (2005), Adie (2002) and Simpson (1999), and also feature in the history of the NUJ by Gopsill and Neale (2007). Reflective journalists can also be found discussing ethics in the pages of *British Journalism Review*, *Press Gazette*, *Broadcast*, *Free Press* (Campaign for Press and Broadcasting Freedom) and the NUJ's *Journalist* magazine, and on the BBC editors' blog at: www.bbc.co.uk/blogs/theeditors.

References

Adie, K. (2002) *The Kindness of Strangers*, London: Headline

BBC (2001) 'Journalists and their critics', at http://www.bbc.co.uk/dna/h2g2/ A500374 (accessed 18 December 2007)

BBC Trust (2007a) *From Seasaw to Wagon Wheel: Safeguarding Impartiality in the Twenty-first Century*, at: www.bbc.co.uk/bbctrust/assets/files/pdf/review_report_ research/impartiality_21century/report.pdf (accessed 18 December 2007)

BBC Trust (2007b) *Impartiality of BBC Business Coverage*, www.bbc.co.uk/ bbctrust/research/impartiality/business_news.html (accessed 18 December 2007)

Bell, M. (1998) 'The journalism of attachment', in M. Kieran (ed.) *Media Ethics*, London: Routledge, pp. 15–22

Bolton, R. (1990) *Death on the Rock and Other Stories*, London: W.H. Allen

Cathcart, B. (2007) 'Baiting the goody-goody', *New Statesman*, 21 June, at www.newstatesman.com/200706250015 (accessed 18 December 2007)

Clarke, B. (2004) *From Grub Street to Fleet Street: An Illustrated History of English Newspapers to 1889*, Aldershot: Ashgate

Curtis, L. (1996) 'A catalogue of censorship 1959–1993', in B. Rolston and D. Miller (eds), *War and Words: The Northern Ireland Media Reader*, Belfast: Beyond the Pale, pp. 265–304

Dyke, G. (2004) *Inside Story*, London: HarperCollins

Frost, C. (2007) *Journalism Ethics and Self-Regulation*, Harlow: Pearson

Gopsill, T. and Neale, G. (2007) *Journalists: A Hundred Years of the National Union of Journalists*, London: Profile

Harcup, T. (2007) *The Ethical Journalist*, London: Sage

Hudson, G. and Rowlands, S. (2007) *The Broadcast Journalism Handbook*, Harlow: Pearson

Jempson, M. (2007) 'The ethics business', *Journalist*, April: n.p.

Keeble, R. (2001) *Ethics for Journalists*, London: Routledge

McLaughlin, G. (2002) *The War Correspondent*, London: Pluto

McQuail, D. (2000) *McQuail's Mass Communication Theory*, London: Sage

Marr, A. (2005) *My Trade: A Short History of British Journalism*, London: Pan

Roy, K. (2002) 'One pair of eyes: Jon Snow, presenter of Channel 4 News, laments the decline and fall of the broadcasting characters', *Journalist's Handbook* 71, Autumn, pp. 33–8

Sanders, K. (2003) *Ethics and Journalism*, London: Sage

Seib, P. (2002) *The Global Journalist: News and Conscience in a World of Conflict*, Oxford: Rowman and Littlefield

Simpson, J. (1999) *Strange Places, Questionable People*, London: Pan

Snow, J. (2005) *Shooting History: A Personal Journey*, London: Harper Perennial

Next steps and staying ahead

Marie Kinsey

23

Introduction

> The most important equipment reporters have is that which is carried around between their ears.
>
> (Randall, 2007: 4)

Journalism is a process of finding things out and telling people about them. Its products are newspapers, magazines, bulletins, programmes, documentaries, features and websites. These products can be accessed via a computer, a mobile phone, a radio, a television or bought over the counter. The world of journalism is, in some ways, more complex and uncertain than it's ever been, but at bottom very little has changed: journalism is about people, the things they do and the things that happen to them. Journalists tell stories, real ones, significant ones – stories that draw in listeners, viewers and readers because they want to know what's happening. Journalism is an intellectual activity: 'Decent journalism, never mind great journalism, is not a matter of technique, it is a matter of intelligence' (*ibid*.: 2007: 232).

Journalism matters because it helps people make sense of the world around them. It rightly attracts scrutiny and criticism, so the best journalists are reflective, thoughtful and never satisfied with their work. They are a little bit obsessive, love talking to people, are tenacious and have a prodigious capacity for hard work. They care about accuracy and truth, are sceptical but not cynical, have an eye for detail and can home in on the important things. They read anything and everything and question it all.

Veteran BBC journalist John Simpson says journalists are instantly recognisable to each other: 'There tends to be a certain unkempt quality about all journalists . . . a hint of vagueness strangely allied to a driving force which can at times be obsessional, the otherness of a confirmed outsider' (Simpson, 2002: 23).

This chapter will examine what it takes to make a good journalist, how to become one and how to survive in a particularly demanding but exciting and thoroughly worthwhile occupation.

Could it be me?

The first thing to ask yourself is why you want to be a journalist. Many people start off by thinking that if they are good at English at school or have studied it at university, then journalism beckons. It's a good start, but there's more to journalism than that. *Sunday Times* journalist Nicholas Tomalin (1969) famously wrote:

> The only qualities essential for real success in journalism are ratlike cunning, a plausible manner and a little literary ability . . . The ratlike cunning is needed to ferret out and publish things that people don't want to be known (which is – and always will be – the best definition of news). The plausible

manner is useful for surviving while this is going on . . . The literary ability is of obvious use.

More than thirty years later this was endorsed by BBC *Newsnight* presenter Jeremy Paxman, who said there's 'no way of improving' it (in Ray, 2003: 8).

The ability to write clearly – and spell properly, even in broadcast – is crucial, but this comes at the end of the journalistic process. Good journalism depends on other things. If you have not asked the questions, checked the facts and identified the story there is to tell, your writing ability counts for nothing. Broadcast writing, as we have seen earlier, calls for a facility with spoken as well as written English. Writing for television is particularly demanding and about as far removed from most people's experience of writing as it is possible to get.

The BBC's Mark Mardell explains what else is needed:

> A determination, even a passion, to cut through the crap and tell people what's really going on, using clear and often memorable language. Someone who always thinks about what they're writing and never uses bolt-together clichés. Someone who aims for clarity above all but never sacrifices truth on its altar. A bloody-minded persistence comes in handy, too.
>
> (In Ray, 2003: 7)

Scratch a journalist and behind that hard-bitten veneer you often find a potent mixture of idealism and scepticism. If you are curious and knowledgeable about the world around you – including the place where you live – interested in people and want to make a difference, then journalism may be for you.

Getting in

Broadcast journalism is not particularly well paid, with salaries in some parts of commercial radio and the independent sector notoriously low, yet people are queuing up to go on courses and many are willing to work for nothing in order to get a foot in the door. It is enormously competitive, which calls for even more determination, persistence and resilience when the rejection letters fall on to the mat, as they will. Author Robert Harris spent years as a journalist: 'If you haven't got the nous to talk your way into journalism, then you probably haven't got the nous to be a journalist' (in Boyd *et al.*, 2008: 6).

There is no substitute for doing your homework and there is no golden path to follow. Whether your ultimate aim is to make award-winning documentaries that challenge the status quo, to report from the world's trouble spots, to commentate at the World Cup Final or to present *Newsnight*, you will have to earn your spurs first and be realistic about where to start. Most often that might be as a runner with an independent production company, in local radio or on local newspapers. Finding a job here, in itself, can be a tall order. You will need to be hungry, committed and determined.

Journalism careers rarely develop with one employer and many journalists move between different media and different types of programming. It used to be common for radio and television journalists to begin their careers in newspapers; that still happens, but it is also possible to start as a local radio or television freelance, or on a short-term contract. Increasingly, new entrants have completed a journalism course, either at university or at college. Along the way they will have undertaken unpaid work experience wherever they can find it.

The route is rarely straightforward. The documentary-maker might have served time on a local newspaper, as a regional television producer, or both. The now-famous television sports commentator might have spent years in local radio.

These days few people are lucky enough to walk into a broadcast newsroom straight from school or university with no previous effort to gain experience. But not everybody decides their career path in their mid-teens; nor should they have to. However, let us assume you are seduced by the prospect of working crazy hours, like a little uncertainty in your life, do not mind breaking dates and think you have what it takes.

The knowledge

In the twenty-first century it would be unwise to rely on one basic set of skills to see you through a whole career. As newspapers develop their websites to the point where traditional broadcast skills become desirable and as broadcasters seek multimedia skills that draw on print writing skills, it is important for the newcomer to build up a suite of expertise and knowledge that crosses boundaries. You do not need to be fully formed or expert in everything before you try for that first job or contract, but the more you can demonstrate, the more attractive you will be. So look for something that makes you stand out in what will inevitably be a crowd.

Every journalism employer in whatever medium wants people who can ask questions, and can recognise, find and tell stories. In radio and television what you sound like when you tell those stories will count for much – if your voice does not fit, you will not get far. Happily, what is not pleasing to the ear of one news editor quite often is to another – stories abound of young journalists being told they have a hopeless voice only to be eagerly employed by another station which thinks it is great.

Here is a checklist of some of the skills you should make a point of developing:

- *How to find things out*: Google and Wikipedia are *not* primary sources of information. They might lead you to a primary source, but learn to use the Internet intelligently. You may not know the answer to every question, but you must know where to find the correct answer – and quickly. Do not be nervous of picking up the phone: personal contact can often yield more than an email or a Web search.
- *Critical thinking*: Watch as much television, listen to as much radio news and current affairs and read as many newspapers and magazines as you can, but engage your brain. Why is the story being told in this particular way? Why was it interesting (or not)? What techniques were most effective? Did the interviewer ask the right questions? Were there gaps in the interviewee's arguments?
- *Understand the industry*: Learn as much as you can about the shape of the media. Read the media pages in the national newspapers and on the Web. Learn about individual organisations, their style, their target audience and their output.

If you want a job at your local commercial radio station, it's pointless expecting to do long, polished documentaries.

● *Understand the medium*: Radio uses sound, television relies on pictures and the Web employs both to create something different. Learn how use of sound can bring a radio story alive and how moving pictures are fitted together to create a narrative. Browse the Internet for examples of stories that use sound, text, still and moving pictures in innovative ways. (For example, '13 Seconds in August', the story of a bridge collapse in the American city of Minneapolis at http://www.startribune.com/local/12166286.html (accessed 2 April 2008) or the Pulitzer Prize-winning 'Remember Me', the story of how an American family coped with terminal cancer at http://www.concordmonitor.com/apps/pbcs.dll/section?category=photos (accessed 2 April 2008)).

● *Technical skills*: If you can, learn how to record audio and shoot pictures and how to use an editing software programme, for audio, video, or both. Build a website using a content management system. Start a blog.

Getting the knowledge – work experience

Far and away the most effective way of building up your knowledge and skills – and deciding whether broadcast journalism is for you in the first place – is to spend a few days in a newsroom, or on a shoot with a documentary crew. Unfortunately, getting work experience can be almost as competitive as finding a job. It does not really matter which branch of the media you target: time in your local newspaper or radio station is just as valuable as a week on the *Ten O'clock News* – in fact, probably more so, because you have a better chance of doing more than make the tea.

Persuading a newsroom to let you in is likely to be your first experience of the type of polite persistence employers demand, and you should not let any number of refusals, ignored emails and unreturned phone calls put you off. Editors are inundated with requests for work experience and look for those who demonstrate determination. If you keep on asking, without making a nuisance of yourself, an editor will start to think you are serious. If you have friends or relatives in the business, use them shamelessly.

Plan your campaign with military precision. Who do you want to target and why? If you are making an approach in writing, find out the name of the editor or news editor and how to spell it correctly (ring the switchboard and ask if you are not sure – a badly spelled, inarticulate letter will go straight in the bin). Explain why you want work experience with that particular newsroom – never send out a general letter to lots of organisations. In your letter demonstrate your knowledge of the company and its output and that you listen, read or watch. Sound enthusiastic and give dates that you would like to attend. Summarise the skills you can already bring and what you hope to learn. Do not write more than a single sheet of A4. If you are sending an accompanying curriculum vitae, make sure the journalism-relevant skills are at the top, along with any other journalism work experience you have done. Do not send a CV of more than two pages, and include only unusual extra-curricular achievements: Grade 3 swimming certificate at the age of twelve is not impressive; but spending six months in a Peruvian village probably is, as long as you can explain what you got out of it.

When you hear nothing, which is very likely, follow up your letter with a phone call after a week or so. Try to speak to the person to whom you wrote, but if they are not available, ask if anyone else can talk to you. Explain that you sent a letter, you are very keen and wondered if the dates you suggested were possible. If you are fobbed off with something non-committal, say you will ring again in a few days. If the dates are not suitable, suggest some new ones. You could also try to make an appointment for a chat. Talking to an editor face to face will give a stronger impression.

Work experience comes with a health warning, particularly if you have already undertaken a few periods and also have a formal journalism qualification. In April 2008 the National Union of Journalists released a survey of over 600 journalists who had qualified in the last five years: over half went on placements after their course had finished and more than 15 per cent did between three and six months continuously. The NUJ's general secretary, Jeremy Dear, said: 'This isn't work experience, it's exploitation. We're all in favour of students getting a feel for life in a newsroom, but in many cases companies are just looking for free labour' (NUJ, 2008).

Getting the knowledge – volunteering, hospital radio and student media

Do not put all your eggs in the work experience basket. While you are trying to set up a placement pursue other avenues. There is a growing number of community radio stations in Britain and volunteering can give you valuable hands-on experience. The same applies to hospital radio, where you can learn how a studio works and how to edit. Most universities and many colleges have their own newspapers, magazines, websites, radio and television channels. Getting involved will give you the freedom to experiment, discover which branch of journalism you enjoy most and build up a valuable portfolio of material. It will almost certainly help your case when you later look for work experience or a job.

Getting the knowledge – a course

> You can't get good journalism on the cheap, or by taking a philistine attitude to teaching aspiring journalists to think.
>
> (Cole, 1998: 79)

It used to be the case that most journalism training was 'on the job', and crusty news editors took a dim view of any young reporter daring to admit they had a degree. It is an attitude that still lingers in pockets, but since the 1970s much formal journalism training has migrated from the industry into universities and colleges, so employers have had to learn how to work with these institutions and what they have to offer. The Universities and Colleges Admissions Service (UCAS) listed 765 three-year undergraduate courses with the word 'journalism' in the title for entry in September 2008, and there were nearly 2,500 courses containing the word 'media'. There are also a number of journalism- and media-related two-year foundation degrees. It is a minefield and you should research with great care.

Opinion is split over whether a good first degree in journalism is better than spending three years studying something you are interested in – be that archaeology or zoology or any subject in between – and following it up with a one-year vocational postgraduate course. The industry is more familiar with the postgraduate courses, which have a longer track record of turning out people who go on to establish successful careers. Employers also like the breadth of knowledge about a specialist subject that a non-journalism first degree brings. The first undergraduate journalism degrees did not launch until the early 1990s. Many successfully equip people for a career in journalism; but more do not, or do not even claim to.

A number of factors will play a part in your decision, not least of which is money. A typical student will graduate in debt to the tune of £20,000 or more. Another five or six thousand pounds on top for a postgraduate course after a general three-year degree is too much for many.

You will need to study the course content with a fine-tooth comb. What is the mix between practice and theory? Who teaches? How much contact time do you get? What production facilities does the institution have? Will you go on work experience? Some courses are accredited by the Broadcast Journalism Training Council (BJTC), an organisation that represents the main broadcast journalism employers, including the BBC, ITV, Channel 4, GCap Media, Independent Radio News, Sky News, the RadioCentre, the National Union of Journalists and Reuters. It is a respected kitemark. BJTC guidelines lay down minimum standards for course structure, content, staffing and facilities (BJTC, 2006) and accredited courses have an excellent track record in helping people towards that first job.

One advantage of a reputable formal course, either postgraduate or under-graduate, is that you will learn law, ethics and public affairs as well as journalism practice and theory. Several broadcast courses will encourage you to take exams set by the National Council for the Training of Journalists (NCTJ), which accredits newspaper courses, as their qualifications in law and public affairs are recognised industry wide. Law training is one of the reasons why employers favour journalism graduates – there is less chance of legal mistakes that could cost an employer thousands.

Yet there is evidence that, as employers have favoured graduates, the pool of journalists is being drawn from an ever narrower section of society – those who are wealthy enough to get through further education and undertake unpaid work experience. A survey by the Journalism Training Forum (Skillset, 2002) found that 96 per cent of Britain's 70,000 journalists are white and middle class. Only 3 per cent of new entrants come from families headed by someone in a skilled or semi-skilled job. 'Can a workforce like this properly reflect and understand society as a whole when it is made up of such a narrow section of it?' (Ray, 2003: 167).

There have been some efforts to tackle this. In 2007 the BBC launched a new six-month journalism training scheme aimed specifically at recruiting good writers with no professional background in broadcasting who could help the Corporation reflect diverse audiences. It attracted 1,400 applications for 21 places (BBC, 2007). The National Union of Journalists has operated the George Viner Memorial Fund since 1986 to fund the training of black and Asian journalists. In 2007 the Guardian Media Group reorganised its Scott Trust Bursary scheme to include students studying broadcast and Web journalism.

Getting on

It is a mistake to think that once you have a qualification under your belt or have managed to find a job that all training and learning suddenly ends. Many organisations will require you to undergo short training programmes and refreshers, and it pays to keep abreast of new developments in the industry.

As your career progresses, it can be useful to carve out a specialist niche for yourself. Previous chapters have examined how sport, finance, political and celebrity journalism work, and it is often the case that a few years as a general journalist will give you the basic storytelling skills you can adapt. The BBC's economics editor, Hugh Pym, began in local radio:

> There's nothing that quite beats working in local papers or local radio. There's not a right or wrong way to do it but in most of my experience you get the general journalistic experience, and then you use maybe previous knowledge from university.[1]

In some cases, he says, it may be possible to use your specialism as an entry route in the first place, bypassing formal training altogether:

> [Business] is one of the few areas where you can get into a network-level job from something completely outside journalism because they do recruit people from management consultancies or research organisations, so you can use your City hat to get in that way. But if you've never done any other form of journalism it may be difficult to move on. What they don't always have, unless you are quite exceptional, is a grasp of what is a story.

It is certainly the case that a background in day-to-day news opens doors you may never previously have considered. Chris Shaw, the senior commissioning editor for news, current affairs and documentary at Channel Five, rates journalistic skills for all sorts of productions:

> The basic disciplines around journalistic law and compliance mean that you are trained to ask the right questions up front . . . The rigour required to produce to deadline – often a very tight deadline – is also invaluable, especially when working on low-cost or fast-turn-around projects which require real energy and efficiency.[2]

The presenter of *Channel 4 News*, Jon Snow, says other forms of programming, like documentary, can be rewarding in different ways: '[Have] a flexible open mind and above all patience. There are fewer instant rewards than news offers, but the larger prize at the end is much greater . . . Be prepared to *do* anything, seize your chances, render yourself irreplaceable fast.'[3]

Fiona Stourton, editorial executive at the independent company Ten Alps TV and Radio says moving to documentary production calls for a desire to tell the bigger picture, but journalists have 'the gift of storytelling . . . making a beginning, middle, end and a headline. Encapsulating an idea or story in a few words is very useful in pitching.'[4]

There may be an obvious link between news and documentary-making, but those small beginnings can lead you to other, more general areas. *Big Brother* creator Peter Bazalgette spent a little time as a BBC news trainee and says journalists make good entertainment producers: 'Being able to analyse any story, get to the core of it and express its essence pithily is really useful in the broader world of entertainment . . . Secondly, to develop a successful product in the world of entertainment requires intense application of forensic skills in relation to story arcs, format plots and so on.'[5]

Peter Kosminsky has directed some of the most controversial dramas seen on British television, including *The Government Inspector* (Channel 4, 2005), which told the story of the late Dr David Kelly, the scientific expert caught in the crossfire between the government and the BBC over the war with Iraq and *Britz* (Channel 4, 2007), the story of British-born Muslim siblings pulled in radically different directions post 9/11. He says:

> What TV lacks is bite – programmes that make life uncomfortable for those in positions of power . . . Drama in particular has become very safe . . . Paradoxically, the skills required to make such programmes are available in abundance – in the newsrooms of our TV and radio stations. A good journalistic instinct, a strong political sense and an understanding of how to go about researching a story that is hidden are exactly the skills required to make mischief with drama and documentary.[6]

And if you thought starting out as a journalist means the top jobs will never be yours, think again. Lorraine Heggessy, chief executive of Talkback Thames and a former controller of BBC1, says training as a journalist was a huge help:

> It gave me all sorts of skills that I have relied on in my various roles: accuracy – get your facts right and check that you have got your facts right; the ability to deliver to deadlines and to make complex decisions quickly; how to absorb a brief on a subject I previously knew little or nothing about. These are the skills that give you a solid foundation on which to build a career in any area of broadcasting.[7]

Conclusion

There is a saying that if you can find a job you love, you'll never have to work a day in your life. This is particularly true of broadcast journalism, where the rewards may not necessarily be financial but where the job satisfaction has the potential to be enormous. Journalists do not exist to be loved or to be popular: they are the 'awkward squad', who ask the questions some would prefer not to answer. David Randall says this about newspapers:

> This paper, and the hundreds of thousands of words it contains, has been produced in about 15 hours by a group of fallible human beings working out of cramped offices while trying to find out what happened in the world from people who are sometimes reluctant to tell us and, at other times, positively obstructive.
> (Randall, 2007: 16)

Much the same could be said about broadcast journalism. But if you like that sort of challenge, go to a newsroom near you.

Notes

1 Interview with the author, 11 January 2008.
2 Interview with Fiona Chesterton, December 2007.
3 *Ibid.*
4 *Ibid.*
5 *Ibid.*
6 *Ibid.*
7 *Ibid.*

References

BBC (2007) *BBC Journalism Training Scheme 2007/2008*, at http://www.bbc.co.uk/jobs/jts/index.shtml (accessed 2 April 2008)

BJTC (2006) *Accreditation Criteria and Procedures for First and Higher Degrees*, at http://www.bjtc.org (accessed 4 April 2008)

Boyd, A., Stewart, P. and Alexander, R. (2008) *Broadcast Journalism: Techniques of Radio and Television News*, 6th edn, Oxford: Focal Press

Cole, P. (1998) Instinct, Savvy and Ratlike Cunning: Training Local Journalists, in B. Franklin and D. Murphy (eds), *Making the Local News: Local Journalism in Context*, London: Routledge

National Union of Journalists (NUJ) (2008) *Work Experience Survey*, April, at http://www.nuj.org.uk/innerPagenuj.html?docid=776 (accessed 18 April 2008)

Randall, D. (2007) *The Universal Journalist*, 3rd edn, London: Pluto Press

Ray, V. (2003) *The Television News Handbook: An Insider's Guide to Being a Great Broadcast Journalist*, London: Macmillan

Simpson, J. (2002) *News from No Man's Land: Reporting the World*, London: Macmillan

Skillset (2002) *Journalists at Work: Their Views on Training, Recruitment and Conditions*, London: The Journalism Training Forum

Tomalin, N. (1969) Stop the Press, I Want to Get On, *Sunday Times Magazine*, 26 October

Conclusion

Jane Chapman and Marie Kinsey

In the Introduction to Part I we referred to the need for a broadcast journalist to acquire a 'toolkit for critical understanding', but the contextual explanations that accompany the practical content of this book have probably left the reader wondering how this can be achieved in the future; or, at least, what the future is likely to hold. For many years now certain undercurrents of change have proved troublesome for many industry stakeholders. One is the future of broadcast journalism in a converged, multi-platform environment. Certainly, the broadcast journalist has to navigate a way through a landscape that is rapidly transforming, influenced by patterns of usage, themselves enabled by technological developments.

Chapter 1 ended with the suggestion that in the future, broadcast journalists will be able to use their skills and their medium to support the interchange of content and ideas between networked communities, but for this an understanding of the needs of communities is required, in other words a social role for broadcast journalism. Regional newspaper groups have already invested heavily in local news provision and therefore have the potential to expand into live, local news bulletins. Thus, digital local video and interactive content are potential growth areas in the future. Here is an area where the social role of the broadcast journalist could be at a premium. Chapter 4 cited the public purposes for this that Ofcom have identified. They can also provide a mission statement for the socially aware broadcast journalist:

- To inform ourselves and others and encourage understanding of the world and the locality.
- To stimulate interest in the arts, science, history and other topics.
- To foster cultural identity and awareness of diversity.
- To support local services and community affairs.

Chapter 3 started with a quote that characterises 'on demand news': 'People can choose the news they want, when they want it. And they can interact with it, rant about it, and contribute to it.' What are the implications of this, especially if we add another factor to the equation – the growth of 'citizens' journalism'? Does it make the professional broadcast journalist redundant in this age of 'Martini media' that can be consumed any time, any place, anywhere? Observers have talked of the demise of mass broadcasting: more precisely, audiences have become fragmented to the extent that it is no longer possible to talk of 'the television audience', 'the radio audience' or 'the Web audience' in clear-cut terms. In Chapter 3 we were reminded that audiences tend to divide news coverage into two categories: interesting and dull. Although this provides another challenge for the broadcast journalist, historically this has always been the case – hence the press baron Northcliffe's instruction to his journalists almost a hundred years ago: 'Bring me a murder a day.'

Contributions from members of the public do not necessarily make professionals redundant: the interviews with a senior editor at Sky in Chapter 7 established that journalists still decide on stories and check amateur footage. Is this editing or moderating? Furthermore, a broadcast journalist can offer visualisation skills as an increasingly important element in the equation, as was stated in Chapter 10: 'The broadcast journalist must complement research skills and wordcraft with an ability to transform a conceptual conundrum into a visual imperative with impact, flair and above all meaning.'

One of the main differences today is the speed of technological change, but in Chapter 2, we were advised not to see this as a panacea: 'The expectation of new managers is that more can be achieved within the same time, that you can "get more news for your money".' No matter how advanced the technologies become, this could well compromise the quality of our work. The challenge is to keep accuracy and high standards of well-researched and responsible reporting as a priority and to guard against the unavoidable financial pressures that may compromise these aims.

Chapter 5 supported the central theme of Manuel Castells' classic argument (1996): that news geography no longer positions 'journalism conceptually in the centre of one society but globally as a communication culture of a world 'network' society. The amount of competition that this provides should not be underestimated: on a quiet day, the BBC 'Interactivity News Desk' receives around 12,000 emails, with 15,000 for a bigger story. No wonder the global communications arena has been characterised as 'cultural chaos' (McNair, 2005: 151). Journalists have to see the news through more than one medium and adjust to a move from individualistic to 'a collective and cross-departmental team based news work' (Deuze, 2007: 148). The positive side is that opportunities to obtain access to as well as to distribute information are greater than ever before. The multimedia newsroom can act as a centre for exploiting these opportunities.

Even in a scenario where the journalist becomes a kind of broker for the processing and distribution of information, news values will still be applied. The complex nature of news values is central to our understanding of the practice, production and output of news journalism. As Chapter 6 implied, application from day to day involves a compromise – between the ideal and the real in newsroom values.

Convergence amounts to more than online journalism using former broadcast features. The space within which online journalists operate is user driven, shared and flexible. The journalist has less control over information. Survival depends on our ability to 'think, and act, in a networked way', according to Chapter 12, where it was argued that new tools, such as improved communication software, are a gift to journalists because of the opportunities for new forms of communication. A good example of manna from heaven is the BBC's weekly *iPM* radio programme, built around a blog. Readers contribute story ideas and story development. Using new media involves a fresh, decentralised approach and a changed role for journalists who do not necessarily have to deliver content or a product, but instead help people make connections with each other and with information.

Online offers speed and depth, and different ways of telling stories that are genuinely innovative, combining text, audio, video and still pictures in ways that television and radio simply cannot do. However, it is not simply at the technical level that online needs to be understood. It seems that the fully digitalised environment is likely to be influenced by political as much as technological factors, linked to pressures at the economic level that influence the ways in which news and current affairs programmes communicate, their content and their style. Chapter 20 correctly identified three major trends that have challenged news programming: the expansion of the PR industry and the increasing 'mediatisation' of news sources themselves;

tabloidisation that has redesigned politicians as celebrities and established a 'continuum of performance'; and the heightened global visibility of major international traumas such as 9/11 that has made journalism 'subject to greater scrutiny and potential control from both governments . . . and from extremist groups with international scope'. Meanwhile, broadcast news is scrutinised, monitored, supplemented – and frequently contradicted – by myriad Internet sources. All of these influences are likely to challenge the confidence of broadcast journalism. This is an occasion when an understanding of news values can help.

As for practical skills, we emphasised in Part II the paramount importance of research, writing, presenting and technical skills because it is no longer possible to dismiss some tasks, such as picture editing, as 'someone else's job'. Video journalists shoot and edit their own material and online journalists need to be familiar with audio and video. Planning and preparation remain essential in research and newsgathering, regardless of the pressure of deadlines, and Chapter 8 ended by stating, 'there will never be any substitute for going there: getting out on location, talking to the people who matter and collecting the sights and sounds of the story'.

The style and approach to interviews as the central features of broadcast journalism have changed over time. At first deference to those in power and a patronising attitude to ordinary people were the order of the day at a time when media awareness was lower than it is now. More recently we have seen a 'hectoring' style for serious interviews and a public relations collaborative approach to celebrity interviews. According to Chapter 9, at present and in the future, 'nothing less than incisive and straightforward questioning by informed and impartial interviewers is acceptable'. There is a chance that some potential interviewees may prefer to go unchallenged via blogs and their own podcasts, and that broadcasters will give audiences more opportunities to influence the line of questioning. Yet, despite all of these trends, we still maintain that interviewing is the paramount skill for a broadcast journalist.

However, the interview cannot be seen in isolation, especially when it comes to the production of packages and longer-form journalism. Writing, interviewing and the recording of actuality can be efficiently realised only if the role of editing and packaging are appreciated from the very conception of the piece. In other words, broadcast journalists need to think holistically. One way of doing this is to consider yourself a 'mojo' (mobile journalist) or a 'backpacker journalist' – a reporter on location equipped with a video camera and a laptop to edit and produce stories. Eventually, all journalists will use the same technology, much of which was previously reserved for broadcasting. Chapter 12 quoted a journalist who said, 'a wired journalist without a camera and connectivity is like a hack without a pencil'.

As the news cycle has speeded up, particularly over the last twenty to thirty years, the amount of change in broadcast journalism is a major preoccupation of most contributors to this book: they have provided first-hand experiences for us to consider. Chapter 16 examined the increase in speculation and comment rather than straightforward reporting of who said what in Parliament. Spin doctors, political advisers and public relations all provide additional hurdles. The journalist needs tenacity and strength of character to withstand the pressures, but the good news is that when it comes to celebrity journalism (Chapter 17), getting it right can be an audience winner. As one reporter said: 'If you put a clip of Clint Eastwood in your headlines, it's a ratings draw and people will watch the rest of the news programme.'

The enthusiasm of individual contributors for their specialities is obvious – and they clearly would like readers to share it. This is probably the most important effect that this book can have. These chapters give an insight into the specialist reporting of sport, business, politics and celebrity that can be a way into journalism as well as a means of developing a career. Also crucial is the message that techniques learned as a broadcast journalist are transferable skills that can be applied to other areas. As Chapter 23 explained, journalism is an intellectual activity. It takes a certain sort of person and demands persistence, determination, resilience and lateral thinking. It can open doors to other jobs in broadcasting that at first sight are not journalistic.

Life beyond the newsroom presents a different sort of challenge, including the need to sell ideas through independent producers. As Chapter 18 concluded, this may not always endear you to your bank manager, but it is often the route that documentary-makers take (Chapter 19) because they are passionate about a particular subject that merits wider communication.

We have maintained a critical approach throughout this book, and this is paralleled by a similar process within the BBC In Chapter 22, one commentator claimed that no other British organisation of any size that engages in journalism puts half as much effort into considering the ethics and propriety of what is produced. This is one reason why the BBC is trusted by the general population. Similarly, we have tried to question why things are done in certain ways rather than simply presenting how they are done. We have wanted ethics to be woven into the spirit of this book, not just into the chapter dedicated to that theme.

Our approach is underpinned by a concern for journalism in the public interest, not merely journalism that interests the public. This has always been the philosophy behind public service broadcasting, but it also offers a wider and timeless appeal as the best possible mission statement for a broadcast journalist – whatever their speciality or transmission platform. Among the variety of messages that the reader takes away, this one has to be the most enduring point of principle that underwrites all the skills and attributes that broadcast journalism requires. It is a rewarding, challenging and important business.

References

Castells, M. (1996) *The Rise of the Network Society*, Oxford: Blackwell

Deuze, M. (2007) *Media Work*, Cambridge: Polity Press

McNair, B. (2005) 'The emerging chaos of global news culture', in S. Allan (ed.), *Journalism: Critical Issues*, Maidenhead: Open University Press

Index